Securing Clou~~d~~ ~~Services~~

A pragmatic guide

Second edition

Securing Cloud Services

A pragmatic guide

Second edition

LEE NEWCOMBE, PH.D

IT Governance Publishing

IT Governance Publishing Ltd
Unit 3, Clive Court
Bartholomew's Walk
Cambridgeshire Business Park
Ely
Cambridgeshire
CB7 4EA
United Kingdom
www.itgovernancepublishing.co.uk

First published in the United Kingdom in 2012 by IT Governance Publishing.

ISBN 978-1-84928-396-0

Second edition published in the United Kingdom in 2020 by IT Governance Publishing.

ISBN 978-1-78778-205-1

PREFACE

Cloud computing represented a major change to the IT services landscape. For the first time, enterprise grade computing power was made available to all without the need to invest in the associated hosting environments, operations staff or complicated procurement activities. Unfortunately, this flexibility did not come without compromise or risk.

Security remains one of the major concerns of chief information officers (CIOs) considering a move to Cloud-based services. The aim of this book is to provide pragmatic guidance on how organisations can achieve a consistent and cohesive security posture across their IT services – regardless of whether those services are hosted on-premises, on Cloud services or using a combination of both.

This book provides an overview of security architecture processes and how these may be used to derive an appropriate set of security controls to manage the risks associated with working 'in the Cloud'. This guidance is provided through the application of a Security Reference Model to the different Cloud delivery models of Infrastructure as a Service (IaaS), Platform as a Service (PaaS) and Software as a Service (SaaS). It also considers the required changes in approach to work securely with the newer Function as a Service (FaaS) model.

Please note that this book is not a hands-on technical reference manual; those looking for code snippets or detailed designs should look elsewhere.

ABOUT THE AUTHOR

Lee Newcombe is an experienced and well qualified security architect. During his career, he has been employed by a major retail bank, two of the Big 4 consultancies and a global systems integrator (twice). His roles have included penetration testing, security audit, security architecture, security design, security implementation, business continuity, disaster recovery, forensics, identity and access management, security monitoring and many other facets of information assurance. He has worked across various sectors, including financial services, retail, utilities and government, from the very earliest days of the UK government G-Cloud programme through to his current role helping FTSE100 companies succeed with their Cloud First strategies. He currently leads the Cloud Security capability in Northern Europe for a global systems integrator.

He is a TOGAF 9-certified enterprise architect and holds numerous security certifications including CISSP, CCSK, full membership of the Institute of Information Security Professionals and is a CESG Certified Senior Information Risk Advisor, having previously been a long-term member of the CESG Listed Advisor Scheme. Lee acted as the chair of the UK Chapter of the Cloud Security Alliance from 2017 to 2019 and has been writing about, presenting on and working with Cloud technologies since 2008.

ACKNOWLEDGEMENTS

Cloud computing, and the enterprise appetite for Cloud adoption, have both matured since I completed the first edition of this book back in 2012. Cloud years are apparently like dog years; that being the case, this second edition has required substantial updates to bring the content up to date. I am extremely grateful to a number of peers for their review comments on the revised manuscript, including:

Ian Bramhill, John Sorzano, Paul Ward, Koby Kulater, Nasir Razzaq, James Relph, Alex Stezycki, Simon Hill, John Ward and Kevin Watkins.

I am also grateful to my ever (almost) patient wife Lynne for her review of the text from a general readability perspective, as well as the expert editing offered by IT Governance Publishing.

Despite the efforts of all of the above, there is always the chance that I have erred in this document – any such technical errors are purely my own!

Finally, many thanks to you, the reader. Books would be very lonely places if left all by themselves; I hope you find something of value within these pages.

CONTENTS

xi

Contents

Contents

Part 1: Securing Cloud services – setting the scene

INTRODUCTION

Part 1 provides the foundation for the rest of this book as it introduces the concepts embodied within Cloud computing, describes the associated security threats and lists a few of the existing industry initiatives dedicated to improving the security of Cloud services.

Part 2 introduces a number of security architecture concepts and a conceptual Security Reference Model. This model is then applied to the different Cloud service models – Infrastructure as a Service (IaaS), Platform as a Service (PaaS), Software as a Service (SaaS) and Function as a Service (FaaS) – to show how the conceptual security services within the reference model can be delivered for each Cloud service model.

If you are already familiar with Cloud computing models, terminologies and associated risks then you could go straight to Part 2, although you may find the contents of Part 1 a useful refresher.

Throughout this book, I have italicised the names of the security services defined within the Security Reference Model (SRM). This is to distinguish between the name of a service such as *identity management* and the wider topic of identity management.

CHAPTER 1: INTRODUCTION TO CLOUD COMPUTING

Cloud computing

One of the more evocative labels for an IT delivery model – certainly more so than the utility computing label to which Cloud owes much of its heritage. However, like its rain-carrying namesake, Cloud computing can be difficult to describe, with many observers having their own perspective on what is, and what is not, Cloud. Many people use Cloud services without realising that they are doing so – iTunes, Facebook and Twitter are all examples of Cloud services. However, these are consumer Cloud services, aimed at individual users, and the security of such consumer services is not discussed within this book.

The purpose of this book is to help those organisations looking to implement Cloud services aimed at the enterprise – the likes of Salesforce, Amazon Web Services, Microsoft® Azure and the Google Cloud Platform – to do so in a risk-managed manner.

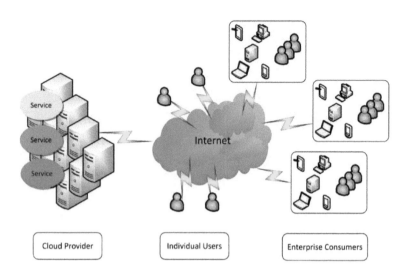

Figure 1: Cloud computing model

Figure 1 shows a high level representation of the Cloud computing model. On the left, we have a Cloud computing provider – essentially a set of servers offering some form of shared IT service. On the right, we have a set of organisations with users and client devices capable of accessing that shared service. In the middle we have the Internet (or some other delivery network) that acts as the transport mechanism enabling the access devices to connect to the shared service. You can also see some individual users sitting on the Internet that are just as capable of accessing those shared services as the larger organisations. The shared service on offer could be anything from the original Amazon Web Services model of access to compute and/or storage resources through to the Salesforce, Concur or SuccessFactors model of access to specific software applications.

Regardless of the service on offer, there are a number of key characteristics that the service must display in order to be truly 'Cloud', these are:

- **Multi-tenant** – the service should (at some level of the technology stack) be shared amongst its users rather than dedicated to the use of a single consumer. In the case of services like Amazon Web Services, multi-tenancy traditionally exists at the level of the physical hardware and the hypervisor,[1] which can host virtualised images serving many consumers.[2] In the case of services such as Salesforce, the multi-tenancy sits at the application level – many different consumers access the same instance of the applications on offer. Consumers are, therefore, separated only by the barriers implemented by the provider within their applications. This is a prime differentiator of Cloud services from a more traditional data centre outsourcing model, where resources would more typically be dedicated to individual clients.

- **Ubiquitous network access** – the service should be available to all over a common network. For public Cloud services, the common network is usually the Internet. For other types of Cloud services, the network

---

[1] Hypervisors are responsible for allocation of physical hardware resources such as compute, storage and communications to virtualised operating system guests hosted on that hardware.

[2] Although bare-metal services dedicated to the usage of a single customer can also be used at additional cost.

could be a more private network such as a government or academic network.

- **Elastic** – the service should be able to respond quickly to spikes in demand, with the Cloud consumer able to add the additional resources needed to maintain service levels during a spike in demand and, then, to rapidly release resources again once the spike has passed. Cloud providers should look to reduce the amount of manual effort required to support this elasticity.

- **Pay per Use** – consumers should be charged for the amount of resources that they actually consume; in the case of infrastructure services this could be by charging per CPU per hour or charging per GB of data stored or transferred. For Cloud providers offering SaaS this could be a case of charging per user per month rather than charging on the traditional basis of a perpetual license.

- **On-demand self-service** – consumers should be able to provision the services they need themselves, without needing to talk to the Cloud provider. In many popular Cloud services, customers can obtain the services they need with only a network connection and a credit card.

That is my view of Cloud, a view heavily influenced by the now de facto definition of Cloud computing produced by the American National Institute of Standards and Technology (NIST). The NIST definition of Cloud computing is discussed in much more detail in *chapter 2*. There are a number of services that seek to use the Cloud label, but which do not display all of the characteristics described above. A number of service providers continue to jump on to the Cloud bandwagon, and many services that would normally just be viewed as a shared service or a virtualised data centre have been relabelled as Cloud services. This relabelling is so common that it earned its own title – 'Cloud-washing'.

This book is not dogmatic about whether or not a Cloud service displays all of the expected characteristics described above; the guidance it provides is also generally applicable to wider classes of shared services.

CHAPTER 2: OVERVIEW OF EXISTING CLOUD TAXONOMIES AND MODELS

Chapter 1 provided an informal introduction to the main concepts underlying the Cloud computing model. This chapter provides a more formal set of definitions and a common terminology to enable a joint understanding of what is meant by terms such as IaaS, community Clouds and deployment models.

There are a number of different definitions of Cloud computing, with probably the most widely accepted being the definition of Cloud computing produced by NIST.[3] The NIST definition describes Cloud computing as being:

> [A] model for enabling ubiquitous, convenient, on-demand network access to a shared pool of configurable computing resources (e.g., networks, servers, storage, applications, and services) that can be rapidly provisioned and released with minimal management effort or service provider interaction. This cloud model promotes availability and is composed of five essential characteristics, three service models, and four deployment models.

The five essential characteristics, as defined by NIST, are:

1. On-demand self-service
2. Broad network access
3. Resource pooling
4. Rapid elasticity

---

[3] *https://csrc.nist.gov/publications/detail/sp/800-145/final.*

5. Measured service

The three service models defined by NIST are the familiar terms of IaaS, PaaS and SaaS. These service models are described in more detail shortly.

The four deployment models within the NIST definition comprise the commonly used terms of public and private Clouds together with the less commonly used models of community and hybrid Clouds (though hybrid Cloud is becoming increasingly popular in the enterprise space). Each deployment model is described more fully a little later on in this chapter.

There are some interesting things to note about the NIST model of Cloud computing, one of which is that it focuses on the three main traditional delivery models of IaaS, PaaS and SaaS. New models have emerged since the publication of the NIST definition, notably FaaS and the different, but often related, model known as serverless computing. As both the FaaS and 'serverless' models are likely to become increasingly popular over the next few years, particularly with respect to the implementation of microservices architectures, we will consider the security of such models in this book.

Whilst this book is relevant to Business Process as a Service (BPaaS), and, indeed, to many of the other *aaS terms that have been coined since the publication of the NIST definition, it is structured so as to consider IaaS, PaaS, SaaS and FaaS in turn. Those deploying other *aaS models should take the relevant guidance and adapt it to their purposes.

Service models

Infrastructure as a Service (IaaS)

In their definition, NIST describe Cloud IaaS as the model where:

The capability provided to the consumer is to provision processing, storage, networks, and other fundamental computing resources where the consumer is able to deploy and run arbitrary software, which can include operating systems and applications. The consumer does not manage or control the underlying cloud infrastructure, but has control over operating systems, storage, deployed applications, and possibly limited control of select networking components (e.g. host firewalls).

The most popular IaaS services are those offered by the 'Big 3' comprising Amazon Web Services (AWS), Microsoft Azure and the Google Cloud Platform (GCP); however, some of the major systems integration companies, such as IBM and HPE, also offer IaaS specifically targeted at enterprise users. You can also find smaller local Cloud service providers (CSPs) offering 'sovereign' Cloud services, i.e. Cloud services hosted and supported from a single host country, which target those organisations with specific regulatory or national security requirements necessitating that data and services remain in-country.

An example of a more focussed IaaS is that of companies offering Disaster Recovery as a Service (DRaaS) whereby organisations can store machine images and data in a Cloud-based service ready for use in a disaster scenario rather than building a secondary data centre. Another example of an IaaS is that of desktop as a service which enables end users to access their company 'desktop' over the Internet, with the desktop infrastructure itself being hosted within a Cloud provider and shared with other clients.

The primary selling point of IaaS is that the Cloud provider has already invested in providing the infrastructure and so end user organisations only have to concern themselves with the operational expenditure of using the service rather than the capital expenditure of building their own services. Consumers, therefore, pay for the capacity that they actually use rather than having to pay for servers sitting idling in their data centres. Furthermore, IaaS enables the speedier deployment of new resources, with new server images being available to consumers in a matter of minutes rather than months, as may be the case for those organisations needing to manage complex procurement and deployment processes. Those resources can then be released again should demand recede, at which point the organisation bears no further costs – a marked contrast to the traditional model. IaaS also promises to release headcount currently assigned to physical server management to tasks that offer more perceived value to the business.

Many enterprises are adopting IaaS for mission-critical production services across a wide variety of sectors. 'Cloud First' is the dominant IT strategy for both the FTSE350 and the UK government. It is now extremely rare to find an organisation that is looking to build new physical data centres; few organisations see building and operating data centres as a core business activity.

There are a number of reasons why some organisations may still be resisting a move to IaaS, with security being one of those factors.

Other factors include:

- It is potentially more expensive to run a 24/7 service, with relatively constant levels of demand, on the Cloud. Clouds tend to be cheaper for short-term or bursty applications – consistent loads can be cheaper to host on-premises, particularly where organisations are not willing to re-architect services to take advantage of the elastic nature of the Cloud.
- Certain legacy technologies, such as mainframes, cannot easily be migrated to the Cloud. Mainframe workloads are now being moved to the Cloud, but this is certainly not as straightforward as moving a virtual machine from VMware ESX to AWS EC2 or Azure. Furthermore, mainframe applications may require substantial data transfers to and from the Cloud provider and this may create greater costs.
- Discomfort with the 'follow the sun' support model of the underlying Cloud platform. Whilst the Cloud provider's physical infrastructure is, obviously, supported in the host geography, the higher levels, such as the hypervisor layer, may be supported from outside the host region. This situation can cause difficulties for those organisations subject to blanket compliance requirements demanding data, services and support be hosted within a specific geography.

Platform as a Service (PaaS)

NIST describe Cloud PaaS as the model where:

> The capability provided to the consumer is to deploy onto the cloud infrastructure consumer-created or acquired applications created using programming languages, libraries, services, and tools supported by the provider.

The consumer does not manage or control the underlying cloud infrastructure including network, servers, operating systems, or storage, but has control over the deployed applications and possibly configuration settings for the application-hosting environment.

The most well-known examples of PaaS include Microsoft Azure, Google AppEngine, AWS Elastic Beanstalk, Heroku and the Force.com platform. In addition to those platforms that allow the Cloud consumer to simply run their code, the PaaS term is also commonly used to describe other services that sit in-between the IaaS and SaaS definitions. Examples of such PaaS services include the Azure data analytics offers and the Service Now platform where customers are able to develop and extend upon the provided service.

PaaS offerings build on the advantages of the IaaS model by taking away the overhead of server administration from consuming organisations. Developers get direct access to the development environment and can increase or decrease their compute resources as and when they need; project delivery is no longer dependent on server installation lead times.

As we shall see later in the book, PaaS is perhaps the hardest of the three delivery models to secure as the responsibilities for delivery of security services is distributed across the provider and consumer much more widely than in the other two service models.

Cloud interoperability and portability is the subject of many industry initiatives, including work by the Open Group,[4]the International Organization for Standardization[5] (ISO/IEC

---

[4] *https://collaboration.opengroup.org/cloudcomputing/i14y/.*

[5] *www.iso.org/standard/66639.html.*

19941:2017) and the Object Management Group[6]; however, both issues remain problematic with no standard being widely adopted by the major Cloud providers. Whilst it constitutes an issue for all Cloud models, the potential risk of lock-in is more pronounced with PaaS than with either IaaS or SaaS. PaaS providers may support specific frameworks, APIs, identity management services and databases that may not be compatible with those offered by other providers or traditional on-premises products. In practice, this makes it very expensive to move from one PaaS provider to another as the developed application must be recoded (ported) to utilise the APIs, frameworks and other features offered by the platform of any alternative provider.

The PaaS model tends to be very attractive to those organisations needing quick delivery of Internet-facing services and those organisations (such as start-ups) that do not have the resources to host or manage their own servers at the operating system level. The PaaS model is also increasingly popular with the enterprise market, particularly in the area of big data analytics and machine learning.

Software as a Service (SaaS)

NIST describe Cloud SaaS as the model where:

> The capability provided to the consumer is to use the provider's applications running on a cloud infrastructure. The applications are accessible from various client devices through either a thin client interface, such as a web browser (e.g., web-based email), or a program interface. The consumer does not manage or control the

---

[6] *www.omg.org/cloud/deliverables/CSCC-Interoperability-and-Portability-for-Cloud-Computing-A-Guide.pdf.*

underlying cloud infrastructure including network, servers, operating systems, storage, or even individual application capabilities, with the possible exception of limited user-specific application configuration settings.

Salesforce.com, a company that offered Cloud services before the term 'Cloud' itself was coined, is without doubt a pioneer in the area of SaaS. Other examples of well-known SaaS applications include Office365, SuccessFactors.com, Google Docs and Concur.

With SaaS, organisations will typically access a specific software application (such as a customer relationship management application) via a web browser. This means organisations only need to consider the business usage of that application and the provision of devices capable of accessing the Internet – concerns around servers, operating systems and application development are no longer relevant. This model can be very attractive to business executives, particularly if the relationship between business and IT representatives has been strained by past perceptions of poor or unresponsive IT delivery.

The SaaS model is probably the most commercially successful of the three delivery models, perhaps in part due to the previous industry flirtation with the Application Service Provider (ASP) model. Enterprises appear to be more comfortable making use of specific services hosted in the Cloud than they are with the idea of making more general purpose usage of Cloud-based services. SaaS can appear to offer genuine business enabling services whereas PaaS and IaaS may appear to the business as simply different ways of doing IT.

There are a number of specific, security-focussed SaaS offerings, including email security, web content filtering, identity as a service, vulnerability assessment and anti-malware to name a few. These 'security as a service' offerings are often pitched as providing security expertise for those organisations that cannot provide such expensive expertise internally.

Function as a Service (FaaS)

As noted earlier, NIST do not currently publish a definition for FaaS or the related term 'serverless'. There are a number of different definitions relating to both terms, but no widely accepted standard; that being the case, I feel little guilt in putting forward my own definitions in this book!

Let us define serverless as:

> The capability provided to the consumer is to deploy functionality onto the Cloud by accessing utility services via the APIs offered by the provider. The consumer does not manage, control or have visibility of the underlying Cloud infrastructure, including its network, servers, operating systems or storage, but has control over the deployed applications.

The key point here is that the consumer has no visibility of the underlying infrastructure as services are accessed purely by application programming interface (API). In other words, whilst physical servers are providing the services within the realm of the Cloud provider, these services appear 'serverless' to the consumer who only ever interacts via API. The canonical example of a serverless technology is AWS S3 (Simple Storage Service); in this case, consumers simply call the S3 API to PUT or DELETE data objects but have no visibility of the underlying infrastructure.

FaaS is a form of serverless technology and an evolution of the PaaS model. The most popular FaaS services are AWS Lambda, Azure Functions and Google Cloud Functions.

We will define FaaS as:

> The capability provided to the consumer to deploy event-triggered, time-limited functions on the Cloud without requiring an overall process to be running at all times. The consumer does not manage, control or have visibility of the underlying Cloud infrastructure including its network, servers, operating systems or storage, but has control over the deployed applications. Scaling is the responsibility of the Cloud provider.

In general, FaaS services charge per number of executions, execution time and related factors, i.e. if a particular function is never triggered then there will be no charge (other than for associated storage of code or data). Functions can be triggered by a variety of events including provider-specific events (e.g. changes to the contents of an AWS S3 bucket), the receipt of an HTTP request or the identification of an event in a data stream. FaaS functions are time-limited; for example, an AWS Lambda function has an execution limit of 15 minutes whilst an Azure Function has a default execution time limit of 5 minutes (configurable to a maximum of 10 minutes) under the Consumption hosting plan option. If a function is not completed within those time limits, it may be terminated by the Cloud run-time.

FaaS services are commonly used to assist in the automation of IT operations, e.g. as part of DevOps initiatives (or, in the context of this book, DevSecOps initiatives), due to their ability to automatically respond to defined events. Another common use case for FaaS is the cleansing of data, e.g. to prevent regulated data from being transferred outside of an assured environment.

FaaS is also becoming one of the primary technologies used to implement microservices architecture, i.e. applications that are decomposed into modular components. Enterprises have the option of containerisation of microservices components or using FaaS, and some of those that have not invested in the likes of Kubernetes and Docker to provide containerisation are now deciding to avoid that complexity and move to FaaS.

The ephemeral and distributed nature of the FaaS model presents a number of novel challenges from the perspective of security that we will explore later in this book (see chapter 12).

Deployment models

Public Cloud

The public Cloud model is the archetypal Cloud model; the services are open to all-comers, individuals, enterprises, governments, your collaboration partners and your competition. The key point is that there are no real security barriers governing who can register to access the shared service. The low barrier to entry (typically a need for a credit card and an Internet connection) is one of the major selling points of the public Cloud model.

NIST define a public Cloud as one where:

> The cloud infrastructure is provisioned for open use by the general public. It may be owned, managed, and operated by a business, academic, or government organization, or some combination of them. It exists on the premises of the cloud provider.

Examples of public Clouds include Amazon Web Services, Microsoft Azure, the Google Cloud Platform, Salesforce.com, Office365 and most other well-known Cloud services.

Private Cloud

The term 'Private Cloud' is one of the more contentious concepts within the area of Cloud computing. Some commentators such as Werner Vogels of Amazon[7] have argued that private Clouds do not exist, with the implication that those organisations which believe themselves to have a private Cloud in fact only have a virtualised data centre. I must admit that the distinction between a virtualised data centre and a private Cloud can be hard to define; however, I do see merit in the idea of a private Cloud. In the public Cloud the economies of scale are realised through the sharing of resources, such as CPU cycles and storage across different organisations. However, in the private Cloud model the economies of scale come from the sharing of resources across different cost centres *within* the consuming organisation.

Of course, in the private Cloud model there are much lower savings on capital expenditure compared to the public Cloud as the consuming organisation must still invest in the IT and physical hosting infrastructure. However, a private Cloud is still likely to be cheaper to operate than a more traditional infrastructure due to the lower footprint of a shared, multi-tenant (between cost centres) virtualised IT estate. A perception that private Clouds are more secure than their

---

[7] *www.ciozone.com/index.php/Cloud-Computing/Beware-of-the-Private-Cloud.html.*

public equivalents is one of the main drivers for organisations to build their own Cloud. The other major driver for organisations adopting private Cloud approaches is a risk-averse interpretation of regulatory requirements. These ideas will be explored later in chapter 6, which discusses some examples of regulatory requirements relevant to Cloud usage.

NIST define a private Cloud as being where:

> The cloud infrastructure is provisioned for exclusive use by a single organization comprising multiple consumers (e.g., business units). It may be owned, managed, and operated by the organization, a third-party, or some combination of them, and it may exist on or off premises.

The major public Cloud providers do now allow their customers to procure dedicated instances and dedicated hardware (i.e. compute resources that are not shared with other tenants); this allows them to offer private Cloud services albeit at greater cost than their multi-tenant offers.

Community Cloud

Community Clouds form the middle ground between public and private Clouds and could be viewed as equivalent to a gated community. Community Clouds are only open to members of the community with rigorous registration procedures to be completed prior to access being granted. Once granted access to the community, there would typically be a set of minimum security controls that member organisations must implement in order to protect the overall community. Community Clouds are more cost-effective than private Clouds as the cost of building and operating the services are shared across all of the organisational tenants.

NIST define community Clouds as being those where:

> The cloud infrastructure is provisioned for exclusive use by a specific community of consumers from organizations that have shared concerns (e.g., mission, security requirements, policy, and compliance considerations). It may be owned, managed, and operated by one or more of the organizations in the community, a third-party, or some combination of them, and it may exist on or off premises.

Secure government Clouds, open only to departments and their executive agencies, are good examples of community Clouds. Other such community Clouds exist in specific private sector industries, notably defence.

Hybrid Cloud

NIST define the Hybrid Cloud model as representing the model where:

> The cloud infrastructure is a composition of two or more distinct cloud infrastructures (private, community, or public) that remain unique entities, but are bound together by standardized or proprietary technology that enables data and application portability (e.g., cloud bursting for load balancing between clouds).

The initial driver for implementing a hybrid Cloud model was the belief that this would ensure the effective management of spikes in demand that would exhaust the resources available to a more private deployment model. For example, organisations hosting a private Cloud could draw upon the CPU resources of a public Cloud should demand become too great for the private Cloud to service. However, the demand for such 'Cloud-bursting' has not proved to be as great as expected.

The hybrid model is now much more popular with those enterprises that are unable to move all of their IT services to the public Cloud, either as a consequence of other choices or of their interpretation of strict compliance requirements. In both scenarios, it is likely that there will be a requirement for data, and potentially for workloads, to transfer across the private and public Cloud environments in a controlled manner.

In my opinion, hybrid Clouds represent the worst of all options from a security perspective; organisations must now cover off all security issues for both the private and public Cloud models. For example, should an organisation be subject to specific compliance requirements (e.g. the EU General Data Protection Regulation (GDPR) in relation to data protection) then they must now ensure that these requirements are met in both the private and the public Clouds. Difficult problems must, therefore, be solved twice, quite likely using different solutions depending upon the Cloud services adopted. The one obvious security advantage of the hybrid approach is the likely improved availability of services provided by the additional capacity hosted on the more public Cloud service. As an example, a number of charities burst to public Cloud services to manage huge spikes in demand following major disasters.

The NIST definitions may be the most widely accepted, but that does not mean that they are the only set of definitions. As you would expect, the major analyst firms, such as Gartner, IDC and Forrester, have all produced their own definitions of Cloud computing and/or Cloud services, as has the ISO. I am not going to detail each of the competing definitions of Cloud services (Google can help you find them if you feel the need); I believe that the NIST definitions are now the clear leader and provide the basis for a common terminology, particularly as they have been adopted by cross-industry groups such as the Open Group and the Cloud Security Alliance.

This chapter has introduced the NIST definitions of Cloud computing – this is important as the terms IaaS, PaaS, SaaS, public, private, hybrid and community will be used many times throughout the rest of this book. Now we have a common terminology, it is time to discuss the security considerations of Cloud adoption.

CHAPTER 3: THE SECURITY BALANCE

This chapter aims to give a pragmatic overview of some of the potential security benefits and potential pitfalls of working in the Cloud. From the security perspective, working in the Cloud typically tends to be neither intrinsically better nor worse than on-premises – just different.

Security benefits

Like beauty, security is very much in the eye of the beholder. Which is a slightly pretentious way of saying that 'good' security is (or at least should be) dependent upon the context of your organisation in terms of the nature of your business, the threats and vulnerabilities to which your business is exposed and the risk appetite of your organisation. What is 'secure' for one organisation may be viewed as inadequate by another organisation with a lower appetite for the acceptance of risk. Security baselines, therefore, vary across organisations; all of which makes it difficult to make categorical statements about security benefits and downsides. Given this variability, I will discuss *potential* security benefits and downsides; you will have to take an honest look at your currently deployed security controls and consider whether each of the benefits listed below would be a real improvement on your current situation.

Data centre security

Designing, constructing and then operating a secure data centre is a costly exercise. A suitable location must be found, preferably one with a low incidence of natural disasters, close enough to transport links (without being too close), conveniently located for staff to commute to work and with excellent utility facilities for communications, power and water. The data centre must then be constructed complete with a secure outer perimeter, secure inner perimeter, appropriate security monitoring devices (CCTV, passive infrared, etc.), strong walls, access control mechanisms (e.g. proximity cards and mantraps), internal monitoring controls and countless other controls. You then need to consider the environmental aspects around cooling, humidity, uninterruptible power supplies, on-site generators (with fuel) and the staff to police and operate the building and the IT hardware that it contains. Or perhaps you do not.

In general, Cloud providers have already invested in state of the art secure data centres, or in the case of many SaaS and PaaS providers, in building upon the secure data centres offered by one of the Big 3 IaaS providers. The task of recouping the initial capital expenditure of construction, and the on-going operational costs, are shared amongst their client-base. The major Cloud providers tend to operate very lean data centres and employ an extremely strict segregation of duties: the few staff with physical access to the servers and storage in a Cloud data centre will have zero knowledge of which clients are operating on that specific hardware. Any threat source seeking to gain unauthorised access to their target's data via physical access will struggle to identify the right hardware to attack. Similarly, the major Cloud providers tend to stripe their customers' data across different storage disks, so an attacker walking off with a physical disk is unlikely to escape with a disk containing only the data of their target. Add in consideration of the use of data encryption at rest, along with the minimal chances of being able to sneak physical hardware out of the secure data centres, and the risk of a compromise of the confidentiality of data via physical access becomes minimal.

One other physical security factor to consider is the nature of the hardware used to provide the Cloud services – yes, even 'serverless' services rely upon physical servers. The major Cloud providers have the scale to procure their own custom hardware, including bespoke hardware security chips. For example, the custom AWS Nitro[8] hardware has various components, including specific elements covering network virtualisation and security, whilst GCP has the Titan[9] chip which provides secure boot capabilities by acting as a hardware-based root of trust. The use of such custom hardware can be a determining factor when choosing between different Cloud providers. Smaller providers using commodity hardware may still be exposed to more common security issues relating to IPMI (Intelligent Platform Management Interface) or the BMC (Baseboard Management Controller). An example of such an issue was the Cloudborne[10] attack that enabled security researchers to install an implant within the BMC and maintain persistence on the hardware after it had been 'freed' for use by other customers of affected Cloud providers.

For those organisations that do not have adequate data processing environments (e.g. those of you with business-critical servers hiding under *that* desk in the corner), then moving services to a Cloud provider will almost certainly

---

[8] *https://perspectives.mvdirona.com/2019/02/aws-nitro-system/.*

[9] *https://cloud.google.com/blog/products/gcp/titan-in-depth-security-in-plaintext.*

[10] *https://eclypsium.com/2019/01/26/the-missing-security-primer-for-bare-metal-cloud-services/.*

provide a benefit in terms of the physical security of your information assets and, potentially, the security of the hardware hosting those assets. For those organisations that already run highly secure data centres, the Cloud will probably not offer as much benefit from a security perspective. However, it may prove more cost-effective to deploy new applications on to a public Cloud if capacity issues demand construction of new data centre floorspace. One common factor driving many organisations to the Cloud is a burning platform of legacy data centres coming towards the end of their life, either due to lease expiry or the inevitable march of technology.

It must be noted that there is an implicit assumption here that the Cloud providers facilities are as secure as expected – would-be consumers should perform appropriate levels of due diligence to ensure that they are comfortable with the locations where their data may be held.

Improved resilience

In most circumstances, it is likely that the top Cloud services will provide more resilience (by default) than the on-premises equivalent. For example, Amazon Web Services offers a number of different Availability Zones[11] within different Regions such that services can be hosted across different Availability Zones (or Regions) in order to improve the resilience of the hosted services. The Microsoft Azure platform now also offers Availability Zones and automatically replicates customer data held within the Azure storage facilities and stores copies in three separate locations to improve resilience. Outside of top tier enterprises, how

---

[11] Essentially different data centres within a specific geographic Region.

many other organisations have multiple data centres (across different geographies) capable of providing similar levels of resilience? Furthermore, if your service undergoes a rapid surge in demand then an on-premises service could find itself struggling to cope whilst additional capacity is procured and installed. Additional instances could be spun up on the Cloud in a matter of minutes (or less depending upon your provider and toolset).

Of course, not everything always works according to plan, and even Cloud providers have service outages despite all their efforts to eliminate points of failure. The 'illusion of infinite resource' is also just that: an illusion. Cloud consumers using smaller Regions can sometimes find themselves unable to provision resources of a specific type due to wider demand. Consumers are well advised to investigate how much information Cloud providers release about past outages so as to judge their levels of openness and competence when managing incidents. An example of a comprehensive post-mortem of an outage of the AWS S3 service can be found at:

https://aws.amazon.com/message/41926/.

One potential use case for Cloud computing is for disaster recovery purposes. Why invest in a backup data centre to cater for an event that may never occur if a Cloud solution could provide an environment to operate within for a short period of time, but at very little cost whilst not in operation? For those organisations that run heavily virtualised environments, the Cloud can be a very cost-effective way of providing disaster recovery capabilities; hybrid technologies have improved dramatically over the last few years making the Cloud a suitable backup option for VMware or Hyper-V hosted workloads. Whilst full-blown Cloud-based disaster recovery may not be possible for some organisations,[12] the Cloud can still be a suitable option for storing backups of data rather than relying on physical storage media.

Improved security patching

Security patching is not straightforward in many organisations: firstly, you need to obtain vendor or researcher security advisory notifications; secondly, you need to identify which of those advisories are relevant to your environment; and, thirdly, you need skilled staff to understand the content of the bulletins or advisories. Once you are confident that you know you have a problem that you need to fix you then get into the real pain of patch testing and the scheduling of when these tested patches are to be applied, particularly if down-time is necessary to business-critical applications. With SaaS and PaaS (in general) consumers do not need to worry about patching of operating systems; this task is the responsibility of the Cloud service providers. Unfortunately, this is not usually the case for the standard IaaS service model, in which consumers must still ensure that their virtual images are up to date with the required patches; however, Managed IaaS models, whereby a Cloud provider or Cloud broker will take on responsibility for such patching, are available.

SaaS consumers also have the added bonus of not having to concern themselves with patches to the applications that they are using; again this is the responsibility of the service provider who would typically patch any issues during their

---

[12] This could be for a number of reasons, one good example being that of organisations running business critical systems on mainframes that cannot be ported to cloud services.

regular updates of functionality unless there is a need for a more urgent fix. PaaS consumers are responsible for fixing any issues in the code that they may have developed and deployed, whilst the provider is responsible for fixing any issues in the shared capabilities that they offer. PaaS consumers do not get to completely forget about security patching.

Overall, SaaS and PaaS solutions can significantly reduce the workload of existing system administrators with regard to the monthly patch process.

Automation and DevSecOps

Real-world consumers are driving rapid evolution of the services and products that they consume, particularly in the online world. This means that Cloud-native organisations are moving from, perhaps, a major release every quarter to multiple releases in a single day. Traditional security checkpoints and processes cannot operate at that speed of delivery. This is where the DevSecOps approach – the embedding of security within the DevOps structure and workflows – and an associated increase in security automation comes into play. Organisations can build security in much closer to the start of the development and delivery lifecycle, hence the emergence of the term 'shift-left'. Security can be embedded in the form of preapproved templates and machine images, the embedding of code analysis tools (static, dynamic and fuzzers) into continuous integration and continuous delivery (sometimes deployment) pipelines, alongside the use of third-party dependency checkers looking at known vulnerabilities and potential license restrictions in any libraries a development team may choose to reuse. This approach stands in stark contrast to the legacy world where developers may be left to their own devices, at least until the penetration test immediately before the scheduled go-live date – which then often needs to be rescheduled to allow the identified weaknesses to be addressed.

Much of this DevSecOps approach can be adopted whether an organisation works on the Cloud or on-premises. Where Cloud comes into its own is the ability to define an infrastructure as code (IaC), i.e. an entire network environment, the constituent servers, security controls and application components can all be defined in code for implementation on an IaaS platform using tools such as CloudFormation, Azure Resource Manager or Terraform templates. Much of the security tooling designed for use in the Cloud can also be driven via APIs, e.g. anti-malware, host-based intrusion prevention systems, firewalling, container security tools, et cetera. Organisations can, therefore, automate changes to their Cloud-based environments, perhaps as part of an automated response to an identified security incident, simply by making code changes and then pushing the updated code through the deployment pipeline (including the embedded security tests). Cloud providers also offer the capability to check for policy drift and, following this, to automatically remediate any such deviations from expected configuration. Whilst some level of automation is possible within virtualised on-premises environments, the Cloud tends to offer a wider range of technologies that can be defined as code; these include compute, storage, security and data warehouses.

Another potential advantage of Cloud and IaC is the opportunity to enforce immutability within their production environments, i.e. to make them unchangeable. This allows organisations to move away from the need to have privileged administrative users in production environments, significantly reducing the risk of outages due to human error. In this model, any errors are investigated in separate environments and then fixed by the DevSecOps teams via the CI/CD pipeline. Further advantages of automation and DevSecOps approaches will be explored later in this book, including chaos engineering and the use of blue/green environments[13] (or red/black if you are using Netflix-derived terminology or tooling, e.g. Spinnaker[14]) to remove the need to patch services in a currently live environment.

Security expertise

Many smaller businesses and start-ups do not have the budget, inclination or identified business need to employ dedicated security staff. A typical large enterprise may require security expertise across a diverse range of technologies such as networking, operating systems, databases, enterprise resource planning, customer relationship management, web technologies, secure coding and others. It can be difficult and/or expensive for these organisations to retain skilled security staff due to the demand for such scarce resources.

Most organisations can benefit from improved security expertise at the provider when operating in the Cloud. The established Cloud providers are well aware of the impact that a serious security incident would have upon their business in the competitive Cloud market, and so have invested in recruiting and retaining high calibre security expertise. At the SaaS level, it should be expected that the providers understand the security of their application extremely well.

---

[13] *https://martinfowler.com/bliki/BlueGreenDeployment.html*.

[14] *www.spinnaker.io/concepts/*.

Similarly, many of the IaaS providers operate customised variants of open source hypervisors and again, they should understand the security at least as well as a consumer would understand their own installed hypervisor.

On the other hand, it would be an exaggeration to suggest that all Cloud providers operate to the highest levels of security. In 2011, a study conducted by the Ponemon Institute and CA[15] canvassed 127 Cloud service providers across the US and Europe on their views with respect to the security of their services. Worryingly, a majority of the surveyed providers did not view security as a competitive advantage and were also of the opinion that it was the responsibility of the consumer to secure the Cloud, and not that of the provider. Furthermore, a majority of the surveyed providers admitted that they did not employ dedicated security personnel to secure their services. Without more information on the providers that took part in this study, it is difficult to judge whether the canvassed providers were truly representative of the attitude of Cloud providers targeting enterprise customers at the time. What is clear is that Cloud service provider understanding of the importance of security as a business differentiator has increased in the years since the Ponemon survey – the market has driven CSPs towards a need to demonstrate their compliance with relevant security standards and sector-specific regulations.

---

[15] *www.ca.com/~/media/Files/IndustryResearch/security-of-cloud-computing-providers-final-april-2011.pdf*.

In all cases, it is advisable to investigate the security expertise available to a Cloud provider prior to adopting their services. Options for investigation include:

- Examination of any security certifications or independent operational reviews of the service (e.g. SOC2 type II reports[16]);

- Investigation of the security materials present on their website or otherwise made available to consumers (sometimes this information is only available under Non-Disclosure Agreements (NDAs)). Major Cloud providers now make much of this information freely available, e.g. Amazon Web Services offers the Artifact[17] service to facilitate download of such materials, whilst the Azure Service Trust Portal[18] and the GCP Compliance[19] page offer customers the ability to obtain assurance reports, which are not covered by NDAs; and

- Investigation of the security individuals employed by the Cloud provider, e.g. looking for past research papers or thought leadership pieces.

---

[16] SOC2 Type II reports examine whether a set of claimed controls are implemented and operated in accordance with those claims. ISAE3402 (International standard) and SSAE16 (US equivalent) replaced the well-known SAS70 style reports.

[17] https://aws.amazon.com/artifact/.

[18] https://servicetrust.microsoft.com/.

[19] https://cloud.google.com/security/compliance/#/.

Knowledge sharing and situational awareness

Cloud providers are in a privileged position whereby they have visibility of the network traffic entering, traversing and leaving their Cloud services, though there are some exceptions, such as situations in which consumers employ encrypted links. This visibility can give the provider the ability to identify an attack against one of their clients and then apply any identified mitigations to the whole of their service, improving the security position of their entire customer base. Although a number of (typically) industry-specific information sharing exchanges do exist with regard to the sharing of identified attack vectors, such forums tend to be limited in scope compared to the vista available to the major Cloud providers. Most organisations will, therefore, obtain more complete protection when using Cloud solutions than when relying on their own knowledge (or that of their partners) to identify active threats. Cloud providers have also now productised elements of their threat intelligence and active monitoring capabilities and they make those capabilities available for incorporation into their customers' overall security management solutions. The best examples of such solutions are AWS GuardDuty[20] and Azure Sentinel[21].

There have been a number of occasions where Cloud providers have informed their clients of a compromise of one of the client's hosted services of which the client themselves were unaware. One example of which I am aware involved a compromised virtual server being used to distribute illegal materials. Some Cloud providers go even further, e.g. AWS helps to secure customer accounts by scanning public code

---

[20] *https://aws.amazon.com/guardduty/*.

[21] *https://azure.microsoft.com/en-us/services/azure-sentinel/*.

repositories like Gitlab and GitHub for the presence of AWS credentials and then informing affected users of any leaked credentials. Consumers can, therefore, benefit from an additional security monitoring and incident response facility.

Improved information sharing mechanisms

There have been many publicised incidents of sensitive information being placed at risk through the loss of removable storage media such as flash drives. The Cloud can be a more secure alternative for the sharing of information, particularly when information is encrypted and decrypted on-premises. Consider the balance of possibilities: what is the most likely event, the compromise of the storage as a service offer of a major provider or the loss of a memory stick?

Renewal of security architecture and segmentation

Moving to any new model of outsourced service provision should encourage a thorough re-examination of the underlying security requirements of the organisation and/or specific service. Business processes and enabling technologies tend to evolve faster than the deployed security solutions. Consider how many organisations still rely upon their stateful inspection firewalls for protection despite their applications interacting using JSON or XML tunnelled over TLS, i.e. effectively bypassing their firewall. The recent Wannacry[22] and NotPetya[23] malware outbreaks both demonstrated the risks of operating flat network

---

[22] *www.kaspersky.co.uk/resource-center/threats/ransomware-wannacry.*

[23] *www.wired.com/story/notpetya-cyberattack-ukraine-russia-code-crashed-the-world/.*

environments with little internal segmentation. A move to the Cloud enables organisations to deploy applications into their own dedicated security domains, reducing the blast radius should any single application be compromised. In other words, should an attacker or a piece of malware compromise an application, the segmentation offered by this approach will prevent the incident impacting the wider organisation. Segmentation can be provided at a variety of levels, from full account level segmentation through to simple deployments into different virtual networks or virtual private Clouds.

A fresh start via a move to a Cloud service can offer an opportunity to renew the overall security architecture – so that it supports rather than hinders the needs of the business – whilst protecting the business from ever more virulent malware. Even if an organisation decides not to move to a Cloud-based service, this process of re-examination of the security architecture and its underlying requirements can still offer real benefits to the organisation.

Potential pitfalls

As with the potential security benefits of moving to the Cloud, the potential pitfalls are also very much dependent upon the relative merits of the current security solutions in place at the would-be Cloud consumer.

Compliance

Compliance is often highlighted as being one of the major potential problem areas for organisations wanting to make use of public Clouds. Chapter 5 discusses some of these compliance and regulatory issues in more detail. Suffice to say, for now, that organisations should take great care to ensure that they remain within their compliance and regulatory regimes. Compliance cannot be outsourced.

Assurance

Cloud providers can sometimes make bold claims about the strength of their security controls; however, it can be very difficult to ascertain whether those claims are valid. From the perspective of the Cloud providers, it is clearly not feasible to allow each and every potential customer to conduct a visit and complete a thorough review of the physical security of their data centres. Similarly, the providers cannot afford the resource to be able to answer a multitude of compliance-centred questionnaires for each potential consumer. Consumers should look for those Cloud providers that have undertaken some form of independent security certification, validation or assurance exercise. Examples include ISO 27001 certification, CSA STAR certification[24] or the results of a SOC2 Type II audit. Now, in isolation, neither an ISO 27001 compliance certificate nor a statement that a SOC2 Type II audit has been undertaken offers much value to consumers. In order to derive any real value from such assessments, would-be consumers must obtain the scope of such exercises, e.g. the statement of applicability for any ISO 27001 certification. The detailed assurance documentation is not always made publicly available by the provider, but it can often be obtained under non-disclosure agreements. This is clearly not as transparent a process as you would typically find in a more traditional outsourcing agreement where the consumer can conduct their own visit and due diligence. However, the need for disclosure control is often a result of

---

[24] *https://cloudsecurityalliance.org/star/#_overview*.

restrictions placed upon the CSPs by the independent firms authoring assurance reports and not as a result of a reluctance to share on the part of the CSPs. The Big Four audit and assurance firms that commonly produce such reports, on behalf of the CSPs, will typically wish to control distribution of their outputs to reduce their own risk from those seeking to place reliance on their reports.

There are other options for obtaining assurance of the services implemented in the Cloud, primarily using vulnerability assessment and penetration testing approaches. AWS, Azure and Google all allow their clients to conduct penetration testing within their own accounts, but not across different accounts. Similar approaches are available for some PaaS services; however, it is not uncommon for SaaS providers to bar any penetration testing of their services.

This does cause concerns for consuming organisations; they may be able to check that their services are correctly configured, but they cannot test the actual barriers separating their virtual environment from those of other tenants within the CSP infrastructure. Consumers must be comfortable with trusting the effectiveness of the controls put in place by their CSPs to segregate their customer environments.

Availability

In theory, Cloud services should offer greater availability than their on-premises equivalents due to their greater geographic diversity and wide use of virtualisation. However, to quote the American Baseball legend Yogi Berra, "In theory there is no difference between theory and practice. In practice there is."

Consumers are well-advised to closely examine the guaranteed availability service levels contained within the contracts of their likely Cloud providers. Service levels tend to be around the 99.5% mark with little in the way of recompense should the providers fail to meet those targets.

In the on-premises world, consumers can aim for higher service levels and implement their own measures to ensure those service levels are met, e.g. backup data centres, uninterruptible power supplies and on-site generators. Just as importantly, organisations can conduct their own disaster recovery exercises by switching across data centres as often as they wish to ensure that the failover processes work correctly. Such testing is not as straightforward for Cloud providers due to the number of clients potentially having their service adversely affected.

Outages in Cloud services are usually widely reported, and this can give an exaggerated impression of the relative stabilities of Cloud services versus on-premises equivalents. Consider how much press attention is paid to outages in the Microsoft Office 365 service[25] compared to an outage in the Exchange infrastructure of any individual organisation.

For smaller organisations, without the luxury of backup data centres, the availability offered by Cloud services is likely to be no worse than that available to them on-premise. For large enterprises that have invested in the hardware to support five 9's availability (99.999%) the public Cloud is unlikely to offer equivalent levels of service for business-critical applications. Private Clouds should be able to meet

---

[25] For example, *www.wired.co.uk/article/microsoft-office-365-down-multi-factor-authentication-login*.

equivalent service levels to traditional deployments, as the private Cloud is dedicated to a single consuming organisation and the consumer can invest as much capital as they need to meet their desired levels of availability.

Organisations considering a move to a Cloud model should confirm any existing rationale underlying expensive high availability requirements with their business stakeholders prior to discounting a move to the public Cloud. It is not uncommon for services to have been assigned high availability requirements 'just to be on the safe side' where business stakeholders have not been able to provide more realistic requirements.

Shadow IT

One of the strengths of the Cloud model is the ease of procurement and implementation, particularly when it comes to SaaS. Any individual with a credit card and Internet access can establish a presence on a Cloud service; this can cause issues in the enterprise space where users may decide to establish such a presence without going through central procurement and IT processes. Such actions can result in business critical processes being delivered by services that enterprise IT has no awareness of, or the transfer of regulated data to inappropriate locations. This lack of visibility and awareness underlies the rationale for the labelling of this phenomenon as 'Shadow IT'. Shadow IT is a common feature in many enterprises as users, or indeed departments or business units, may get frustrated with central IT or procurement and decide to proceed under their own steam. We will cover the use of Cloud Access Security Broker (CASB) technologies to both identify and, then, control Shadow IT later in this book (chapter 11).

Information leakage

The ongoing skills shortage in the area of Cloud computing, and Cloud security in particular, can lead to Cloud usage being poorly secured. This impact is most commonly seen in the number of publicised security incidents relating to poorly secured S3 buckets. It should be noted that S3 buckets are not accessible from the Internet by default; every time you read about yet another organisation leaking information from their S3 buckets it is as a result of somebody, somewhere, having taken the necessary action to open up access to that specific bucket. However, it is fair to say that information stored within an S3 bucket is more at risk of compromise from the Internet than the same information stored within an on-premises Storage Area Network (SAN). A SAN will typically be behind numerous layers of defence which means that a simple single misconfiguration is unlikely to render stored information available to all.

Whilst information leakage is typically discussed in the context of S3 buckets, or very similar storage services, these are not the only sources of potential risk. Consider also Internet-accessible code repository tools such as GitHub and BitBucket. As with S3, such tools can be adequately secured if the relevant security specialists have the skills. However, if the security specialists lack the required skills, organisations can find their source code available to all; in the days of infrastructure as code, organisations can find themselves a single username/password compromise away from losing their entire environment. In short, sensitive information can be stored safely in the Cloud; however, the Internet-native nature of Cloud services will often mean that there are fewer layers of defence in place to mitigate the risk posed by a simple misconfiguration.

Lock-in

Vendor lock-in is a problem with traditional IT; it's a little more pronounced with the Cloud model.

Although significant effort has been invested to improve interoperability of, and portability between, Cloud services, it is still not straightforward to move an IT service from one Cloud to another. The Distributed Management Task Force's Open Virtualisation Format[26] (OVF) is supported by a number of the well-known on-premises hypervisor vendors (e.g. VMware, XenSource, KVM, Dell, IBM, etc.) and related OVA (Open Virtual Appliance) files; essentially, a compressed archive of OVF files can be imported and exported onto the AWS Cloud via their VM Import/Export capability.[27] It is not as straightforward to import or export such images via the other main IaaS Cloud providers. A cynic could argue that it is not in the commercial interests of IaaS providers to make it straightforward for their consumers to switch providers. Third-party tooling is available to manage the migration of workloads across different Cloud providers to provide a degree of portability, e.g. RightScale.[28] An alternative approach is to look to containerise workloads using tools such as Docker, and, then, look to move these containers between Cloud providers as necessary.

Unfortunately, lock-in is not limited to virtual machine image or container formats. What about data? Many Cloud provider cost models involve making it considerably more

---

[26] www.dmtf.org/standards/ovf.

[27] https://aws.amazon.com/ec2/vm-import/.

[28] www.rightscale.com/.

expensive to take data out of their Clouds than it is to place data within their Clouds. For example, AWS currently charges consumers up to $0.09 per GB[29] for data transfers out of their Clouds using a tiered pricing model. AWS do not charge for data transferred into their Cloud (other than the storage costs once the data has been transferred). This becomes more of an issue for any consumers that use an IaaS-hosted application to generate data in which case they may have significantly more data to get out than they put in.

The question of data export is also an issue for consumers of PaaS and SaaS services where data may be stored in specific formats or again be more expensive to export than import. However, data export is not the largest lock-in threat for PaaS. Applications must be coded differently to run on different PaaS services due to the variance in the languages they support and in platform capabilities; for example, an application coded to run on Microsoft Azure would not run on the Force.com Apex platform. Even where PaaS providers make use of the same underlying language (e.g. C#, Java, Ruby, etc.) the available libraries or APIs may vary. This issue is even more pronounced when it comes to FaaS: FaaS applications will typically be tightly bound to the underlying serverless capabilities of the platform, e.g. for storing of state data, persistence of data, access control, observability, et cetera. PaaS and FaaS consumers must, therefore, be cognisant of the costs involved in porting their applications when considering the trade-offs between agility, functionality and portability.

---

[29] This refers to the pricing available from *https://aws.amazon.com/s3/pricing/* for the EU (London) Region on 3 March 2019.

Switching SaaS providers is more straightforward than switching either IaaS or PaaS providers; consumers must be able to export their data from their existing provider and be able to transform this data into the form expected by a new provider. By 'data' I don't just mean business data, data such as audit data and access management information must also be preserved such that security and/or compliance holes are not created through the switch of providers. Finally, consumers must be aware of the potential impact of switching SaaS providers on the back-end business processes. If an organisation has tailored their business processes to reflect the capabilities of their existing SaaS provider, then changing that provider could require substantial reworking of the relevant business processes. Such a reworking is likely to have an adverse impact upon the dependent business services during the changeover period.

In any type of migration or portability scenario, enterprises must not forget the need to have suitably trained resources able to operate the new platform appropriately; this training of existing staff, or hiring of new staff, does not come without cost, particularly when the number of such specialist resources may be limited.

Multi-tenancy

There can be no denying that multi-tenancy adds risk to Cloud services in comparison to traditional on-premises deployment models. Whether sharing takes place at the data, compute, network or application layer, sharing is still taking place. This means that there is a boundary between your service and those of other tenants that would not be there in a traditional deployment. For a private Cloud, organisations may not care that different business units now share a boundary. For a public Cloud, organisations may be greatly concerned that they could be sharing a boundary with their most hostile competitors or other highly capable threat actors.

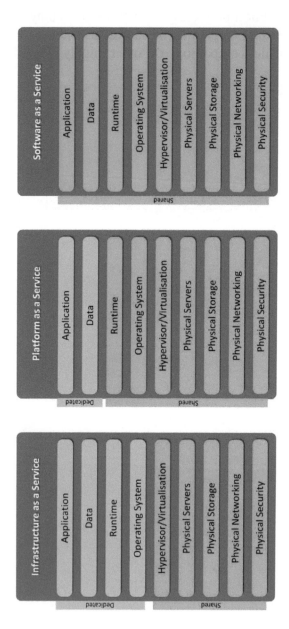

Figure 2: Levels of sharing

Figure 2 illustrates the increasing levels of resource sharing as you move up the IT stack from IaaS through to SaaS, with the barriers between the different tenants sitting in different places depending upon the chosen delivery model.

The issue of multi-tenancy is most commonly discussed at the infrastructure level, particularly with regard to hypervisor security. If an attacker can use a weakness in the hypervisor to jump from their virtual machine into yours then there is little that you can do to protect yourself. Hypervisor security is also, obviously, an issue for any PaaS or SaaS service that relies on server virtualisation to host their services. Hypervisors should not be viewed as security barriers; hypervisors are primarily there to enable organisations to consolidate their physical servers and to offer increased agility in terms of server deployment. Server virtualisation has been subject to extensive research by the security community (e.g. the work of Joanna Rutkowska et al at *www.invisiblethingslab.com*). Hypervisors have not escaped from such scrutiny unscathed. In 2009 Kostya Kortchinsky of Immunity Security discovered a means of executing code in the underlying VMware host from a guest machine.[30] This issue was fixed in subsequent releases of the VMware hypervisor, but the principle was proved – hypervisor hacking is not just a theoretical threat.

More recently, security researchers have turned their attention to security at the hardware level, i.e. the ability to exploit weaknesses within physical RAM or the CPU itself.

---

[30] *www.blackhat.com/presentations/bh-usa-09/KORTCHINSKY/BHUSA09-Kortchinsky-Cloudburst-SLIDES.pdf*.

Bitflipping attacks against RAM, such as Rowhammer,[31] can be used to escalate privileges to Ring 0 (the kernel), whereas, CPU weaknesses, such as those labelled Meltdown and Spectre,[32] can lead to arbitrary memory reads. In a Cloud context, this could lead to an attacker escaping their VM to read memory contents belonging to other tenants operating on the same physical hardware. This is a risk that Cloud consumers can seek to manage by only using dedicated hosts within IaaS Clouds, at additional cost; alternately, they can explicitly accept the risk on the basis that the major CSPs have access to excellent threat intelligence and will usually be part of any such vulnerability embargo process whilst fixes are developed. This was the case during the Meltdown and Spectre remediation process: the major CSPs had fixes in place, where these were available, in advance of smaller players and traditional, on-premises enterprises.

There are other forms of multi-tenancy, each with their own threats. Storage can be shared but organisations need to be aware of the risks associated with iSCSI storage.[33] Back-end databases can be shared, in which case organisations need to be comfortable that the security controls within the underlying database are sufficiently strong. For example, Salesforce.com is driven off a shared back-end database per POD (point of deployment, essentially an instance of the Salesforce.com application) with each customer having a

---

[31] *http://dreamsofastone.blogspot.com/2016/05/row-hammer-short-summary.html*.

[32] *https://googleprojectzero.blogspot.com/2018/01/reading-privileged-memory-with-side.html*.

[33] For example, *www.isecpartners.com/files/iSEC-iSCSI-Security.BlackHat.pdf* (old, but a worthwhile read).

specific Organization ID (OrgID) used to separate out their data through partitioning.[34] Networks can be shared using a variety of virtualisation technologies; Cisco for example offer Virtual Routing and Forwarding (VRF) and Virtual Device Context (VDC) technology in addition to the well-established Virtual LAN (VLAN) technology. All of which leads to increased sharing of physical network equipment and cabling.

As well as the direct threats to confidentiality posed by attackers breaking through whatever multi-tenancy boundary is relevant to your service model, multi-tenancy also comes with some second-order threats. For example, suppose you share a service with another tenant that undergoes a massive spike in demand (e.g. through a distributed denial of service attack (DDos)). The Cloud only gives an impression of infinite resource, there are still physical limits on the compute, network bandwidth and storage availability; such a DDoS could exhaust the available bandwidth taking out your own service as collateral damage. This is more of a risk with smaller, often local providers that do not have the scale of the global Cloud providers and their individual Cloud distribution networks. Another, real world, example of second-order damage occurred when the FBI suspected a customer of DigitalOne, a Swiss-based service provider, of being related to their investigation of the Lulzsec hacking crew. Rather than simply taking the three servers suspected of being involved in the illegal activity, FBI agents unwittingly removed three enclosures of servers effectively

---

[34]*www.salesforce.com/au/assets/pdf/Force.com_Multitenancy_WP_101 508.pdf.*

knocking several DigitalOne customers off the Internet[35]. Whilst law enforcement seizures of equipment are a relatively rare event, it is something that Cloud providers should be able to cater for, e.g. through appropriate disaster recovery mechanisms.

There is no alternative to having multi-tenancy at some level in a true Cloud service – it is this level of sharing and increased utilisation of shared resources that drive the underlying economics providing the savings associated with Cloud models. Even if dedicated hardware is used, the networking and back-end storage will still likely be shared, alongside some level of infrastructure support.

Cloud consumers need to ensure that they understand where their new boundaries lie when they work in the Cloud and implement suitable controls to secure, or at least monitor, these new boundaries.

Visibility

Cloud consumers do not have the same levels of visibility to the network traffic that they are used to in more traditional deployment scenarios. Consumers cannot install physical network taps in public Cloud providers to provide full packet capture capabilities, particularly in PaaS or SaaS environments[36]. Cloud providers will perform their own network monitoring activities in order to protect the services that they offer; however, Cloud consumers must be prepared

---

[35] *https://bits.blogs.nytimes.com/2011/06/21/f-b-i-seizes-web-servers-knocking-sites-offline/.*

[36] IaaS consumers do have some options to use cloud provider offerings such as Azure Network TAP or VPC Traffic Mirroring to capture network traffic as discussed in Part 2 of this book.

to sacrifice a level of network visibility if moving towards Cloud services.

Inflexible and/or inadequate terms and conditions

Most public Cloud providers offer standard 'click wrap' terms and conditions that users sign up to when they create their accounts. Unless your organisation is of significant scale or importance, there is little opportunity to negotiate individual terms and conditions more suited to your own individual requirements. This is an area where private and community Clouds offer more protection and more flexibility than their public equivalents.

Research by Queen Mary's College of the University of London[37] shows that the standard terms and conditions of the major public Cloud providers typically offer little in the way of protection to the consumer in the event of the service provider failing to protect their service or data. Whilst this research is now fairly old in Cloud terms (published in 2011), the underlying themes remain relevant and little new research has been conducted in this area since.

A survey[38] of Cloud provider terms and conditions conducted by Queen Mary researchers found that "most providers not only avoided giving undertakings in respect of data integrity but actually disclaimed liability for it". Most providers include terms making it clear that ultimate responsibility for the confidentiality and integrity of

---

[37] *www.cloudlegal.ccls.qmul.ac.uk/research/*.

[38] *www.cloudlegal.ccls.qmul.ac.uk/research/our-research-papers/cloud-contracts/terms-of-service-analysis-for-cloud-providers/*.

customer data remains with the customer. Furthermore, many providers explicitly state that they will not be held liable to their consumers for information compromise, e.g. even the current Amazon Web Service AWS Customer Agreement (as updated on 1 November 2018) (*https://aws.amazon.com/agreement/*) disclaims any liability for:

ANY UNAUTHORIZED ACCESS TO, ALTERATION OF, OR THE DELETION, DESTRUCTION, DAMAGE, LOSS OR FAILURE TO STORE ANY OF YOUR CONTENT OR OTHER DATA.

Interestingly, given the general concern around the location of data within Cloud services, the Queen Mary researchers found that 15 of the 31 surveyed providers made no mention of the geographic location of data or protection of data in transit between their data centres within their terms and conditions.

One other important point regarding Cloud provider terms and conditions is the recompense available to consumers should their Cloud services be unavailable. Such recompense is usually extremely limited (typically in the form of service credits), and bearing no relation to the actual business impact of such an outage on the Cloud consumer. Consumers are, therefore, well-advised to maintain tested disaster recovery plans even when implementing using Cloud-based services.

On the positive side, the Queen Mary research found no evidence of Cloud providers attempting to claim ownership of Intellectual Property that consumers may upload to the Cloud. This was an issue that dogged the adoption of Cloud computing at the outset, and authoritative research in this area had been lacking.

CHAPTER 4: SECURITY THREATS ASSOCIATED WITH CLOUD COMPUTING

The previous chapter illustrated some of the potential benefits and pitfalls associated with the security of Cloud computing.

This chapter highlights some of the threat actors that may be in a position to attack a Cloud-based service. Some of the threat actors discussed in this chapter are taken from the NIST list of important actors for public Clouds available from:

www.nist.gov/itl/cloud/actors.cfm.

Alternative threat actor lists are available from the likes of CESG/NCSC via the now withdrawn HMG Information Assurance Standard 1 (NCSC currently points towards NIST SP800-30[39] as an example threat taxonomy), and as part of the Information Security Forum (ISF) IRAM v2 risk assessment methodology.[40]

The threat actors discussed in this chapter, and illustrated in Figure 3, should be considered during the risk *analysis* phase prior to any move to a Cloud-based service.

---

[39]*https://nvlpubs.nist.gov/nistpubs/Legacy/SP/nistspecialpublication800-30r1.pdf.*

[40] The Common Threat List (only available to ISF members) *www.securityforum.org/news/isf-updates-risk-assessment-tools/.*

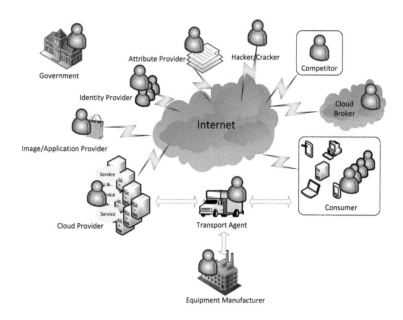

Figure 3: Cloud threats

Cloud provider staff

Whenever a service is outsourced, the client is reliant upon their service provider to abide by the provisions of their contractual arrangements. This situation is little different when dealing with Cloud providers. Consumers are still reliant upon the Cloud provider to abide by their security commitments. These commitments should include appropriate employment checks, activity monitoring, segregation of duties and internal disciplinary procedures. Cloud providers should also be willing to provide details of the internal approvals processes; these are privileged access controls and monitoring processes that have been implemented to control the access of staff to customer data and services. Certain providers have also devised solutions to allow their customers to exercise a degree of control over support access to their services, including Lockbox in the Microsoft Cloud environment[41] and the ServiceNow SNC Access Control plug-in.[42]

Cloud consumers are well-advised to examine their provider's published staff security commitments prior to trusting their data to the provider.

Contractual commitments aside, there is still a risk that a member of service provider staff could act maliciously or accidentally to compromise the security of their clients' data. Whilst there are controls, such as on-premises encryption or tokenisation, that clients can implement to protect their data from a compromise of confidentiality (and from some integrity attacks), there is little that they can do to protect against risks to availability. Should a privileged member of staff at a service provider turn rogue there are few technical controls available to prevent them accessing or destroying data or disabling services.

However, this is also little different to the situation with internally hosted systems: Cloud employees of consuming organisations or traditional outsourcers can also turn rogue. There is one factor that may increase the likelihood of Cloud service provider staff turning rogue; threat sources such as organised crime or intelligence agencies may be more likely to target Cloud provider staff. These members of staff may

---

[41] Lockbox is a long-standing feature of Office 365. Similar functionality is now available in Azure *https://azure.microsoft.com/en-gb/blog/approve-audit-support-access-requests-to-vms-using-customer-lockbox-for-azure/*.

[42] *https://docs.servicenow.com/bundle/london-platform-administration/page/administer/security/concept/c_SNCAccessControl.html*.

present such threat sources with access to more data or services than would be the case when targeting internal staff or employees at more traditional service providers.

Image/application providers

One of the major productivity benefits of deploying services into the Cloud is the number of preconfigured machine images (e.g. Amazon Machine Images (AMIs)), Docker[43] containers and applications that are available for almost immediate use. Many AMIs are now available from Amazon themselves and many more from other EC2 users; these AMIs come with pre-built capabilities for web serving, database hosting, security scanning and many other options.

Security researchers, such as Sensepost, have already demonstrated that it is possible to upload AMIs containing instructions of which the AMI consumers were unaware[44]. Fortunately, the Sensepost example simply used GNU Wget to obtain a file from Sensepost to allow the researchers to track download and usage of their uploaded AMI. It is likely that other backdoored AMIs will be, and perhaps already are, more harmful in nature.

As well as the threat of purposefully malicious backdoored AMIs, there is also the threat of AMIs that were not appropriately sanitised prior to being published. Work by Bugiel et al.[45] has shown that a large proportion of AMIs

---

[43] *www.docker.com/.*

[44] *www.defcon.org/images/defcon-17/dc-17-presentations/defcon-17-sensepost-clobbering_the_cloud.pdf.*

[45] *www.trust.informatik.tu-darmstadt.de/fileadmin/user_upload/Group_TRUST/PubsPDF/BNPSS11.pdf.*

contain the SSH (Secure Shell) user authentication key of the AMI Publisher. This is dangerous for Cloud consumers as such authentication keys give the AMI Publisher access to the virtual machines of the Cloud consumer. I would surmise that it is most likely that not all of these backdoors were left in by accident. Amazon does provide guidance[46] on the steps that should be taken to remove credentials prior to uploading AWS AMIs to the Marketplace; however, this guidance is only pertinent to those not intentionally looking to cause mischief. Whilst I have used the term AMI, the same concerns are relevant to the sharing of pre-built server images whatever the IaaS provider. Similarly, the use of Docker containers for implementation on IaaS or pre-built applications for deployment onto PaaS platforms may also suffer from similar issues relating to backdooring.

However, trust in the supply chain is not a new issue. Organisations must always place trust in the servers, storage, network equipment and the software that they choose to deploy. Organisations will typically perform a certain amount of due diligence and testing before purchasing IT assets and then deploying them. This approach should also be adopted before deploying pre-packaged machine images, applications, blueprints or other templates in Cloud-based environments.

Equipment manufacturers

As explained earlier in this book, the security research community has an increasing interest in exploring the security issues associated with the physical hardware

---

[46] *https://docs.aws.amazon.com/marketplace/latest/userguide/product-and-ami-policies.html.*

underlying all Clouds (and indeed all IT), from the CPU to the BMC via DRAM (Rowhammer) attacks. In conjunction with increased concerns about nation state threat sources seeking to compromise the supply chain (including through the use of physical implants or the deliberate inclusion of physical design flaws), equipment manufacturers should also be viewed as potential threat actors. Cloud consumers must also consider that threat and risk level attribution by national security services to specific vendors may be affected by the contemporary nature of global trade relations between those issuing the guidance and those producing the hardware.

Competitors

There is nearly always a driver to keep certain information assets away from your competitors. These assets could be your latest findings from research and development, your client list or something more prosaic such as your staff directory. When services are hosted internally then organisations can be confident that they understand the barriers preventing access by their competitors.

These barriers become a little less formidable when services are outsourced. IT hardware may still be dedicated to individual clients; however, to drive cost-efficiencies, the service desk and support staff may well be shared across the client-base of the provider. Similarly, multiple client IT systems may be managed by a common management network and operations centre. Even with a traditional outsourcing arrangement, organisations may find themselves sharing aspects of their service with their competitors.

When moving to a Cloud model, the barriers become even less formidable. An organisation and its competitors could now be operating their services on the same physical servers, having their data stored on the same physical SANs and using the same applications or run-times as their competitors. Competitors may, therefore, see Cloud services as a more likely source of competitive information than more traditional deployment models.

Organisations should however bear in mind that the more traditional industrial espionage methods, such as financial inducements and blackmail, targeted at individuals are likely to be just as successful with obtaining information stored on-premise as they are with information stored within the Cloud. As an interesting side note, some businesses refuse to adopt Amazon Web Services as they see the wider Amazon business itself as being a competitor either now or in the near future; I have personal experience with several retail and insurance businesses that have displayed such beliefs.

Crackers/hackers

Crackers have already proven themselves to be a genuine threat to Cloud services – consider the compromise of the Sony PlayStation Network (PSN)[47] as a prime example. In April of 2011 Sony decided to close the PSN whilst they investigated, and recovered from, an attack which compromised the user account information of millions of PSN users. In May of 2011, Sony estimated that this breach of security was going to cost the business around $170m. More recently, Uber (the taxi firm) were compromised in 2016[48] after hackers obtained sensitive credentials relating to their Cloud-hosted services from the GitHub account of one

---

[47] *www.bbc.co.uk/news/technology-13206004*.

[48] *www.wired.com/story/uber-paid-off-hackers-to-hide-a-57-million-user-data-breach/*.

of their developers. The hackers got away with the names and driver's license information of 600,000 Uber drivers, together with the names, email addresses and phone numbers of 57 million Uber users.

Hackers may pose a more direct threat to services deployed on Cloud systems than those deployed on-premises. Side-channel attacks may allow an attacker to identify the physical hardware hosting their target's virtual images; at this point, the attacker can attempt to bring up their own virtual machine on the same physical hardware. A hacker would still require a mechanism like Rowhammer or a Spectre-style CPU-level attack to break the virtualisation barrier(s); however, work by Ristenpart et al.[49] has shown that the side-channel analysis reconnaissance is not merely a theoretical problem. So, whilst hackers and crackers are a threat to systems wherever they are hosted, more attack vectors exist with respect to services hosted on a Cloud service.

Insiders

Insiders, such as company employees (shown in the consumer element in Figure 3), have long been considered by security professionals to be one of the major threat sources to organisations. Insiders tend to be trusted (to some extent) and so granted access to applications and data. Insiders are, therefore, in a position where they could deliberately, or accidentally, release, modify or destroy valuable data. This aspect of insider access to data is independent of IT delivery model and so equally applicable to Cloud services.

---

[49] *www.cs.tau.ac.il/~tromer/papers/cloudsec.pdf*.

Cloud does, however, present a new mechanism by which insiders could knowingly, or unwittingly, compromise the data or services of the organisation to which they belong. Cloud services are extremely straightforward to sign up to and use; all that is typically needed is a credit card and an Internet connection. It is a trivial exercise for an insider to deploy a Cloud service, inadvertently opening up new mechanisms for business data to be exfiltrated or for attackers to infiltrate back-end systems. From the perspective of compliance with the GDPR, it is extremely difficult for an organisation to maintain a complete information asset register, and then apply the necessary controls to those information assets, if they are not aware of the locations where their employees are storing and/or processing personal data.

However, this is not a new pattern of behaviour; similar behaviours were displayed during the rise of the client/server model and during the early days of wireless networking. Proactive and technology-aware members of staff would implement their own systems or wi-fi networks as they found that they could get the IT services they wanted without having to suffer the delays often associated with central IT teams – a phenomenon commonly known as 'Shadow IT'. Cloud computing displays many similar characteristics to these previous disruptive technologies; Cloud services can be quick and easy to deploy, promising more efficient delivery of the services required by business users. Unresponsive or overly risk-averse IT departments can, therefore, exacerbate the threat posed by insiders establishing their own shadow IT services.

Governments

Cloud computing is a global phenomenon: Cloud services are offered from data centres across the world. Many governments have the legal authority to seize data from data centres hosted within their territories. Some governments have even enacted legislation granting them access to data hosted outside their jurisdiction if the organisation hosting the data concerned has a subsidiary based within their jurisdiction[50]. Such legislation is usually justified as being required for counter-terrorism purposes or for fighting the distribution of child pornography. Some nations do not attempt to justify their access rights and simply take advantage of their position in order to maintain order within their populations. Often, the service providers are under legal obligations not to inform the data owners of any such data seizure.

One example of a major data seizure is that of the US government's seizure of payment data from SWIFT, the organisation which facilitates the transfer of funds between banks. It was reported that the US government compelled SWIFT to provide details of archived inter-bank transfers conducted through SWIFT for the previous 4 years. The output from the Belgian Commission for the Protection of Privacy (CPP) investigation of the events can be obtained from:

www.dataprotectionauthority.be/sites/privacycommission/fi les/documents/swift_decision_en_09_12_2008.pdf.

---

[50] For example, the United States of America has both the Patriot Act and the CLOUD Act: *https://en.wikipedia.org/wiki/CLOUD_Act.*

It is clear that the ability of sovereign states to seize data is not limited to data hosted by Cloud service providers. However, it is equally apparent that governments do represent a threat to the privacy of business data, the threat is simply exacerbated by the Cloud model where data could be located in more jurisdictions than would be typical with other deployment options.

In addition to governments making use of the extraterritorial powers that they have granted themselves, there are also extralegal mechanisms that they may adopt to gain access to Cloud-hosted data. Cloud service providers and Cloud management brokers are tempting targets for nation state and nation state aligned hacking groups. For example, the CloudHopper/APT10[51] incident resulted in the compromise of at least nine managed services providers, with the APT10[52] group widely believed to be a Chinese government grouping. Cloud service providers and those offering Cloud-management services must design their services in the knowledge that they will be attacked by highly capable threat actors.

Transport agents

Some organisations have a requirement to transfer large amounts of data for storage and/or processing at their Cloud provider. The usual mechanism for transferring data between the consumer and the Cloud is over the Internet. This is clearly impractical for large datasets. Cloud providers like AWS have recognised this limitation and, consequently, offer services that enable consumers to save their data onto a

---

[51] *www.ncsc.gov.uk/news/apt10-continuing-target-uk-organisations.*

[52] *www.fireeye.com/current-threats/apt-groups.html#apt10.*

hard drive and mail or courier this hard drive to the provider. AWS customers looking to transfer huge quantities of data can even make use of a dedicated 'snowmobile'[53] consisting of a truck pulling a 45 ft long container with sufficient storage for up to 100PB of data. However, whilst not all CSPs will offer snowmobiles, the ability to transport data via hard drive import/export is increasingly common.

Consumers taking advantage of this service require a means of getting their hard drives to the Cloud providers, and transport agents fulfil this function.

Transport agents, therefore, represent a viable threat to the security of the Cloud consumer's data. They are in possession of storage hardware containing large amounts of consumer data which may or may not be protected by encryption, and so must be subject to appropriate security controls, e.g. due diligence, vetting and monitoring.

Identity providers

The use of identity federation techniques is a common recommendation of Cloud security papers, speakers and this author. Identity federation enables organisations to manage their Cloud users' identities on-premises or using Cloud-based Identity Providers (IdPs), and can provide seamless access to applications whether they are hosted on the Cloud or on-premises. If organisations do not want to manage their own identities, they can rely upon public, third-party identity providers (such as Facebook, LinkedIn, Google and Microsoft) via their support for OAuth2 or similar standards. Whilst it would be a brave business that relied upon such providers to secure access to their internal systems, a case

---

[53] *https://aws.amazon.com/snowmobile/.*

can certainly be made to use such providers for consumer-facing Internet services requiring little by way of identity validation or verification. Such a case could be built around improving the end user experience through providing them with greater control over their personal information through enabling them to use identity providers of their own choice.

If an organisation makes the choice to use an external identity provider to secure a Cloud-based application, then they must recognise that a compromised (or malicious) identity provider represents a serious threat to their service.

Note: it is not only human actors that have identities, systems and services also require identities and these identities can also be compromised.

Attribute providers

Similar arguments to those just expressed with regard to Identity Providers can be made with regard to Attribute Providers, i.e. providers of specific attributes associated with an identity. For example, a user may be authenticated to an application using Facebook Connect, but the application may then require further details associated with that identity to make fine-grained access control decisions. Such details (attributes) can be stored within, and made available by, a different service provider. This can allow an organisation to split authentication and authorisation data whilst also minimising the effect of a single compromise on the privacy of their end users.

Note: End users could choose to store a minimum set of data with their identity providers and with each attribute provider to minimise the impact of a compromise of any single provider.

Of course, a compromised (or malicious) attribute provider then represents a threat to the security of the relying application.

Cloud brokers

Some organisations may want to deliver their IT using multiple Cloud service providers to benefit from additional resilience, variable pricing or to meet perceived regulatory compliance requirements around business continuity and exit planning. However, they may not want to have to worry about the quirks of each service that they use. The role of the Cloud broker[54] is to sit between the client and their Cloud services. Brokers can present a single interface for their clients to use to build and operate their services whilst handling the complexities of actually running these services on a variety of Clouds in the background. Cloud brokers can also simply act as Cloud-based systems integrators for those clients looking to outsource Cloud management, even if they only use a single provider.

Cloud brokers are, therefore, in a trusted position and represent a potential threat to organisations making use of their services.

This chapter introduced a number of different entities that could represent a threat to an organisation's Cloud-based services. Knowledge of potential threats enables organisations to build barriers that are effective against the methods likely to be employed by each relevant threat. Organisations can use the threat descriptions within this chapter to check that the security controls that they have

---

[54] Sometimes known as Cloud service brokers or Cloud management brokers.

implemented cater for the threats that they have identified as being within scope.

CHAPTER 5: PRIVACY AND REGULATORY CONCERNS

Alongside security, compliance with legislative and regulatory requirements ranks as one of the most commonly cited concerns by those considering a move to Cloud computing.

This chapter provides a brief overview of the data privacy concerns impacting adoption of Cloud services, primarily those imposed by the EU through the GDPR. There is also a brief discussion of mechanisms to achieve compliance with the Payment Card Industry Data Security Standard (PCI DSS) when operating in the Cloud.

This chapter is not intended to provide comprehensive advice on the legality or compliance status of any particular Cloud solution – organisations should always consult their own legal counsel prior to storing or processing personal data, or other regulated data, using a Cloud service.

Data protection issues

The area of privacy and data protection is commonly viewed as a major concern by those considering a move to Cloud computing. Where there is a requirement to keep personal data within specific geographical borders, it's not unreasonable to be concerned when that data seems to disappear into a globally diverse Cloud. Similarly, if you are worried about certain unfriendly governments gaining access to your data, then again you will be concerned that your data may find its way into their jurisdictions once it is within 'the Cloud'. This section considers the implications of the EU

GDPR.[55] Whilst the GDPR is a regulation, and so directly applicable across all member states without transcription into national law, the regulation does contain a set of derogations whereby member states have scope to make their own provisions, e.g. in the processing of special categories of data. I am not a lawyer, and organisations should consult their own legal advisors before placing personal data into the Cloud. Once it is gone, it is gone.

I will start with a quick overview of the jurisdiction of the GDPR as there are some important scoping issues worthy of discussion. The protections offered by the GDPR apply to "natural persons, whatever their nationality or place of residence, in relation to the processing of their personal data".[56] The scope is also extraterritorial, as outlined in the following extracts[57]:

> Any processing of personal data in the context of the activities of an establishment of a controller or a processor in the Union should be carried out in accordance with this Regulation, regardless of whether the processing itself takes place within the Union[.]

> [P]rocessing of personal data of data subjects who are in the Union by a controller or a processor not established in the Union should be subject to this Regulation where the processing activities are related to offering goods or services to such data subjects[.]

5: Privacy and regulatory concerns

The processing of personal data of data subjects who are in the Union by a controller or processor not established in the Union should also be subject to this Regulation when it is related to the monitoring of the behaviour of such data subjects in so far as their behaviour takes place within the Union[.]

There is an exemption in the scope of the Regulation that is relevant to consumer Cloud computing: the 'household' exemption. This excludes data processing carried out by individuals in the course of purely personal or household activity. This exemption is clearly defined in the following passage[58]:

This Regulation does not apply to the processing of personal data by a natural person in the course of a purely personal or household activity and thus with no connection to a professional or commercial activity. Personal or household activities could include correspondence and the holding of addresses, or social networking and online activity undertaken within the context of such activities. However, this Regulation applies to controllers or processors which provide the means for processing personal data for such personal or household activities[.]

In other words, those using Facebook to manage groups, such as family groups, are exempt from the Regulation; however, Facebook themselves are not.

---

[58] https://eur-lex.europa.eu/legal-content/EN/TXT/?uri=celex%3A32016R0679.

As a starting point, we need to define some common terms used in data protection discussions, the definitions below are taken from Article 4 of the GDPR:

Controller:

"the natural or legal person, public authority, agency or other body which, alone or jointly with others, determines the purposes and means of the processing of personal data; where the purposes and means of such processing are determined by Union or Member State law, the controller or the specific criteria for its nomination may be provided for by Union or Member State law".

Processor:

"a natural or legal person, public authority, agency or other body which processes personal data on behalf of the controller".

Personal Data:

"any information relating to an identified or identifiable natural person ('data subject'); an identifiable natural person is one who can be identified, directly or indirectly, in particular by reference to an identifier such as a name, an identification number, location data, an online identifier or to one or more factors specific to the physical, physiological, genetic, mental, economic, cultural or social identity of that natural person".

In most circumstances, a Cloud consumer storing or processing the personal data of their staff or customers in a Cloud solution would be the data controller. The Cloud provider would typically be viewed as a data processor. However, this may not always be the case. The EU Data

Protection Supervisor has argued in the past that, dependent upon the level of control of processing offered, Cloud providers could also be acting as data controllers. This is particularly applicable to SaaS providers who more or less dictate how their customers can process personal data through the services that they offer. This interpretation is yet to be tested in the courts.

For now, we will work with the assumption that Cloud providers are data processors and Cloud consumers are data controllers.

Cloud consumers are, therefore, obligated to protect the personal data that they wish to store or process in the Cloud in line with their relevant data protection legislation. The GDPR has seven key principles:

1. Lawfulness, fairness and transparency

2. Purpose limitation

3. Data minimisation

4. Accuracy

5. Storage limitation

6. Integrity and confidentiality (security)

7. Accountability

The GDPR describes these principles in the following way[59]:

> (a) processed lawfully, fairly and in a transparent manner in relation to individuals ('lawfulness, fairness and transparency');

---

[59] https://ico.org.uk/for-organisations/guide-to-data-protection/guide-to-the-general-data-protection-regulation-gdpr/principles/.

(b) collected for specified, explicit and legitimate purposes and not further processed in a manner that is incompatible with those purposes; further processing for archiving purposes in the public interest, scientific or historical research purposes or statistical purposes shall not be considered to be incompatible with the initial purposes ('purpose limitation');

(c) adequate, relevant and limited to what is necessary in relation to the purposes for which they are processed ('data minimisation');

(d) accurate and, where necessary, kept up to date; every reasonable step must be taken to ensure that personal data that are inaccurate, having regard to the purposes for which they are processed, are erased or rectified without delay ('accuracy');

(e) kept in a form which permits identification of data subjects for no longer than is necessary for the purposes for which the personal data are processed; personal data may be stored for longer periods insofar as the personal data will be processed solely for archiving purposes in the public interest, scientific or historical research purposes or statistical purposes subject to implementation of the appropriate technical and organisational measures required by the GDPR in order to safeguard the rights and freedoms of individuals ('storage limitation');

(f) processed in a manner that ensures appropriate security of the personal data, including protection against unauthorised or unlawful processing and against accidental loss, destruction or damage, using appropriate technical or organisational measures ('integrity and confidentiality').

The accountability principle is defined in Article 5(2), which states,

> The controller shall be responsible for, and be able to demonstrate compliance with, paragraph 1 ('accountability').

In contrast with the previous iteration of data protection law in the European Union, there is no specific principle relating to the transfer of personal data outside of the European Economic Area. This does not mean that the GDPR does not concern itself with such transfers, rather that there is now an entire Chapter (Chapter V) dedicated to transfers of personal data to third countries or international organisations.

I am only going to discuss those elements of the GDPR that are directly impacted by a move to Cloud computing services, i.e. Principle (f) (on data security) and Chapter V (on the international transfers of data). Other elements of the regulation are no less important but they should already have been considered by any existing processing of personal data. Principle (f) compels data controllers to implement good practice with regard to the security of the personal data that they hold. Cloud consumers should ensure that they consider this legal obligation when they are conducting their due diligence activities in relation to their choice of Cloud provider. Cloud consumers should be able to convince themselves (and others) that their chosen Cloud providers have sufficient security controls in place to satisfy the good practice requirements of Principle (f).

The most obviously relevant articles of the GDPR to Cloud computing are those contained with Chapter V. The GDPR forbids the transfer of personal data to countries that do not provide a similar level of legislative protection to personal data to that of the EU unless some form of compensating arrangement is in place. Personal data can be transferred freely within the European Economic Area (EEA) and also to a number of countries that the EU has approved as having adequate[60] data protection controls – this list currently consists of Andorra, Argentina, Canada, Faroe Islands, Guernsey, Isle of Man, Israel, Japan, Jersey, New Zealand, Switzerland, Uruguay and the US (limited to the Privacy Shield framework). EU-based Cloud consumers sending data to other countries must implement one of the approved routes for international data transfer before storing or processing data within Clouds hosted outside of the EEA.

There are a number of available options for enabling the international transfer of data outside of the EEA including:

- The use of Binding Corporate Rules (BCRs);
- The use of model, standard contract clauses provided by the EU[61]; and
- An in-house assessment of adequacy.

Organisations wishing to use US-based Cloud providers could also consider making use of a Cloud provider that has signed up to the provisions of the Privacy Shield framework agreed between the US Department of Commerce and the European Commission. The Privacy Shield framework acts as a mechanism for those organisations signing up to the framework to achieve adequacy from a GDPR perspective.

---

[60] *https://ec.europa.eu/info/law/law-topic/data-protection/international-dimension-data-protection/adequacy-decisions_en.*

[61] *https://ec.europa.eu/info/law/law-topic/data-protection/international-dimension-data-protection/standard-contractual-clauses-scc_en.*

There is a sister agreement between the US and Switzerland that provides a similar route towards adequacy. However, organisations looking to make use of the Privacy Shield framework should remember that certain industries (e.g. financial services) are excluded from the provisions of Privacy Shield. Privacy Shield is enforced by the US Federal Trade Commission (FTC) and the Department of Transportation (DOT). The financial services sector and law firms are not within the jurisdiction of either the FTC or the DOT and, consequently, they cannot take advantage of the Privacy Shield agreement. US organisations signing up to the Privacy Shield self-certify that they adhere to the framework's requirements and they must also publicly commit to abiding by those requirements. Signing up to the framework is optional; however, once an organisation has signed up to the framework, and made their public commitment, that commitment becomes enforceable under US law.

EU or EEA organisations wishing to use the Privacy Shield framework should also remember that the US Patriot Act and the CLOUD Act trump the requirements of the framework; consequently, if those organisations view US government access as undesirable, they should not rely upon the Privacy Shield to provide reliable protection.

Payment card industry issues

Another common compliance requirement often raised in the Cloud context relates to the Payment Card Industry Data Security Standard (PCI DSS). The PCI DSS[62] aims to set a minimum baseline of security controls (documented as 12

---

[62] *www.pcisecuritystandards.org/documents/PCI_DSS_v3-2-1.pdf.*

high level requirements and significantly more low level requirements) necessary to adequately secure payment card account data within an organisation. This standard is subject to regular updates as deemed suitable by the PCI DSS Council.

Each payment card issuer (e.g. Visa, MasterCard and American Express) defines different tiers of merchants, usually categorised by the numbers of payment card transactions performed per year. Each merchant level is subject to different specific audit and reporting requirements. Level 1 tends to be the top tier across the issuers, and so Level 1 merchants face the most stringent audit and reporting requirements. Merchants processing more than 6 million payment card transactions annually are categorised as Level 1 by Visa and MasterCard.[63] American Express set the bar significantly lower at 2.5 million transactions per year, whilst JCB is even lower at 1 million. American Express[64] also only have 3 levels of merchants compared to the 4 levels of Visa and MasterCard. Some of the PCI DSS requirements that can cause issues in Cloud deployments include requirements for regular vulnerability assessments and an ability to conduct a physical audit of the hosting environment. Penalties for breach of compliance can include substantial fines (e.g. $500,000 per incident) through to possible removal of a non-compliant merchant's ability to process cards issued by the affected card issuer(s).

---

[63] *www.visaeurope.com/receiving-payments/security/merchants*; *www.mastercard.us/en-us/merchants/safety-security/security-recommendations/merchants-need-to-know.html*.

[64] *www.americanexpress.com/uk/merchant/support/data-security/information.html*.

5: Privacy and regulatory concerns

A number of Cloud service providers now claim compliance with PCI DSS[65]; accordingly, consumers using such services can have some confidence that those providers will operate in line with the relevant requirements. However, consumers must ensure that they have complete knowledge of the scope of the provider's compliance so that a cohesive and demonstrably compliant consumer solution can be implemented. The PCI Security Standards Council have published a useful supporting guide discussing Cloud aspects of PCI compliance over at:

www.pcisecuritystandards.org/pdfs/PCI_SSC_Cloud_Guid elines_v3.pdf.

Organisations could also explore alternative options to the storage of payment card information such as the use of third-party payment providers. This can remove most of the PCI DSS burden from the organisation itself as it never actually has sight of the data in-scope for PCI DSS.

This book does not set out to develop a generic solution that evidences compliance with PCI DSS. Rather I'll be showing how security architecture methodologies can be used to result in production of an architecture that takes account of requirements sourced from PCI DSS.

---

65 For example, AWS: *https://aws.amazon.com/compliance/pci-dss-level-1-faqs/*; Azure: *www.microsoft.com/en-us/trustcenter/compliance/pci*; GCP: *https://cloud.google.com/security/compliance/pci-dss/*.

Financial services and the Cloud

A wide range of organisations look to the financial services sector for guidance on what is and what is not reasonable from a security perspective. The rationale for this is that if a service is secure enough for banking it must be good enough for most other sectors. This may be a reasonable assumption for those sectors that do not have particularly strict regulatory requirements. Within the UK, a number of financial services organisations are now enthusiastically adopting Cloud services, whilst the main regulator, the Financial Conduct Authority, is itself a major user of Cloud-based solutions. The FCA issued its guidance on the usage of Cloud computing in 2016[66] and this encouraged a wider take-up of Cloud services across the sector. UK financial institutions adopting such services must also consider the wider requirements of the FCA Handbook, particularly the SYSC8[67] controls on material outsourcing. The European Banking Authority (the EBA) released its own draft Cloud recommendations in 2016, with the final draft of those recommendations[68] coming into effect on 1 July 2018 – from a UK perspective, this deprecated the FG16/5 guidance previously issued by the FCA for those firms within the EBA's scope.

The FCA and EBA recommendations are broadly similar and are, in general, pragmatic in terms of recognising the wider shift towards the usage of Cloud services. However, there are

---

[66] *www.fca.org.uk/publication/finalised-guidance/fg16-5.pdf*.

[67] *www.handbook.fca.org.uk/handbook/SYSC/8/1.html*.

[68] *https://eba.europa.eu/documents/10180/2170121/Final+draft+Recommendations+on+Cloud+Outsourcing+%28EBA-Rec-2017-03%29.pdf*.

areas of the guidance that are unclear and potentially problematic. One long-standing area of concern surrounds the issue of right to access and audit, for both the institutions themselves and their supervisory authorities. It is still uncertain whether the EBA expects Cloud consumers to require providers to contractually guarantee access to data centres in the event of an incident. The practicality of acting on such a right is unclear given the distributed nature of Cloud services, and it is also unlikely that Cloud consumers would wish to see representatives of other Cloud provider clients having access to the underlying physical hardware. Some major Cloud providers do offer their financial services clients additional contract terms and conditions, with a view to addressing the requirements of the relevant regulators. We are still awaiting a firm precedent with respect to the scope of the access rights requirements.

Another area of potential concern in the EBA recommendations relates to the contingency planning and exit strategy requirements. For example, recommendation 27 states:

> An outsourcing institution should also ensure that it is able to exit cloud outsourcing arrangements, if necessary, without undue disruption to its provision of services or adverse effects on its compliance with the regulatory regime and without detriment to the continuity and quality of its provision of services to clients. To achieve this, an outsourcing institution should:
>
> (a) develop and implement exit plans that are comprehensive, documented and sufficiently tested where appropriate;
>
> (b) identify alternative solutions and develop transition plans to enable it to remove and transfer existing activities

and data from the cloud service provider to these solutions in a controlled and sufficiently tested manner, taking into account data location issues and maintenance of business continuity during the transition phase;

(c) ensure that the outsourcing agreement includes an obligation on the cloud service provider to sufficiently support the outsourcing institution in the orderly transfer of the activity to another service provider or to the direct management of the outsourcing institution in the event of the termination of the outsourcing agreement.

Given the difficulties associated with Cloud portability we have already discussed, meeting these requirements for sufficiently tested cross-provider contingency solutions can prove to be expensive if full replication is required. This is an area in which financial services firms currently seem to be taking a more pragmatic interpretation of 'sufficiently tested'.

However, Cloud is, overall, an increasingly popular option in the financial services sector, with many of the challenger banks being Cloud-native, and some of the better known asset management firms being enthusiastic adopters of the SaaS-First model.

Others

This chapter has briefly touched upon the Cloud-relevant issues relating to data privacy, PCI DSS and financial services regulation. This is not an exhaustive set of regulatory or legislative compliance requirements. I believe that the subject of regulation would be worthy of a series of books in its own right. For example, see the Bloor Report available for download at:

www.bloorresearch.com/research/eu-compliance-and-regulations-it-pro/.

This report discusses 33 different sources of regulatory and compliance requirements relevant to IT delivery, which only encompass those which were relevant to the EU in 2010. The situation has certainly not become any simpler in the years since this report was issued.

Government organisations must also be aware of any specific compliance requirements that have been devised by their specific home governments. The US government, for example, have set up the FedRAMP[69] initiative for Cloud providers looking to service the US administration, whilst the UK National Cyber Security Centre (NCSC) has published a set of Cloud Security Principles, which Cloud consumers within the UK public sector must seek to deliver.[70]

The best advice is to consult with your legal counsel and compliance colleagues to ensure that all relevant sources of requirements have been considered and adequately implemented (in line with your organisational appetite for risk) prior to launching new services.

---

[69] *www.fedramp.gov/*.

[70] *www.ncsc.gov.uk/guidance/implementing-cloud-security-principles*.

Part 2: Securing Cloud services – in practice

INTRODUCTION

Part 2 is the meat of this book, providing pragmatic advice on deploying Cloud services in a risk-managed fashion.

This book uses security architecture techniques to drive a consistent, cohesive and comprehensive approach to securing Cloud services. Part 2, therefore, begins with an overview of the security architecture processes that can be used to derive the necessary security controls associated with a proposed Cloud deployment. I then introduce a Security Reference Model (SRM) which provides the basis for discussion of the delivery of security controls across the different Cloud service models.

CHAPTER 6: INTRODUCTION TO SECURITY ARCHITECTURE

Chapter 6 introduces the concepts of security architecture, drawing on well-established enterprise architecture methodologies to derive logical services that deliver consistent levels of security regardless of the technologies used to implement those services. One of the main advantages of adopting this approach is the complete traceability from business requirement to technical component. This allows the business to understand how their risks are managed and the consequences of any move to Cloud-based services.

What is security architecture?

The international software architecture standard ISO/IEC 42010[71] defines architecture as:

> The fundamental organization of a system, embodied in its components, their relationships to each other and the environment, and the principles governing its design and evolution.

Architecture can, therefore, be thought of as an abstract view of a system (including organisations and enterprises) in terms of its component parts and how these parts interact with themselves and the outside world.

---

[71] *www.iso.org/iso/iso_catalogue/catalogue_tc/catalogue_detail.htm?cs number=50508.*

By slightly adapting the ISO/IEC 42010 words we can think of security architecture as:

> The fundamental *security* organisation of a system, embodied in its components, their relationships to each other and the environment, and the principles governing its design and evolution.

In essence, security architecture should provide a holistic view of the security controls relevant to the enterprise or solution. Furthermore, the architecture should demonstrate how these controls are adequate to meet the underlying requirements and identified risks. Conversely, the security architecture should also be able to demonstrate:

- Where requirements or risks are not being adequately managed; and
- Where controls may have been implemented but do not demonstrably meet a documented requirement or manage an identified risk.

Finally, a fully formed security architecture should be able to identify the physical security components in place in an organisation, thereby identifying duplicate security services and driving the consolidation of such services, as well as reducing ongoing expenditure. The goal of the security architecture should be to enable, and not hamper, the needs of the business.

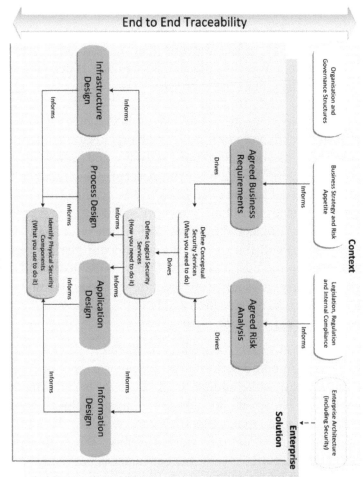

Figure 4: Security architecture process

Figure 4 shows how a security architecture process can be implemented. This process is applicable at either individual solution or enterprise levels. For the solution architecture, I would expect any existing enterprise architecture (including security aspects) to form a further element of the 'context' layer at the top of the figure. This element is dotted within the diagram to reflect the fact that an enterprise security architecture may not be present, particularly if deriving such a beast is the aim of the exercise.

The importance of the context layer cannot be overstated. A security architecture must reflect the organisation in terms of supporting its goals, structures, activities and acknowledging the risk appetite of the business. A security architecture that attempts to enforce an overly risk averse approach on a fairly relaxed business will fail. A security architecture that ignores existing governance structures and which is derived in an ivory tower will fail. A security architecture that blocks all attempts by the business to meet their stated goals will fail, spectacularly. A security architecture must demonstrate how it fits within an organisation and help the business to meet its needs to stand a chance of success.

This is not to say that a security architecture cannot attempt to improve upon existing governance structures or seek to educate key stakeholders with a view to altering risk appetites. However, to do so it must include suitable mechanisms for managing such change rather than simply wishing that the context were different. We will explore different security governance approaches and their applicability in the agile and Cloud environments later in this book (chapter 8); failures in governance underlaid a number of the failed enterprise-wide Cloud adoptions that I have encountered over the years.

Once the security architect is fully versed in the context, the next stage is to ensure that there is an agreed set of business requirements that the organisation is looking to fulfil via the system under consideration. These requirements should also include the key non-functional requirements around service levels (e.g. availability) and hosting. Similarly, the architect should ensure that a risk assessment of the service has been conducted. Both the requirements and the risk assessment must be informed by the context and, crucially, the set of requirements and identified risks must be agreed by the business. This agreement is critical to achieving successful adoption of the security architecture. Business agreement of the capabilities the security architecture must provide and of the risks that it must mitigate helps to smooth adoption of the security architecture by design teams and, in due course, by the end user population.

Once a set of requirements and risks has been agreed, it is then time for the security architect to use their skills and experience to derive a set of architectural services capable of meeting the needs of the organisation.

The process described in Figure 4 could be viewed as being somewhat old-fashioned and tethered to a 'Waterfall model' of project delivery. This is certainly not the case; for example, Figure 5 illustrates a number of options for using the various steps described to support more iterative and agile ways of working.

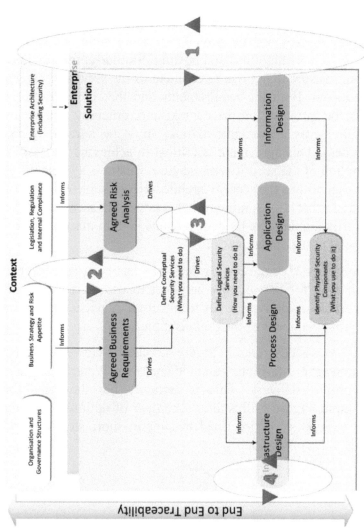

Figure 5: Security architecture process – Agile

Different organisations will choose different styles of iteration; indeed, an individual global enterprise may choose a number of different styles of iteration across different parts of their business. The global analyst firm Gartner has suggested a bimodal[72] approach towards the organisation and delivery of enterprise IT, with Mode 1 relating to areas that are more predictable and well-understood and more straightforward to transform. Mode 2 is intended to service the need for more exploratory and experimental activities targeting delivery in areas of uncertainty. The bimodal approach has achieved some traction within enterprise environments. Enterprises considering the bimodal approach may also wish to be aware of the Pioneers, Settlers and Town Planners (PST) model[73] suggested by Simon Wardley; this seeks to address the potential 'missing middle' between the two extremes of the bimodal approach whilst trying to avoid the stigma that can arise when working in a Mode 1 environment. Whether adopting bimodal, PST or other flexible organisational structures, it is vital that the security architecture approach is adapted to meet the need(s) of the organisation.

Let us look more closely at the four different iteration options shown in Figure 5. In Option 1, the entire solution is being delivered via an iterative approach. This is the option to use for a true 'scrum-based' approach to solution delivery; in this case, product owners are embedded within the delivery team to provide the context information that the rest of the team requires. When dealing with enterprise security architecture,

---

[72] *www.gartner.com/it-glossary/bimodal/*.

[73] *https://blog.gardeviance.org/2015/03/on-pioneers-settlers-town-planners-and.html*.

organisations may wish to consider the more discrete iterations labelled 2, 3 and 4. This would allow the enterprise to continually keep their 'conceptual architecture' up to date via Iteration 2, but it would also decouple the delivery of both the 'logical' (iteration 3) and 'physical' (iteration 4) elements of the architecture. The decoupling of the logical and physical elements is particularly relevant in a Cloud-based agile environment – DevSecOps teams may choose to update the physical components delivering security capability on a regular basis (iteration 4) so long as they maintain alignment with the wider enterprise security architecture.

What is a service?

What do I mean by the term 'architectural service'?

I will be adopting some of the thinking associated with service-oriented architecture (SOA) to drive the security architecture processes used in this book. In line with the wider SOA approach, I use 'architectural service' to describe a self-contained set of discrete and repeatable functionality. These chunks of functionality can then be coordinated (or *orchestrated* in the SOA terminology) to deliver flexible capabilities. To put this into a security context, you could consider a security monitoring capability being provided through an orchestrated set of services including logging, analysis, reporting and event management services.

Now, unfortunately, I cannot pretend to have invented the idea of security architecture, solution architecture or enterprise architecture. Example enterprise architecture frameworks include the Zachman Framework[74] and The

---

[74] *www.zachman.com/about-the-zachman-framework*.

Open Group Architecture Framework (TOGAF)[75] amongst others. In the security space we have the well-respected Sherwood Applied Business Security Architecture (SABSA)[76]. The Open Group and the SABSA Institute have worked together to document how the security aspects of the TOGAF methodology can be bolstered through adoption of SABSA. The methodology I use in this book does not draw directly on any of the processes defined within the aforementioned publications; rather it draws upon their shared underlying philosophies such as their aim of increasing the alignment of technical IT delivery with the needs of the business stakeholders. Don't worry if you either don't agree with the SOA philosophy or do not have great experience with any of the aforementioned approaches – you will still find some value in the contents of this book.

Architectural layers

I have adopted the layers of abstraction defined within Capgemini's Integrated Architecture Framework (IAF)[77] for use within this book. I have already stressed the importance of agreeing the wider organisational and regulatory context of the architecture work; this effort is represented within the contextual layer sitting at the top of the architectural layers shown in Figure 6.

---

[75] www.opengroup.org/togaf/.

[76] www.sabsa.org/.

[77] https://agilearchitect.azurewebsites.net/useful_material/iaf/.

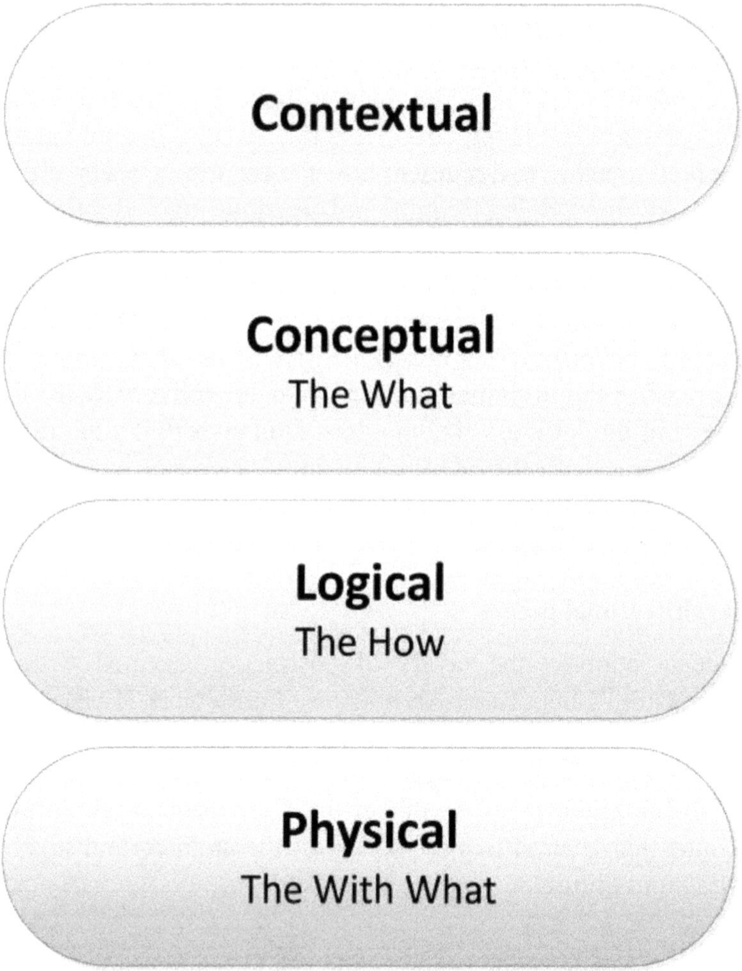

Contextual

Conceptual
The What

Logical
The How

Physical
The With What

Figure 6: IAF layers

A particular strength of the IAF approach is its ability to use the conceptual, logical and physical layers (as shown in Figure 6) to represent an easily understood route from defined business requirement through to defined technical solution.

Conceptual – the what

The conceptual layer of an architecture defines *what* services are necessary to deliver the outcomes expressed within business strategies, drivers, goals. These services must also be defined in line with agreed architecture principles and other elements described by the context. In the case of a conceptual security architecture, I usually define a set of security services that can be traced back to agreed business requirements and which aim to mitigate the risks identified by an agreed risk assessment. As an example of a conceptual security service, let us describe a requirement to limit access to resources to those with authorisation. In order to prevent unauthorised access to resources, there must be some kind of a filter in place. At the conceptual layer then, we can define a *filter* service that only allows authorised access to resources. Note that we have not defined what the protected resources are (e.g. networks, operating systems, applications, specific information objects, etc.) or how the *filter* service should work; we have only defined what the *filter* service must do.

Logical – the how

The logical layer describes *how* to deliver the conceptual services needed through the derivation of a set of independent logical services and the interactions (contracts) between these services. These logical services remain product-agnostic and simply define how the overall architecture should work to meet the needs of the business.

In the case of a logical security architecture, I map these logical security services on to the conceptual services so as to ensure that traceability is maintained. Revisiting the example of the conceptual *filter* service, we must now consider how a *filter* service could work. For this derivation, we'd need to know the resources to be protected and the threats to guard against. At a high level let's assume that we'd need a logical *network filter* (to protect against network attacks), a logical *operating system filter* (to protect against unauthorised use of OS commands) and a logical *database filter* (to protect against unauthorised access to data). It's clear at this point that we also need a whole set of *identity management* and *authorisation* services to provide the *filter* service with the necessary information as to the access rights of users to services and data, but I'll keep our example simple for now! Note that these logical security services remain product-neutral – we know how these services should work and the protection that they should provide, but we have not defined the products used to implement them.

Physical – the with what

The physical layer is the layer at which we concern ourselves with the products, processes and application components needed to implement our security services. The logical layer provides us with a set of functional requirements, non-functional requirements, service levels and interface requirements; the physical layer defines physical components able to meet those requirements. In the Cloud world, 'physical' can also mean virtualised appliances; it does not necessarily mean physical hardware, just the actual instantiation of a logical security control.

For example, if our logical layer includes a *network filter* that must be able to deliver enterprise-class performance, we could consider delivering that logical service using a Fortinet Fortigate 6300F firewall.

These physical components can then be mapped on to the logical services, which are mapped to the conceptual services which are, in turn, mapped on to the underlying business requirements and risks. This approach enables architects to provide complete traceability from the business requirements through to the physical component.

The other main point to note is that it is only at the physical layer that we concern ourselves with actual specific technologies. So, from a Cloud perspective, the conceptual security architecture should be the same regardless of whether the business service is being implemented on-premises or on-Cloud – the goals and aims for the service are independent of the method of IT delivery. The logical layer will also often be independent of physical delivery, subject to consideration of the technical feasibility of delivery! What this means is that the Cloud security architect can then concentrate on finding suitable technical means to deliver the necessary security services (to the levels defined at the logical layer) using appropriate Cloud-relevant components.

Advantages of security architecture

What advantages are offered by following a security architecture approach like the one outlined in this chapter?

Improved traceability from business requirements to security solutions

The security services within an enterprise security architecture are derived from a set of agreed business requirements and the output from an agreed risk analysis. This enables complete traceability between the business requirements (and/or risks) and the security services. Traceability can then be continued through to the physical security product (or process) that implements the architectural security service. This provides an organisation with complete traceability end-to-end from the initial business requirements to the implemented solution. Such traceability is extremely valuable for managing change and for the purposes of internal, and external, audit.

Improved sponsorship and governance

Sponsorship from senior business stakeholders is essential to the success of any piece of architecture work, including enterprise security architecture. Such sponsorship encourages participation from the wider organisation and helps to enforce implementation. Sufficient executive sponsorship and ownership of Cloud strategy is essential for the success of an enterprise Cloud adoption. A failure to have adequate ownership and the associated governance increases the risk of an uncontrolled and/or inconsistent adoption of Cloud services, including the risk of Shadow IT. I am aware of one global organisation in which the failure to adequately assign the ownership and governance of Cloud strategy led to a significant problem with Shadow IT: at one point they discovered that over 6000 SaaS applications were in active use instead of the around 400 applications that they believed were authorised and catalogued in their asset management system. As discussed earlier, organisations can adopt a variety of different approaches towards IT delivery (e.g. bimodal), including the delegation and distribution of control to business units. However, the key to success is to make sure that the delegation and distribution of control are performed in an informed manner, with the threat of a suitably empowered executive ready to intervene should such controls not be adopted in line with expectations. Even where control is delegated, an enterprise may wish to set a few fundamental principles to guide behaviours. For example, enterprises may wish to use principles like a SaaS-First approach; to ensure, as a principle, that all tooling be API-enabled; to prefer Cloud provider native tooling to third party tooling; or to adopt the principle that agility and capability should be preferred to portability. These principles are merely examples, and organisations should define principles suitable for their own needs; the aim of these suggestions is to provide a set of common guardrails rather than a list of definitive solutions.

Improved project success rate

Reuse of security architecture patterns reduces the amount of design work required per project and acts as an accelerator reducing the overall cost of development. In addition, if an organisation reuses existing physical components then there is less risk of unexpected problems with unfamiliar technologies delaying project implementation. The development of a set of pre-approved infrastructure templates and CI/CD pipeline tooling for reuse allows security teams to focus on and address project-specific concerns.

Reduced risk of breaches of compliance requirements

An enterprise security architecture should incorporate the compliance requirements (legal, regulatory and internal) within the context. This enables the organisation to derive a holistic approach to information security. As the compliance requirements are embedded within the architecture, they flow through into individual solution delivery (Cloud or on-premises) alongside the other business requirements.

Ensures security is embedded at the earliest stage of development

A common problem with project delivery is the late incorporation of security requirements into the project development lifecycle and the lack of integration of security architecture with delivery processes of other architecture domains such as application, information and technology. This can often lead to expensive design changes and the shoe-horning of inappropriate security products into the solution. Through enterprise security architecture, attendant governance processes and the adoption of DevSecOps approaches, the organisation can ensure that security requirements are considered early in the design lifecycle alongside any potential reuse of existing security services.

Reduced operational expenditure by consolidation of services

The building of shared security services reduces the complexity and diversity of the technical security products implemented by the organisation. Why manage five different firewall products when two or three would provide the diversity and security required? Why sustain three different identity directories and four different authentication mechanisms? Enterprise security architecture enables the identification of 'champion' products, or at least reusable services, and elimination of the ones that provide little or no value to the organisation, reducing the overall cost of management of the security service. The identification and monitoring of relevant metrics can help to demonstrate the improved cost-effectiveness.

Increased agility of the business to react to new or increased threats as a result of new business strategies or requirements

A fully traceable enterprise security architecture provides organisations with excellent situational awareness including a comprehensive understanding of the true threats, vulnerabilities and risks to which they are exposed and the controls that have been implemented to manage those risks. This understanding enables businesses to consider new approaches to IT delivery (or delivery of new IT services) in full knowledge of the real risks, impact and cost that they currently face. The enterprise security approach enables lingering fears relating to the security of Cloud services to be countered through a reasoned, business-focused approach to risk management.

This chapter has introduced some fundamental concepts regarding security architecture. The next chapter takes these concepts and begins to apply them to the security of Cloud computing.

CHAPTER 7: APPLICATION OF SECURITY ARCHITECTURE TO CLOUD COMPUTING

Chapter 6 introduced some fundamental concepts of security architecture. In this chapter we begin to apply some of these concepts to the area of Cloud computing. The use of a security architecture methodology allows organisations to approach Cloud-based deliveries with the confidence that their security concerns have been identified and appropriately managed. Rather than acting as a blocker, we can use security as a mechanism for enabling organisations to take advantage of the undoubted benefits of Cloud computing.

Security Reference Model

I shall use a Security Reference Model that I have used elsewhere to act as a framework for the discussion of approaches to securing Cloud services. This Security Reference Model (SRM) is shown in Figure 7.

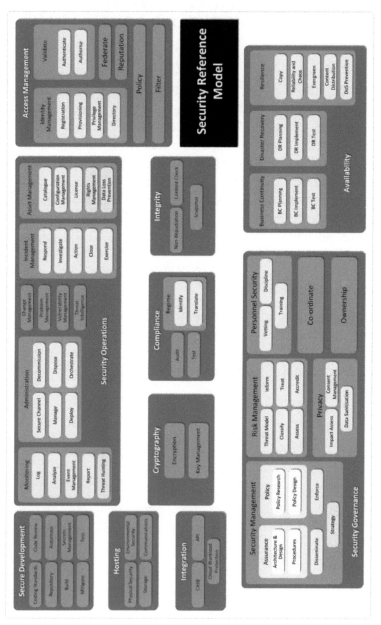

Figure 7: Security Reference Model (SRM)

Using the terminology defined in chapter 6, the SRM shown in Figure 7 is a collection of conceptual security services. This SRM is based on a framework I derived for a real system, but has been extended and modified many times over the years to provide a more comprehensive, generic set of services. Now, there are other existing reference architectures with regard to Cloud computing, notably those provided by NIST[78] and by the Cloud Security Alliance (CSA)[79]. As worthwhile and well-written as these existing models are, they are not sufficiently granular for the purposes of this book. In addition to the architecture provided in their guidance document, the CSA have also issued their Trusted Cloud Initiative architecture[80] which is more granular in nature. However, from a personal perspective I believe that it has jumped straight to the logical level and so loses some of the flexibility provided by working at the conceptual level, and makes tracing back to underlying business requirements more problematic.

The original iteration of the security services within the SRM were derived from the examination of a set of organisational, legislative, regulatory and other requirements together with the output from a business-focussed risk assessment and guidance from a set of agreed security principles. The requirements were grouped together using areas of

---

[78] NIST Cloud Computing Security Reference Architecture *https://collaborate.nist.gov/twiki-cloud-computing/pub/CloudComputing/CloudSecurity/NIST_Security_Referen ce_Architecture_2013.05.15_v1.0.pdf.*

[79] *https://cloudsecurityalliance.org/research/working-groups/enterprise-architecture/#_overview.*

[80] *https://cloudsecurityalliance.org/artifacts/tci-reference-architecture-v2-0/.*

commonality (e.g. requirements relating to audit) to form a series of conceptual services. The output of the risk assessment exercise was used to validate the set of conceptual services, i.e. did the set of services provide an appropriate set of security barriers to mitigate the identified risks? Alterations were made to the services where they were not thought to be sufficient to mitigate the identified risks. This led to a set of conceptual services that the relevant business stakeholders were able to accept as being sufficient to meet both their business requirements and their non-functional requirements arising from the risk assessment. Significantly, this original set of services did not include all aspects of application security within its scope; as a result, the SRM has been through a number of iterations to make it more generic and to keep up with developments in the field, such as the move towards DevSecOps. The SRM now acts as a useful tool for sanity checking that the most common aspects of information assurance have been catered for in any particular design. It must be noted that not all services will be relevant to all applications – the purpose of the SRM is to help its users ensure that there is adequate coverage of those areas that are within scope.

For the rest of this book we will be using the SRM to examine potential technical and/or procedural mechanisms for delivering the conceptual services it defines in the context of an application to be delivered using Cloud services.

Security service descriptions

Figure 7 provides a useful representation of a set of conceptual security services, although the SRM would undoubtedly be more useful if there was a description of what each of the security services is there to provide. These descriptions are provided within Table 1.

Table 1: Service Descriptions

Service Name	Level	Service Description
Secure Development	0	Responsible for delivery of a secure codebase for the Cloud-based application.
Coding Standards	1	Responsible for providing developers with the guidance needed to produce secure code.
Code Review	1	Responsible for peer or automated review of the code produced by developers against the coding standards.
Repository	1	Responsible for secure storage of code.
Automate	1	Responsible for automation of development activities.
Build	1	Responsible for build of code.
Secrets Management	1	Responsible for secure creation, storage and retrieval of application secrets.
Mitigate	1	Responsible for addressing issues raised during testing activity.
Test	1	Responsible for active code testing of modules before incorporation into the main branch.
Integrity	0	Responsible for ensuring that the application runs with integrity.
Non-Repudiation	1	Responsible for ensuring that actions can be attributed to those

Service Name	Level	Service Description
		performing the action (system, process or individual).
Content Check	1	Responsible for ensuring that the information being processed, stored or transmitted does not contain malicious content.
Snapshot	1	Responsible for providing snapshots of known good configurations (function, operating system, application, etc.).
Hosting	0	Responsible for ensuring that the physical infrastructure and operating, processing and hosting of the Cloud application are secure.
Physical Security	1	Responsible for ensuring that the physical infrastructure is in a physically secure environment.
Environmental Security	1	Responsible for ensuring that the physical infrastructure is in a physical environment suitable for IT equipment.
Storage	1	Responsible for providing data storage facilities.
Communications	1	Responsible for providing voice and data communications facilities.
Compliance	0	Responsible for ensuring that the Cloud application meets the legislative, regulatory and internal policy requirements.
Audit	1	Responsible for assurance that the application is designed, built,

Service Name	Level	Service Description
		operated and decommissioned in line with organisational standards.
Test (C)	1	Responsible for delivering security testing requirements to ensure that the application does not contain known or easily discoverable vulnerabilities.
Regime	1	Responsible for defining the compliance regime that the application must deliver against.
Identify	2	Responsible for identifying the legislative, regulatory and internal policy requirements.
Translate	2	Responsible for translating the compliance requirements into the context of the application.
Availability	0	Responsible for ensuring that the application is available when required.
Business Continuity (BC)	1	Responsible for ensuring that the business functions provided by the application can continue in the event of the application itself not being available.
BC Planning	2	Responsible for designing the mechanisms needed to provide adequate levels of necessary business services in the event of a BC invocation.
BC Implement	2	Responsible for delivery of the requirements of the BC plan.

Service Name	Level	Service Description
BC Test	2	Responsible for testing that the BC plan is effective.
Disaster Recovery (DR)	1	Responsible for ensuring that IT services can be brought back online within a reasonable timescale after a disaster.
DR Planning	2	Responsible for designing the mechanisms needed to bring back agreed levels of IT service (RPO) within an agreed time frame (RTO).
DR Implement	2	Responsible for delivery of the requirements of the DR plan.
DR Test	2	Responsible for testing that the DR plan is effective.
Resilience	1	Responsible for ensuring that the service is available as expected.
Copy	2	Responsible for replication of data (including infrastructure as code) across zones, sites or geographies.
Reliability and Chaos	2	Responsible for active testing of resilience through controlled 'failure' of components.
Evergreen	2	Responsible for ensuring currency of environment.
Content Distribution	2	Responsible for ensuring content is made available from a variety of locations.

Service Name	Level	Service Description
DoS Prevention	2	Responsible for protection of a service from (distributed) denial of service attacks.
Cryptography	0	Responsible for delivery of any cryptographic services needed to operate or manage the application.
Encryption	1	Responsible for delivery of encryption services.
Key Management	1	Responsible for ensuring that encryption keys are appropriately managed.
Access Management	0	Responsible for ensuring that only authorised access to data and resources is permitted.
Identity Management	1	Responsible for ensuring that identities are managed securely.
Registration	2	Responsible for ensuring that identities are only created upon appropriate presentation of valid authorised credentials.
Provisioning	2	Responsible for creation and status amendment of identities and associated credentials.
Privilege Management	2	Responsible for ensuring that identities can be assigned the privileges necessary for their function.
Directory	2	Responsible for storing identity and privilege information.

Service Name	Level	Service Description
Validate	1	Responsible for checking that access requests are valid.
Authenticate	2	Responsible for checking that the presented credentials match those associated with the claimed identity.
Authorise	2	Responsible for checking whether the authenticated identity is authorised to perform the requested action.
Federate	1	Responsible for trust infrastructures between federated identity partners.
Policy (AM)	1	Responsible for providing the policy information required for the other *identity management* services to operate.
Filter	1	Responsible for enforcing the access control decisions provided by the *validate* services.
Security Governance	0	Responsible for providing an appropriate governance framework and associated standards.
Security Management	1	Responsible for providing appropriate security management capabilities.
Assurance	2	Responsible for ensuring that services are designed in line with organisational security standards.

Service Name	Level	Service Description
Architecture and Design	3	Responsible for providing architecture and design security assurance.
Procedures	3	Responsible for providing security assurance of operating procedures.
Policy (SM)	2	Responsible for production of organisational security policies.
Policy Research	3	Responsible for incorporation of latest compliance, technology and business developments into policy.
Policy Design	3	Responsible for production of organisational security policies.
Disseminate	2	Responsible for dissemination of organisational security policies.
Enforce	2	Responsible for providing the organisational functions to enforce the provisions of the security policies.
Risk Management	1	Responsible for ensuring services are designed, built, operated and decommissioned in line with the relevant risk appetite.
Threat Model	2	Identifies the threat sources and threat actors relevant to the service.
Classify	2	Ensures that information assets are classified according to organisational policies.

Service Name	Level	Service Description
Inform	2	Responsible for involving all relevant stakeholders in risk management.
Assess	2	Responsible for assessment of the risks associated with the service in scope.
Treat	2	Responsible for development of the approaches to manage each identified risk.
Accredit	2	Responsible for judging whether a system can be accredited for operation.
Personnel Security	1	Responsible for managing the risk that staff may present to the security of the service or data.
Vetting	2	Responsible for validating the identity and references of a candidate. Includes conducting any other pre-employment checks in line with policy (e.g. criminal record and financial checks).
Discipline	2	Responsible for disciplining any breaches of security policy.
Training	2	Responsible for providing employees with the training necessary to fulfil their duties in a secure manner.
Coordinate	1	Responsible for coordination of the security services within the architecture.

Service Name	Level	Service Description
Ownership	1	Responsible for allocation of the ownership of security responsibilities.
Privacy	1	Responsible for addressing matters relating to privacy.
Impact Assess	2	Responsible for completion of privacy impact assessment.
Consent Management	2	Responsible for management of data subject consent status.
Data Sanitisation	2	Responsible for sanitisation of data from tokenisation to anonymisation.
Security Operations	0	Responsible for secure operation of the service.
Monitoring	1	Responsible for monitoring of the output and performance of the security services.
Log	2	Responsible for logging of predefined security event information.
Analyse	2	Responsible for analysis of the logged security information, e.g. to highlight potential security incidents.
Event Management	2	Responsible for management of events (e.g. ignore, escalate or report).
Report	2	Responsible for production of regular reports or other exports of

Service Name	Level	Service Description
		information from the monitoring service.
Threat Hunting	2	Responsible for active identification of threats operating within the environment.
Administration	1	Responsible for secure system administration.
Secure Channel	2	Responsible for secure transit of management traffic.
Decommission	2	Responsible for secure decommissioning of services.
Manage	2	Responsible for system administration.
Dispose	2	Responsible for secure disposal of hardware.
Deploy	2	Responsible for secure deployment of services.
Orchestrate	2	Responsible for orchestration of services or functions.
Change Management	1	Provides security input into the *change management* process.
Problem Management	1	Provides security input into the *problem management* process.
Vulnerability Management	1	Responsible for the active identification and management of security vulnerabilities.

Service Name	Level	Service Description
Threat Intelligence	1	Responsible for the identification of threats to the organisation or service.
Incident Management	1	Responsible for the management of security incidents.
Respond	2	Responsible for formation of the initial response team.
Investigate	2	Responsible for investigation of the security incident.
Action	2	Responsible for deciding and enacting the appropriate course of action.
Close	2	Responsible for closure of the security incident, including documentation of any lessons learned.
Exercise	2	Responsible for active testing of incident response processes.
Asset Management	1	Responsible for management of the IT assets associated with the service.
Catalogue	2	Documents the IT assets associated with the service.
Configuration Management	2	Provides a managed approach to the recording of IT asset configuration.
License	2	Responsible for ensuring that all IT services are appropriately licensed.

Service Name	Level	Service Description
Rights Management	2	Enables control of usage of information within or outside the service.
Data Loss Prevention	2	Prevents unauthorised export of information from the service.
Integration	0	Responsible for integration of security controls in hybrid environments.
CASB	1	Brokers security controls across multiple Cloud environments.
API	1	Provides API interfaces to security functionality.
Cloud Workload Protection	1	Provides a portable wrap of security protection to Cloud workloads.

Table 1 describes each of the different services included within the SRM. The Level column simply refers to a level of granularity – lower level services can be grouped together to provide the higher level services. For example, in order to provide a *secure development* service, it is necessary to consider aspects such as *coding standards, code review, automation, repository, secrets management* and *unit testing*. As stated previously, the SRM is a generic model; experienced security architects are likely to offer different approaches towards delivery of the top level services based on their own experiences and expertise. The SRM is a useful tool; however, I am not positioning it as the holy grail of information assurance!

Service levels and contracts

In our discussions of the SRM so far, there has been no real indication of how the services interact to form a cohesive security solution. Furthermore, there has been no description of how the generic conceptual services can be moulded to provide solutions that are appropriate to a specific purpose or situation. I use a service oriented approach to architecture whereby the security services are as decoupled as possible. This means that each service can be altered without affecting the operation of the relying services – provided that the interfaces presented to other services remains commonly understood. In order to make a security service useable, it must provide an interface that consuming services can access. The mechanism for defining the operation of each of the security services is that of a service contract, as described within the Open Group TOGAF methodology. A template TOGAF-style service contract is shown in Table 2.

Table 2: Service Contract

Attribute Type	Attribute	Description
General	Reference	Unique identifier of the contract.
General	Name	Descriptive name of the relevant service.
General	Description	Description of the service concerned.
General	Source	Origin of the contract artefact,

Attribute Type	Attribute	Description
		e.g. document or requirement.
General	Owner	Owner of the artefact: the individual or governance body that provides authoritative validation of the details of the contract.
General	Version	Version of the contract.
Business	RACI	Lists those who are: • 'Responsible'; • 'Accountable'; • 'Consulted'; or • 'Informed' with respect to the operation of the contract.
Business	Functional requirements	Specific set of bulleted items listing exactly what activities the service performs.

Attribute Type	Attribute	Description
Business	Importance to the process	Description of the criticality of this service to the business – it should be using a common set of criteria and criticality definitions.
Business	Quality of information required	Description of the data quality requirements with regard to information objects input to the service and the data quality requirements of the data output by the service.
Business	Contract control requirements	How the contract will be monitored and controlled, e.g. to ensure that it remains aligned to changing business requirements.
Business	Quality of service	Defines allowable failure rate for the service.

Attribute Type	Attribute	Description
Business	Service level agreement (SLA)	Defines the service levels expected of the service.
Non-functional	Throughput	Defines the throughput that the service must be able to process, e.g. volume of transactions.
Non-functional	Throughput period	Defines the period of time in which the expected throughput will occur, e.g. yearly, monthly, daily, hourly, etc.
Non-functional	Growth	Defines the rate of expected growth in usage of the service (per a defined period, e.g. 10% over 12 months).
Non-functional	Service times	The times during which the service must be operational, e.g. office hours (for example, 9am to 5pm).

Attribute Type	Attribute	Description
Non-functional	Peak Profile (short term)	Description of peak usage on a short-term basis, e.g. 9am to 10am each day.
Non-functional	Peak Profile (long term)	Description of peak usage on a long-term basis (e.g. month end, annual events, etc.).
Technical	Invocation	Description of how the service can be invoked, e.g. service end points for technical services.
Technical	Invocation preconditions	Description of the conditions that must be met in order to invoke the service, e.g. authentication requirements.
Technical	Information objects	Describes: • The information objects that can be passed to the service for processing.

Attribute Type	Attribute	Description
		• The information objects output by the service.
Technical	Behaviours	Criteria and conditions for successful operation, including dependencies. Lists any likely child services invoked in order to fulfil the purpose.

It can be seen from Table 2 that service contracts can be used to define the activities that the service conducts, the information objects it consumes and the information objects it creates. Furthermore, Table 2 shows that the service levels and non-functional requirements are defined by the service contract. This is where the services can be customised to match each deployment situation; a service requiring 24-hour operation with zero downtime will likely require a different technical implementation than one with more relaxed requirements.

Service contracts are incredibly important when defining any form of IT architecture, including security architecture. Service contracts define the levels of service provided by each security service. These service levels will often dictate the set of technical solutions that can be used to deliver each security solution. More importantly, these service levels will often enable a security architect to discount candidate security solutions that simply cannot deliver the required service levels.

I will not talk much more about service contracts in this book. Service contracts must be tailored to meet the specific needs of your application, as this book provides generic guidance it is not desirable to provide a set of service contracts for each security service. Definition of a set of appropriate service contracts, including the required granularity, is one of the critical tasks for your security architect.

Service models and the Security Reference Model

So far, we have talked a lot about the SRM but have yet to discuss its relevance in the context of Cloud computing. The remainder of this chapter uses the SRM to describe some of the differences inherent to the Cloud service models. We will take a hypothetical business application that an organisation is looking to deliver using Cloud services. The actual nature of the application is irrelevant, it simply needs to be an application that could be provided via IaaS, PaaS, SaaS or FaaS models. We will then discuss how the *primary* delivery responsibility for each of the security services within the SRM varies across the service models.

IaaS

Figure 8 illustrates the security responsibilities of the consumer and provider when an application is hosted upon an IaaS Cloud. Appendix A lists each of the SRM security services and provides a rationale for the assignment of primary delivery responsibility per service model.

In the following diagrams, red implies that delivery of the service is primarily the responsibility of the Cloud service provider, green implies that delivery of the service is primarily the responsibility of the Cloud consumer whilst yellow means that the delivery responsibility is split between both provider and consumer.

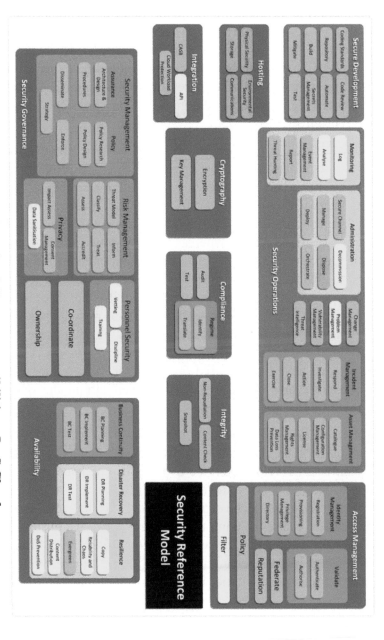

Figure 8: Security delivery responsibilities – IaaS Cloud

Figure 8 is quite clear in showing that the consumer retains primary responsibility for delivery of the vast majority of the security services within the SRM when deploying an application onto an IaaS Cloud. As should be expected, the Cloud provider has primary responsibility for those elements of service delivery relating to the physical hosting environment.

There are a number of services where the delivery responsibility is split between both service provider and consumer. The *filter* service is a good example of joint delivery responsibility; the provider must implement technical controls to *filter* network access to the underlying Cloud infrastructure, whereas the consumer is responsible for implementing appropriate *filter* components within their virtual network and within their application. From a security perspective, the areas of joint responsibility are those where issues are most likely to occur due to a misunderstanding about responsibility handover points. In the *filter* example, it is vital to ensure that all areas where a *filter* service is required have been catered for by either the provider or the consumer and that no gaps have been left in the overall security posture.

Availability is another example of joint delivery responsibility. The service provider will typically provide contracted levels of service availability, perhaps including transparent failover across data centres. However, the consumer must still be cognisant of availability requirements over and above the contracted requirements and ensure that the application can deliver these enhanced requirements. This may include designing in the ability to failover from one Cloud service to another in the event of a major incident at the main Cloud provider.

Note: This is a nontrivial requirement and, in general, it should only be considered where there are strong regulatory requirements that demand this level of workload portability.

PaaS

PaaS is a much more complicated scenario, as shown in Figure 9.

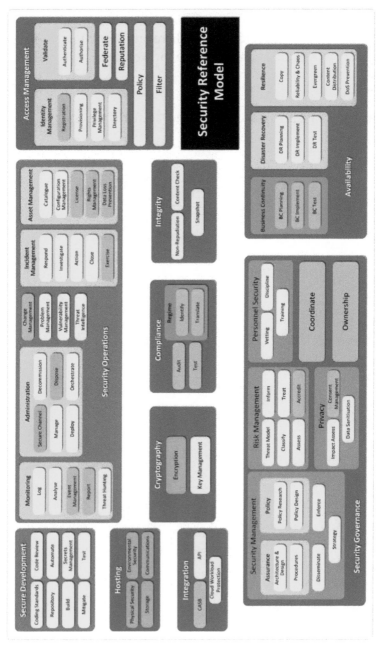

Figure 9: Security delivery responsibilities – PaaS

Given the nature of common PaaS services it should be expected that the vast majority of security services must be delivered jointly by the provider and the consumer. In this example, we are assuming that the PaaS provides a set of security APIs for the purposes of authentication and authorisation, e.g. Azure Active Directory via the Microsoft Graph API. This explains why the primary delivery responsibility for the *validate* services within the *access management* service grouping of the SRM are assigned to the provider. The consumer must call such security APIs correctly, but the coding and maintenance of these APIs are the responsibility of the provider. Consumers of PaaS services should look to those PaaS providers who can demonstrate the adoption of a secure development lifecycle.

Given what I said earlier regarding the areas of joint responsibility being the areas of most concern from a security perspective, it should not surprise you that I view PaaS as the hardest of the service models to secure. After all, almost all of the security services must be delivered jointly and the interfaces and hand-off points between provider and consumer defined and controlled.

Even with the PaaS model, the consumer retains primary responsibility for a small number of services; most importantly this includes the *compliance* service grouping. Whilst the provider may claim to provide services in line with a set of requirements such as PCI DSS, the consumer would still suffer the consequences of any breach of compliance. It remains primarily the responsibility of consumers to protect themselves from breaches of compliance, regardless of the service model.

FaaS

Figure 10 shows that the situation of FaaS is extremely similar to that of PaaS when it comes to security – this is one of the reasons why I tend to view FaaS as an evolution of PaaS rather than as a completely new model.

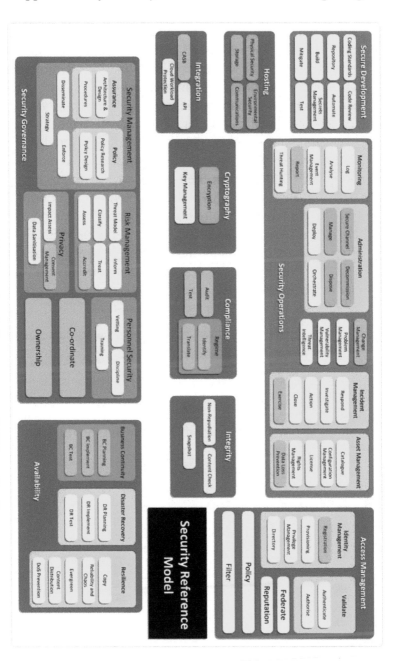

Figure 10: Security delivery responsibilities – FaaS

The main differences between the FaaS model and the PaaS model relate to the ephemeral nature of FaaS functions and their increased reliance upon Cloud provider deployment, management and orchestration mechanisms. As with PaaS, FaaS consumers remain responsible for the security of the code that they create; however, that code will typically make use of back-end services and event triggers offered by the Cloud provider. Significantly, the ephemeral nature of FaaS places more emphasis on the Cloud provider to ensure that they adequately clear down hosting environments prior to using that environment to host functions belonging to a separate customer. Whilst FaaS is very similar to PaaS, the delineation of responsibilities is, in general, somewhat cleaner in the FaaS model – the FaaS consumer is only responsible for the definition of the code to run and does not have to concern themselves with the run-time.

Note: This is not the case when the consumer chooses to use the Bring Your Own Run-time[81] capability offered by some FaaS providers.

SaaS

Figure 11 shows the responsibility split for the final service model under consideration: SaaS.

---

[81] For example, *https://docs.aws.amazon.com/lambda/latest/dg/runtimes-custom.html.*

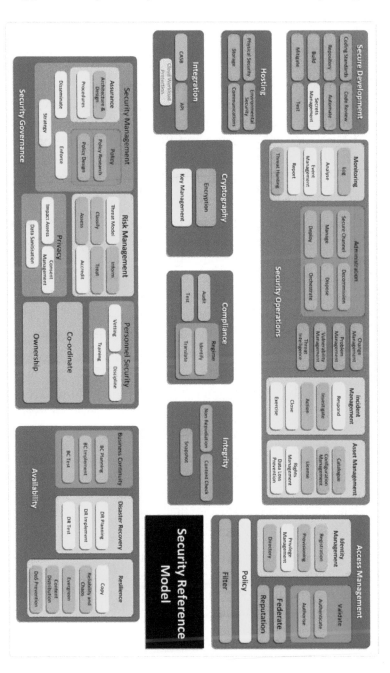

Figure 11: Security delivery responsibilities – SaaS

With SaaS, many more of the security services are now being delivered by the provider. This includes the *secure development* services as the application itself is now developed (or at least tailored and operated) by the provider. You can argue whether or not the fact that more services are delivered by the provider makes SaaS more secure than PaaS or FaaS, depending upon your level of trust in the provider. I would argue that it makes SaaS intrinsically *easier* to secure than PaaS or FaaS, but that this does not necessarily make SaaS intrinsically *more* secure than PaaS or FaaS.

There are some areas of joint responsibility, even with the SaaS model. For example, the *registration* and *privilege management* services are both jointly delivered. The consumer must register their own users and must manage the privileges of their users within the application; however, both registration and privilege management must be performed using capabilities delivered by the provider.

Conclusion

The aim of this chapter was to show how security architecture methodologies can be used to enable organisations to move towards Cloud computing.

The discussion regarding the SRM has shown how security architecture can be used to identify potential areas of concern within the different service models, i.e. those areas where gaps may appear between the services delivered by the provider and those retained by the consumer.

In summary, the last two chapters have provided a high-level approach to the definition of a set of technical and procedural requirements to appropriately secure a Cloud service, based on architecture techniques. The most important components of this approach include:

- Deriving and agreeing the business and non-functional requirements relating to security;
- Performing a risk assessment of the application;
- Identifying any existing or required security principles;
- Identifying a set of conceptual security services derived from the requirements set, the risk assessment and the security principles;
- Drawing up a series of service contracts relating to the identified services;
- Elaborating the conceptual services into a series of logical services; and
- Determining appropriate technical and procedural controls to deliver the logical services, in line with the requirements of the service contracts.

This approach results in the production of a Cloud service that is demonstrably secured according to the needs of the business.

The next four chapters of this book delve into a little more detail in terms of the practical resources and mechanisms available to secure Cloud services. The services described within the SRM are explored for each of the service models and example mechanisms for delivering these services are proposed.

CHAPTER 8: SECURITY AND THE CLOUD

This chapter begins with a brief overview of the existing guidance available to those with an interest in Cloud security. I then propose mechanisms for delivering those security services within the SRM – see Figure 7 – that are common to all three traditional Cloud service models, and where the delivery of those services is not overly impacted by the choice of service model.

Finally, this chapter also discusses the relative merits of the different Cloud deployment models from a security point of view.

Existing guidance

Cloud computing has been growing in popularity and acceptability over the last decade or so; more than enough time for a number of different organisations to produce guidance in the area of Cloud security. The most established guidance document is arguably that produced by the Cloud Security Alliance (CSA)[82]; this group was originally formed in 2009 by a small number of individual volunteers but it now comprises hundreds of corporate members and tens of thousands of individual members. The CSA document, "Security Guidance for Critical Areas of Focus in Cloud Computing" is in its fourth iteration at the time of writing,

---

[82] https://cloudsecurityalliance.org/. In the interests of transparency, I should note that I chair the UK Chapter of the Cloud Security Alliance at the time of writing.

and now presents a relatively mature set of guidance across 14 different domains from architecture through to incident response. The CSA guidance is a must-read document, not least because it also represents a major element of the syllabus for the Certificate of Cloud Security Knowledge (CCSK), the vendor-neutral Cloud security certification offered by the CSA. The guidance within the CSA document has evolved over the years and is now more practical and deliverable than that offered by previous iterations. In addition to the security guidance document and the CCSK, the CSA also hosts around forty other initiatives relating to Cloud security, with the most prominent including:

- Cloud Controls Matrix (CCM);
- Consensus Assessments Initiative Questionnaire (CAIQ);
- Top Threats; and
- CSA Security, Trust and Assurance Registry (STAR).

Of all of the CSA initiatives, I would particularly recommend readers to investigate the CCM, CAIQ and STAR. The CCM has practically become a de facto standard for organisations building secure Cloud services, whilst the CAIQ is the most common approach used to ascertain compliance with the CCM. The CAIQ is also widely used because it includes a mapping of the CCM onto other well-known information security standards, such as COBIT, ISO 27001 and PCI DSS – this mapping across the standards is useful even outside of the Cloud context.

The CSA STAR[83] initiative is one of the more valuable repositories of Cloud security information on the Internet. Its registry allows Cloud providers the opportunity to describe how they deliver the security elements of their offers using the format of completed CAIQs. There are three different levels of assurance available, from simple self-assertion (Level 1) through to continuous independent assurance (Level 3). STAR Level 2 introduces the use of independent third-party auditors to certify compliance with the CCM. This can be achieved through either STAR Attestation, which blends SOC 2 requirements from the AICPA Trust Service Principles (AT 101) and the CCM, or STAR Certification, which blends the requirements of the ISO/IEC 27001:2013 with those of the CCM. Most of the major Cloud providers across all service models now have an entry on the registry, which can be found here:

https://cloudsecurityalliance.org/star/registry.

CSA STAR entries often represent the most comprehensive view of Cloud provider security capabilities available to those charged with conducting the due diligence activities associated with Cloud adoption – they are only rivalled by SOC2 Type II reports. Organisations are strongly recommended to review the STAR entries prior to procuring or building upon a Cloud service.

---

[83] *https://cloudsecurityalliance.org/research/initiatives/star-registry/.*

The CCSK certification is now in its fourth iteration; it tests candidates' knowledge of the latest version of the CSA security guidance document together with knowledge of "Benefits, risks and recommendations for information security", a risk assessment document [84] produced by the European Network and Information Security Agency (ENISA) and the CCM. This risk assessment document is only one of a number of interesting publications that ENISA have produced. Another ENISA document containing some worthwhile guidance is the "Security and Resilience in Governmental Clouds"[85] document which includes a Strength, Weakness, Opportunity, Threat (SWOT) analysis with regard to the different deployment models, in a government context. The main landing page for ENISA's work on Cloud can be found at:

www.enisa.europa.eu/topics/cloud-and-big-data/cloud-security.

I have made extensive use of the work of NIST within this book, primarily their definitions of the Cloud service and delivery models. NIST also have a proud history of producing security guidelines, particularly in the area of operating system security. As you may expect then, given their work with Cloud computing and security, NIST have produced their own special publication on the security of Cloud computing: Special Publication 800-144, entitled "Guidelines on Security and Privacy in Public Cloud

---

[84] *www.enisa.europa.eu/act/rm/files/deliverables/cloud-computing-risk-assessment/at_download/fullReport*.

[85] *www.enisa.europa.eu/act/rm/emerging-and-future-risk/deliverables/security-and-resilience-in-governmental-clouds*.

Computing"[86] provides a good overview of the security issues associated with the use of public Cloud computing services.

Governments have been eager adopters of Cloud services, with the UK government adopting a strategic principle of Cloud First back in 2013. Unsurprisingly, governments have stringent security requirements, particularly with respect to classified data; for this reason, government guidance is a good source of inspiration for those organisations looking to implement secure Cloud services. The UK National Cyber Security Centre (NCSC) has published a widely adopted set of 14 Cloud Security Principles[87] and associated implementation principles. The principles are wide-ranging and cover both largely Cloud-specific issues, such as 'separation between users' (i.e. multi-tenancy considerations), and more traditional security elements, such as 'identity and authentication' in the context of Cloud usage. The US government has also been a keen adopter of Cloud services, and the US approach towards adoption of Cloud has been guided by the FedRAMP approvals process. There is a comprehensive collection of Cloud security guidance available for those organisations seeking to comply with FedRAMP available from the FedRAMP website.[88] As with the NCSC Cloud security principles, the FedRAMP guidance is widely applicable outside of the government arena.

---

[86] *https://csrc.nist.gov/publications/detail/sp/800-144/final*.

[87] *www.ncsc.gov.uk/collection/cloud-security?curPage=/collection/cloud-security/implementing-the-cloud-security-principles*.

[88] *www.fedramp.gov/documents/*.

The final vendor-neutral organisation that I will mention here, in the context of generic advice, is the Open Group. One of the first Open Group outputs in the area of Cloud security was the "Security Principles for Cloud and SOA" whitepaper produced by the Cloud computing workgroup[89]. This whitepaper presents a series of security principles, in the format recommended by TOGAF 9, designed to guide the secure development of service-oriented architectures implemented in the Cloud. The security principles it describes are also often relevant to other forms of Cloud deployments. A more recent output is the Cloud Computing Ecosystem Model[90]which provides guidance to architects developing enterprise architectures that include the use of Cloud services.

That concludes my brief round-up of some of the existing guidance (and wider initiatives) with regard to the security of Cloud computing. The next few pages provide some more detailed guidance on how a number of security services common to all service models may be implemented.

Common security services

In general, the security services defined within the SRM will be delivered differently per service model. However, a number of the security services are technology-agnostic and so independent of Cloud service model. This section provides guidance on how these more procedural and/or organisational services may be provided.

---

[89]*https://publications.opengroup.org/review/product/list/id/89/category/66/*.

[90]*www.opengroup.org/cloud/cloud_ecosystem_rm/index.htm*.

Hosting

In the SRM, the hosting service grouping is composed of the following services:

- *Physical Security*
- *Environmental Security*
- *Storage*
- *Communications*

Regardless of service model, these *hosting* services will always be delivered by the Cloud service provider (CSP).

Consumers should ensure that the physical security mechanisms employed by the CSP are sufficient to meet their requirements. This should not just be limited to the external perimeter security; consumers should ensure that the CSP data centres also include adequate internal security mechanisms, including internal access controls, internal security monitoring (CCTV, passive infra-red intruder detection systems, logging of access to sensitive security zones, et cetera) and suitable procedures governing visitor access. Consumers are unlikely to be able to conduct their own physical audits to confirm that these controls are in place and they will usually be reliant upon independently assessed assurance mechanisms, e.g. SOC2 Type II reports, ISO 27001 certification or CSA STAR entries. In addition to the external and internal physical security of the building, consumers should also content themselves that the CSP data centres are located in areas that are secure from multiple perspectives. Issues that should be considered include:

- **Environmental threats** – earthquakes, volcanic eruptions, flooding, severe weather;

- **Civil unrest** – are the data centres located in stable political locations?
- **Government intrusion** – are the data centres located in countries where government access represents an acceptable threat?
- **Transport** – flight paths.
- **Resource availability** – is there a sufficient pool of skilled resource available?

Some CSPs do not help themselves by keeping information regarding the location and physical security mechanisms of their sites out of the public domain. Consumers should be wary of CSPs that are unwilling to share such information, particularly if such information is still not available under non-disclosure agreements.

As with the physical security aspects, consumers should (where possible) ensure that they are content with the environmental controls implemented by the CSP. In the context of the SRM, environmental controls refer to those controls used to maintain a suitable environment for the IT equipment in terms of cooling, resilient and redundant power supplies and humidity controls. Those organisations with specific carbon reduction, or other 'green' targets, may also be interested in the efficiency ratings of the CSP data centres. Again, this information is not always available from the CSPs. However, a number of CSPs make the efficiency of their data centres a key point of pride and a selling point, e.g. Salesforce.com[91] and Google Cloud[92].

---

[91] *www.salesforce.com/company/sustainability/*.

[92] *https://cloud.google.com/sustainability/?hl=sr*.

Another key element of the *hosting* service grouping offered by CSPs, of all description, relates to *storage*; it concerns whether IaaS, PaaS, SaaS or FaaS consumers are likely to need to store data within the CSP Cloud, and, consequently, within the CSP data centres. Whilst consumers may be able to secure their data via on-premises encryption or tokenisation (depending on the Cloud service), in other cases consumers will be reliant upon the storage security provided by the CSP. Where possible, consumers should content themselves with the mechanisms used by the CSP to secure their data when stored within the CSP Cloud. This should include examination of:

- The access controls to the underlying storage systems;
- The mechanisms separating data belonging to different consumers;
- The support mechanisms for the storage (this should include ascertaining whether customer data can be taken off-site should storage failure require investigation by the storage vendor); and
- The capabilities provided to consumers to remove their data from the CSP and how such 'deleted' data is managed by the CSP.

The final *hosting* service within the SRM is *communications*. Consumers should ensure that the CSP data centres have multiple communications links to ensure that their service remains available in the event of a network failure. As with the other hosting elements described in this section, such information is not always going to be available from the CSPs. In the event that such information is not available from their CSP, consumers must balance the risk of the service (or services) not meeting their requirements against the expected benefits of the Cloud service. Such a lack of information should not lead to automatic disqualification of potential CSPs, *unless* the consumer has specific critical requirements that demand absolute certainty of the mechanisms used to deliver those requirements.

Compliance

Compliance is still perceived to be one of the major barriers to the adoption of Cloud services within enterprises, particularly in more risk-averse and/or more heavily regulated sectors. However, Cloud services are now widely adopted within government and are increasingly being adopted by financial services organisations; this shows that perceived compliance issues can be overcome, at least within the risk appetites of the organisations concerned. In the UK, many of the retail banking giants are increasingly adopting Cloud services, for example HSBC Bank is now working on the principle of Cloud First,[93] whilst Lloyds Bank is adopting a more hybrid approach via IBM, AWS and Google. Whilst some of this adoption may be driven by increasing comfort with the Cloud model, it is also likely that the established banks are starting to feel the pressure of competing with more agile challenger banks that are typically more Cloud native in their approach. OakNorth, for example, is a poster child for Cloud in the financial services sector and has built its core banking systems on AWS.[94]

---

[93] *www.computerweekly.com/news/450418305/HSBC-adopts-cloud-first-strategy-to-solving-big-data-business-problems*.

[94] *www.finextra.com/newsarticle/28952/oaknorth-moves-core-banking-backbone-to-amazon-web-services-cloud*.

Chapter 5 discussed some of the compliance issues associated with Cloud computing, particularly with regard to data privacy and issues relating to compliance with PCI DSS requirements. Compliance is not a trivial subject to address, particularly for global enterprises. For example, the following link lists the data protection legislation of over 50 countries:

www.informationshield.com/intprivacylaws.html.

It is my view that compliance as a whole cannot be outsourced, which is why I have suggested that *compliance* remains the primary delivery responsibility of the client regardless of service model within Figures 8, 9, 10 and 11. I do not dispute that consumers may outsource the delivery of their IT services to providers offering compliant services, or that certain activities relating to the assurance of Cloud services may also be outsourced. However, should the consumer or provider suffer a breach of compliance the consumer would still suffer the consequences such as loss of reputation and potential fines. The organisation always retains accountability for their own compliance and so, in my reference model, they also retain responsibility for ensuring that their services are delivered in a secure manner.

Whilst a growing number of CSPs can legitimately claim to offer services that are compliant with standards such as PCI DSS (subject to very specific scopes), the consumer will still suffer the consequences should the systems that they build on such services become non-compliant. Such a situation could easily arise due to a misunderstanding of the scope of the compliance achieved by their CSP. Cloud consumers cannot insulate themselves entirely from the impacts of being found in breach of their compliance requirements.

Within the SRM, the *compliance* service grouping consists of five services:

1. *Audit*
2. *Test*
3. *Regime*
4. *Identify*
5. *Translate*

So, how does this work in practice? Of these services, by far the most important, and hardest to deliver, is the *regime* service. This is the service that is responsible for defining the compliance regime and so sets the boundaries for the activities that are acceptable. In order to set the compliance regime, two different conceptual services are suggested: the *identify* and *translate* services. These two services perform two different, but equally critical, tasks in terms of defining the compliance regime. The *identify* service is responsible for identification of all of the different compliance requirements; such requirements can be sourced from national legislation, industry regulation, organisational policies and other sources. I would recommend that the set of source requirements be validated by a qualified legal advisor to provide assurance that the set is defensibly comprehensive. Once a set of requirements has been identified, it is then necessary to place these requirements into context. For example, principle (e) of the GDPR requires that personal data be:

> kept in a form which permits identification of data subjects for no longer than is necessary for the purposes for which the personal data are processed; personal data may be stored for longer periods insofar as the personal data will be processed solely for archiving purposes in the

public interest, scientific or historical research purposes or statistical purposes subject to implementation of the appropriate technical and organisational measures required by the GDPR in order to safeguard the rights and freedoms of individuals ('storage limitation')[.][95]

What does this text mean in the context of your application? How do we get from legalese to a testable requirement? The purpose of the *translate* service is to turn the typically generic language used in legislation and regulation into something relevant to the task at hand.

Now, you may be thinking that this all sounds like the production of mountains of paperwork that would severely impact upon the agility, flexibility and time to market that a move to Cloud is supposed to provide. At this point, I should highlight that I do not think it would be necessary for the *compliance* service as a whole to be delivered by every single Cloud project. ICT delivery projects rarely occur within an organisational vacuum, and most organisations should already be aware of their compliance requirements; in this situation, the *translate* service becomes critical for individual project and/or service delivery. That is to say that the key task is to translate the existing, known compliance requirements into testable requirements tailored for the Cloud-based service currently under consideration.

---

[95] https://ico.org.uk/for-organisations/guide-to-data-protection/guide-to-the-general-data-protection-regulation-gdpr/principles/.

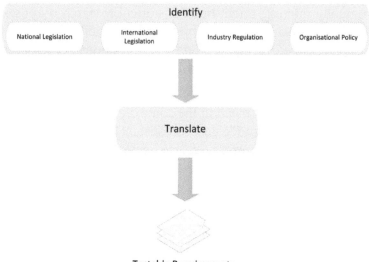

Figure 12: Compliance process

This process of generating a set of testable requirements is shown in Figure 12. Once you have a set of requirements, you can then test whether or not the Cloud services under consideration can meet those requirements. It is vital that the consumer pays close attention to the service levels promised by the provider alongside the liabilities and penalties for failure to meet these targets. There is little incentive (other than reputation management) for Cloud providers to meet strict service levels if their standard terms and conditions limit their liabilities for failing to meet the advertised service levels. Consumers should be wary of the advertised service levels and be comfortable with the possibility of the service levels not always being met. If you are comfortable with the likely *actual* service levels (and many reputable providers offer the capability to monitor their service level history), then you can go ahead and design your service with the comfort that your compliance requirements can be met – so long as you do your own job adequately.

Aside from the use of the SRM, there are some more straight-forward, practical steps that enterprises can take to adhere to strict data protection rules. The simplest mechanism for ensuring that your data does not leave the legal regime of your choice is using a local Cloud supplier, i.e. one hosted within your own country, often referred to as 'sovereign' Cloud providers. For example, there are a number of Cloud suppliers[96] within the UK that only operate data centres within the UK; such suppliers are not going to place your data at risk of being transferred overseas (although there is no guarantee that IP packets between your on-premises systems and the Cloud provider will not be routed overseas). An alternative route would be for the consumer to build their own private Cloud and host this Cloud within the location of their choice. Of course, this latter option requires more initial investment and would not be suitable for those looking to take advantage of the full range of services available from public Cloud providers. The major Cloud providers are now offering some options that work as a compromise between on-premises and on-Cloud models; these include 'Cloud in a box' preconfigured hardware for deployment on-premises, such as Azure Stack or AWS Outposts, which organisations adopting a hybrid Cloud model may find worthy of consideration.

Security governance

The *security governance* service grouping is one of the largest within the SRM catering for:

---

[96] For example, UK Cloud: *https://ukcloud.com/*.

- *Security management*;
- *Risk management*;
- *Privacy*; and
- *Personnel security*.

The security governance grouping also includes a service called *ownership*. *Ownership* relates to the need for those organisations deploying in the Cloud to ensure that the ownership of specific responsibilities and accountabilities has been assigned. I have seen numerous Cloud strategies fail due to a lack of appropriate ownership. Symptoms of such a lack of ownership may include:

- Rampant Shadow IT due to a lack of governance and control;
- An abundance of Cloud environments across a variety of authorised Cloud providers due to the lack of a standard approach to deployment;
- A lack of accountability for the success or failure of Cloud projects;
- A lack of clear principles, policies, standards or other ways of working;
- The proliferation and duplication of tooling and management structures.

Enterprises adopting Cloud must define their ownership structures as early in the Cloud adoption process as they can. These ownership structures can be delegated and distributed; there does not need to be a single centralised owner. However, there does need to be a single centralised view of that ownership structure. Some possible ownership roles include:

- Cloud strategy;
- Cloud risk;
- Cloud architecture; and
- Cloud operations.

Once allocated, it is the responsibility of the role owners to ensure that the wider enterprise (or their allocated business units) is able to maintain a level of control and accountability around success and failure.

There is also one more service included within the *security governance* grouping and that is *coordinate*. Whilst the primary responsibility for delivery of the security services described within the SRM may change depending upon the chosen service model, the *coordinate* service must always sit with the consumer. The purpose of the *coordinate* service is to ensure that all of the other security services relevant to the application work together as a cohesive unit regardless of who bears primary responsibility for delivery. I strongly recommend that consuming organisations assign responsibility for coordination of security across on-premises and on-Cloud services to a named individual or team, perhaps the Cloud risk owner listed earlier. This will help to ensure that a close interest is maintained in the cohesiveness and effectiveness of the overall security architecture (Cloud and on-premises).

The *security management* service is an interesting one in the context of Cloud, digital transformation and DevSecOps. If your enterprise is adopting multi-model IT, perhaps the Gartner bimodal approach or Wardley's PST model, then your approach to security must be cognisant of the need to support these different modes of working. For example, for Mode 1 services, typically those that are more stable, a traditional security management structure may be appropriate (see Figure 13 below).

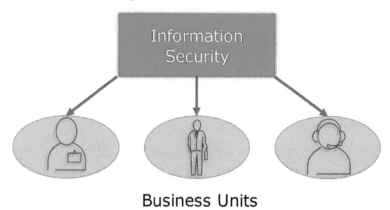

Business Units

Figure 13: Mode 1 – Traditional approach

In this situation, the central information security team may retain responsibility for policy and standard setting, monitoring compliance with those policies and standards, and for the delivery of security operations. This is very much the traditional security approach to the security function: providing projects and programmes with the security requirements that they must deliver – the 'thou shalt' approach. This approach does not scale to the agile, multiple releases per day way of working featured in Mode 2. A new approach is required.

Business Units

Figure 14: Mode 2 – Distributed approach

Figure 14 represents a more appropriate way of working in these more dynamic environments. In this model, much of the responsibility for and control of security is delegated to the business units and project teams, though they may still work to a set of common security principles and tooling. This delegation may take the form of 'security champions' embedded within individual delivery teams. Depending upon the scale and nature of your approach and project, such champions could be embedded at the level of 'tribes', 'squads' (if using the Spotify model) or individual scrum teams. The aim of this approach is to provide the development teams with access to the security input that they need at the time and level that they need it. The security champions themselves do not always need to be full-time security professionals, they simply need to be aware of the security requirements for their area and have strong links to the centralised security capability (and wider security community or guild) should they need further advice and guidance. When this expertise is embedded in the individual teams, they are able to progress to delivery much more rapidly than is common in the more traditional model – in contrast to the 'thou shalt' approach, this approach is closer to 'we will'. Larger enterprises will likely find themselves needing both approaches to provide the right security approach and oversight to the various modes of operation: a single approach to security is unlikely to be appropriate.

Cloud deployment models

The next few chapters of this book consider each of the Cloud service models in turn and describe mechanisms for delivering the security services described within the SRM. However, these chapters do not consider the different Cloud deployment models. To fill this rather obvious gap, I am going to use the remainder of this chapter to talk about the security characteristics of the different deployment models.

Public Cloud

Public Cloud is the deployment model most commonly associated with Cloud computing. The security implications are very much encapsulated by its name – public. Public Cloud services are open to all: competing enterprises, individual users, malicious users and any other interested party. The Public Cloud model is shown in Figure 15.

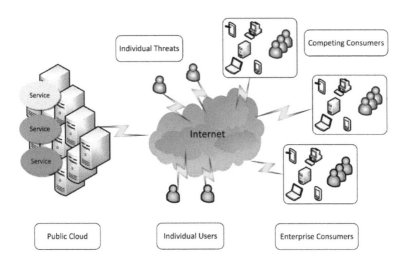

Figure 15: The public Cloud model

The different customers of the CSP are separated only by the mechanisms that have been implemented by the CSP; an insecure Cloud service could effectively bridge across their customer base. So, in the public Cloud model, there are shared networks, hypervisors, access control services, storage and (depending on service model) shared platforms and applications.

A naïve consumer may have neglected to secure their communications to their 'trusted' Cloud provider; it is vital that consumers realise that they are often connecting to their CSP over the untrusted Internet and secure such connections appropriately. This book provides guidance on how to secure FaaS, SaaS, PaaS and IaaS, so I will not go into the details of how to secure connectivity here; the point of this section is to highlight the differences between the different deployment models.

Major public Cloud providers are often global in nature with data centres spread across the world to provide resilience and redundancy and to deliver acceptable performance levels to local users. Such CSPs will often claim to be able to limit the transfer of data between these data centres so as to enable their clients to meet compliance requirements relating to data location. However, there is often no cast-iron guarantee (e.g. acknowledgement of liability) should such CSPs accidentally allow data to leak from one data centre to another. There is also often a lack of clarity regarding the support model for the physical infrastructure providing the public Cloud service. Some of the well-known Cloud providers have a 'follow the sun model'; this means that support staff are located outside of the geographical region of the data centre itself. This leads to a lack of confidence amongst some potential consumers regarding their ability to limit data presence to specific locations and it helps to explain much of the concern that surveys often report with regard to compliance issues in the Cloud.

Of course, the public Cloud model does have some security benefits to provide to their consumers. Firstly, the CSP has likely heavily invested in security already, particularly at the PaaS and SaaS levels. This is an investment in property, technology, personnel and process that consumers can take advantage of and do not need to resource themselves. A second advantage of the public Cloud model is the wide visibility of security incidents that these CSPs may have across their client base. There have been a number of anecdotal incidents whereby CSPs have noticed something amiss with their clients' activities, e.g. sudden increases in network traffic indicating where client services have been hacked and used to distribute illegal content. Such wide-ranging situational awareness can be a positive feature for many clients, particularly if the client does not have the staff or the contacts to be able to identify security threats currently active 'in the wild'. Security monitoring services like Azure Sentinel and AWS GuardDuty obtain threat intelligence from across their entire Cloud infrastructures; consequently, potential malicious activity has a higher visibility with these than most enterprises operating on-premises.

Meanwhile services such as GCP Backstory[97] and AWS Detective[98] provide enterprises with searchable archives of past security log entries that provide valuable insight when investigating the root cause and/or history of security incidents.

In summary, consumers considering the public Cloud model must be wary of compliance issues and be confident in the compensating mechanisms that they have adopted to protect themselves from other tenants accessing the service.

Private Cloud

The private Cloud model is the diametrical opposite of the public Cloud model. A private Cloud is dedicated to the use of a single consumer. However, there is no requirement for the private Cloud to be hosted and operated by the consumer. A private Cloud can be outsourced to a traditional service provider; the service provider may then operate the Cloud service from the premises of their client or from their own data centres. Figure 16 outlines the private Cloud model.

---

[97] *https://cloud.google.com/blog/topics/inside-google-cloud/the-security-moonshot-joins-google-cloud*.

[98] *https://aws.amazon.com/detective/*.

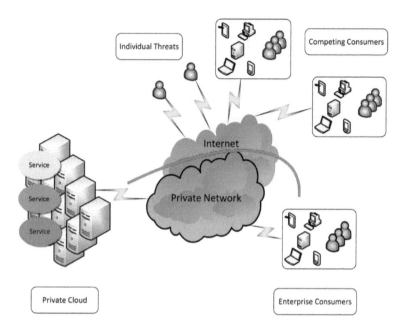

Figure 16: The private Cloud model

Figure 16 shows the two potential access mechanisms for a private Cloud, either over the consumer's own WAN or, in the case of a hosted Cloud, perhaps over the Internet. The red line within the diagram represents the barriers preventing the threat actors from accessing the private Cloud. Unlike in the public Cloud model, there is no multi-tenancy across different consumers. There may, however, be multi-tenancy implemented across different organisational units within the consumer. Indeed, this is where consumers may derive their cost-savings from adoption of the Cloud model; different organisational units or services can now purchase compute or network resource from the private Cloud rather than having to invest in a multitude of discrete technology stacks.

From a security perspective, there is little doubt that the private Cloud model offers consumers the most control. The consumer can dictate their own requirements and engage in detailed dialogue and negotiation with prospective CSPs. This is in direct contrast to the public Cloud model, where it is often difficult (or impossible) for consumers to negotiate any deviation from a provider's standard terms and conditions or service levels. The flexibility offered by the private Cloud model, therefore, enables consumers to implement the exact security solutions that they require, subject to the traditional constraints around cost! Consumers can also dictate the location of the infrastructure and so manage their own compliance risks.

The private Cloud model is not without issues however. If the private Cloud is only for one consumer, with a set of particular security requirements, then the consumer will need to invest in the property, technology, personnel and processes needed to meet those requirements. If the consumer is planning on operating their own private Cloud (rather than outsourcing its operation), then they must also accept the need to provide the necessary security resources.

The other main issue with private Clouds, from a security perspective, relates to availability. Whereas public Cloud services can present the illusion of infinite compute and storage resources, this is an illusion that a private Cloud cannot sustain. An organisation building a private Cloud must still provision enough IT equipment to be able to cater for the maximum usage spikes; this will likely leave the organisation with the traditional issue of over-capacity whereby resources sit idle awaiting the next spike.

Hybrid Cloud

The hybrid Cloud model applies to any combination of the other three deployment models. For example, a service delivered using both private and public Cloud resources would be described as a hybrid Cloud. Figure 17 outlines the different combinations of the other Cloud deployment models that can form a hybrid Cloud.

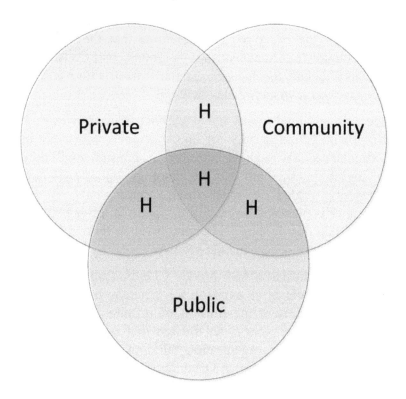

Figure 17: The hybrid Cloud options

It can be seen from Figure 17 that there is at least one configuration for a hybrid Cloud that does not involve public Cloud services. This configuration would entail the use of private Clouds in combination with community Clouds. I point this out as it is easy to forget that the hybrid approach does not necessitate the use of a public Cloud. It should also be noted that the term 'hybrid Cloud' is increasingly being used to refer to situations in which a consumer deploys a service across a variety of different Cloud providers. However, I will continue to use the more traditional NIST definition in this book.

Figure 18 uses a representation very similar to that which I used for the private Cloud model within Figure 16.

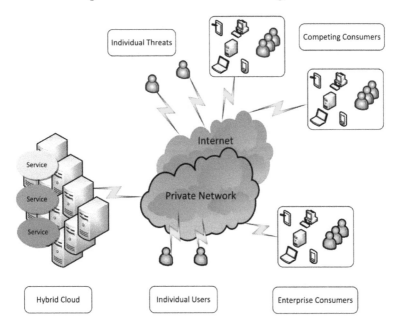

Figure 18: The hybrid Cloud model

The major difference from Figure 16 is that I have removed the barrier between the Cloud resources and the threat actors. This brings me to the crux of the major problem I see with the hybrid Cloud model. It is the worst of all worlds from a security perspective, especially when considering the combination of private and public Cloud models. Not only do consumers need to invest in all of the security resources associated with operating a private (or community) Cloud, but they must also implement the controls needed to operate in the public Cloud. This issue is not necessarily as problematic now as it was in the past – there are a growing number of Cloud workload protection tools (e.g. Guardicore) that enable organisations to use common security tooling across on-premises and on-Cloud environments.

So what reasons are there for an organisation to adopt the Hybrid Cloud model? There are two primary reasons organisations adopt the hybrid model:

1. They may have a desire to keep their most sensitive data on-premises but also want to make use of Cloud services for their less sensitive or commodity services; or
2. They may have some legacy services that are nontrivial to migrate to the public Cloud, e.g. mainframes.

A third driver relates to the over-capacity issue I touched upon when talking about the private Cloud model. Rather than purchasing capacity that may only be used very rarely, an organisation may choose to maintain a presence on a public Cloud service and 'burst' to the public Cloud for additional capacity when their private Cloud becomes over-stretched. In this approach, an organisation's sensitive data remains within their private Cloud with only the occasional foray into the public Cloud. Of course, from a compliance perspective, an occasional breach remains a breach. This may be one reason why such Cloud-bursting is less common in practice than was envisaged in the early days of Cloud.

A final driver for the adoption of a hybrid approach may occur when a consuming organisation wishes to adopt a 'best of breed' approach; in this case, they may choose to use public SaaS services *tied* together with some private IaaS services (e.g. storage or shared identity repository).

From a security perspective, placing data into the public Cloud immediately raises all of the issues associated with operating in the public Cloud: multi-tenancy, data remanence (how does the public Cloud provider manage data that has been deleted by the consumer?) and the potential leaking of data across geographic boundaries. It is vital that those organisations adopting the hybrid model in order to keep their sensitive data on-premises maintain strong barriers between their private Cloud and the outside world.

In terms of the security benefits that the hybrid model offers over and above the public Cloud model, these are perhaps limited to the ability to retain sensitive data within the more enclosed deployment model (e.g. private) whilst still taking advantage of the capabilities of public Cloud services for other services. This does come at the cost of increased complexity, including the likelihood of the duplication of security tooling across the public and private Clouds.

Community Cloud

A community Cloud sits somewhere between the public and private Cloud models. A community Cloud caters for a closed community of organisations, typically bound by a common security and compliance regime. An excellent use case for a community Cloud could include government Clouds or more niche areas such as Cloud services aimed at law enforcement, health or education. Figure 19 illustrates the community Cloud model.

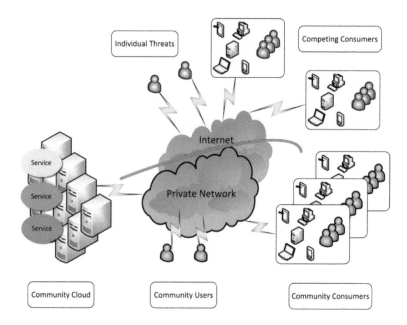

Figure 19: The community Cloud model

As with the private Cloud model, there are a series of barriers preventing access to the Cloud services to those outside of the authorised community. The Cloud services could be hosted within a commercial CSP data centre, or within a data centre belonging to a member of the community or, perhaps, within a shared data centre established by the community. The network links between the members of the community and the relevant data centres could be provided by a private network or through use of the Internet.

Community Clouds have the obvious advantage over their public Cloud equivalents that the community gets to define their own shared security requirements and to dictate the location of the data centres. Another advantage of the community Cloud model over the public model is that it caters for a closed community and so Joe Public (or Joe Hacker) will find it more difficult to compromise the service.

As the community model sits between the public and private models it, by definition, sits somewhere between those models in terms of availability of capacity. Public Clouds present the illusion of infinite resource and private Clouds lead to either over or under-provisioning; community Clouds can help their users to cater for usage spikes through allocation of the resources not currently allocated to other members of the community. This is obviously based on the assumption that not all members of the community experience the same spike in usage at the same time (which is not as unlikely as it may sound if talking about community Clouds for the emergency services).

One downside of the community Cloud approach is the need for the members of the community to establish trust with each other, and also to agree to a common governance structure and approach with respect to their community Cloud. Internal politics can be hard; politics within occasionally competing communities can be harder. A community Cloud requires either a central or distributed governance body to define their requirements and to negotiate the terms and conditions and service levels expected of the CSP. This governance body must then procure the service and, once it is in operation, manage it right through to decommissioning, if this is necessary.

Overview of Cloud deployment models

Table 3 summarises the discussion about the merits of the different Cloud deployment models from a security perspective.

Table 3: Deployment Models

Deployment Model	Strengths	Weaknesses	Candidate Users
Public	• Provider security resources (personnel and technology) in place; • Wide visibility of security incidents; and • Impression of infinite resources.	• Multi-tenancy; and • Compliance concerns.	• All enterprises with limited exceptions (e.g. national security, nuclear); and • Critical National Infrastructure).
Community	• Compliance (Cloud service designed to meet a common regime); • Known (closed) community of users; and • Can be hosted by the community or outsourced.	• Requires a central body (or committee) to manage the service; • Requirement to procure and implement the Cloud service; • Requirement to trust other members of the	• Government; • Other organisations with a shared security regime, e.g. industry groupings; and • Academia.

Deployment Model	Strengths	Weaknesses	Candidate Users
		community; and • Need to provide 'community' security resources.	
Private	• Complete control by the consumer; • Compliance; • Closed set of users; and • Can be hosted by the consumer or outsourced.	• Need to invest in the initial implementation of the service; • Requirement to provide their own security resources; and • Less ability to scale (burst) than either public or community Clouds.	• Financial services; • government departments and agencies; and • Enterprises with large existing investments in data centres and technology.
Hybrid	• Potential to keep sensitive data on-premises whilst using public	• Worst of both worlds: consumers need to secure their service both	• Financial Services; and • Mainframe users.

Deployment Model	Strengths	Weaknesses	Candidate Users
	Cloud where appropriate.	on-Cloud and on-premises; • Complexity; and • Multi-tenancy.	

In general, the amount of security control over a Cloud deployment available to the consumer decreases in the order shown below:

1. Private Cloud
2. Community Cloud
3. Hybrid Cloud
4. Public Cloud

As a principle, I would tend to argue that hybrid Clouds should be viewed as being as secure as the most public aspect of the Cloud services concerned, e.g. a hybrid Cloud of a private and public Cloud should be viewed as being as secure as the public Cloud concerned, although this does depend upon the strength of the barriers between the two.

CHAPTER 9: SECURITY AND INFRASTRUCTURE AS A SERVICE

In this chapter, I describe how the security services defined within the SRM, shown in Figure 7, can be delivered by those implementing an application upon an IaaS Cloud. There are many IaaS providers offering a variety of different types of service. A non-exhaustive list of the different types of IaaS currently available is provided below:

- Compute as a Service
- Storage as a Service
- Backup and Recovery/Disaster Recovery as a Service
- Virtual Desktop Infrastructure (VDI) as a Service
- Container Management as a Service

And here is a partial list of public Cloud providers offering IaaS services:

- Amazon (*https://aws.amazon.com/*)
- Azure (*https://azure.microsoft.com/en-gb/*)
- Google (*https://cloud.google.com/*)
- Digital Ocean (*www.digitalocean.com/*)
- UKCloud (*https://ukcloud.com/*)

Many traditional systems integrators also offer Cloud services; some, such as IBM, offer their own Cloud technology for use as a public Cloud, whilst others, such as Capgemini, focus more on the integration of the public Cloud services offered by dedicated Cloud service providers. Many traditional enterprise vendors are also adopting their software to make it Cloud native; a good example of this approach is VMware which has worked with AWS to offer the 'VMware Cloud on AWS'[99] service – this allows their customers to operate across both on-premises and AWS using their familiar VMware tooling.

Cloudian (*https://cloudian.com/solutions/cloud-storage/storage-as-a-service/*) is a good example of an IaaS provider offering a specific infrastructure service; it offers SaaS that enables enterprises, and others, to store their data in the Cloud.

In many ways the task of securing IaaS services is extremely similar to that of securing traditional on-premises services. The prime differences being that the services are hosted by the CSP and that the underlying networks, compute and storage resources are most likely shared with other consumers to a greater degree than seen in traditional outsourcing models.

IaaS and the SRM

The rest of this chapter is dedicated to explaining how the services described within the SRM can be delivered when deploying services on an IaaS Cloud. Please remember that the SRM refers to the security services associated with an application to be hosted on a Cloud service; bear this in mind when you consider the scope of the services discussed next.

---

[99] *https://aws.amazon.com/vmware/*.

Secure development

Within the SRM, the *secure development* services remain the primary responsibility of the consumer as shown in Figure 8. After all, the CSP is only providing an infrastructure for the consumer to build upon.

One of the major drivers for organisations adopting Cloud services is the need to enable wider digital transformation: typically a move towards more agile development processes and aligning with DevOps ways of working. This book uses the term DevSecOps to refer to the inclusion of security considerations within the DevOps process, but other authors may prefer the term SecDevOps. The traditional security approach – providing a set of requirements at the beginning of an application development lifecycle and then coming back immediately before go-live to conduct a full penetration test – simply does not scale in the digital, Mode 2, environment. It is plainly impractical to conduct a full penetration test of every application release if your DevOps teams are pushing multiple releases per day. Similarly, security should not be viewed as a blocker, acting as a chokepoint at various points during the development lifecycle, e.g. architecture review, design review, code review, secure build review, operations review, penetration test, et cetera. Few organisations have the quantity or quality of security resources to be able to fulfil all of these requirements in a reasonable time frame. DevSecOps is one approach to address those issues.

DevSecOps is all about embedding security controls as close to the start of the development lifecycle as possible, which is often referred to as 'shifting left' because we move security controls towards the start of a project timeline. For example, if security teams are able to embed code analysis tools earlier in the process, this can reduce the risk associated with not being able to conduct a full penetration test at go-live time, whilst it also takes pressure off the developers by giving them more time to fix identified issues. Nobody wants to be the developer receiving a vulnerability report from the penetration testers brought in on the day the application was due to go live. Similarly, if the security team is able to pre-approve deployment environments and build templates (e.g. CloudFormation, Terraform or Azure Resource Manager templates and EC2 images, et cetera.), then they can leave the developer teams to get on with their project without needing to get in the way. Security teams can move towards a strategy of 'trust, but verify' and focus more on strategic security issues and incident resolution rather than spending time on tactical issues relating to project-specific builds.

The major IaaS Cloud providers are aware of this need to support secure ways of working and the deployment of 'secure by default' environments. AWS, for example, has the concepts of the Control Tower[100] and the Landing Zone,[101] with the former representing a means of deploying the preconfigured, deployable and secure multi-account architecture represented by the latter. Azure is not as mature as AWS in terms of preconfigured secure deployable templates; however, Microsoft has documented its concept of an Azure Scaffold,[102] which is essentially a guide to putting in place the structures (e.g. account hierarchies) needed to operate securely in the Cloud. The Azure

---

[100] *https://aws.amazon.com/controltower/.*

[101] *https://aws.amazon.com/solutions/aws-landing-zone/.*

[102] *https://docs.microsoft.com/en-gb/azure/cloud-adoption-framework/reference/azure-scaffold.*

Blueprints[103] service will likely allow Microsoft to copy the AWS Landing Zone concept in the near future, whilst the Lighthouse[104] service allows consistent management across accounts (similar in some ways to AWS Control Tower). In the meantime, enterprises are able to make use of the Azure Blueprints service to create their own in-house standard secure environments.

Figure 20 illustrates what a secure, repeatable AWS environment may look like; it is derived from the AWS Landing Zone approach but is not the default Landing Zone.

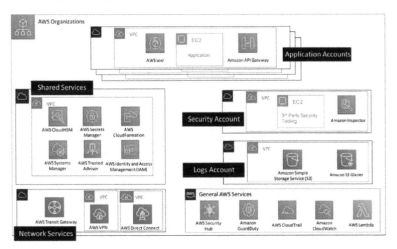

Figure 20: Example AWS architecture

This example architecture adopts the approach of account-level segmentation, i.e. every single application is deployed into its own AWS account so as to limit the impact ('blast radius') of any compromise to that single application and

---

[103] *https://azure.microsoft.com/en-gb/services/blueprints/*.

[104] *http://azure.microsoft.com/en-gb/services/azure-lighthouse/*.

account. The NotPetya outbreak of 2017 highlighted the need to improve internal segmentation in order to avoid the kind of catastrophic spread of malware suffered by the likes of Maersk.[105]

The segmentation offered by account-level segregation is a massive security improvement compared to the traditional flat network architecture found in many enterprises. Other key features of the architecture shown in Figure 20 include the use of a shared services account; this enables the various applications to use a common set of services and to avoid having to duplicate these services across each account. Depending on your preference, some of these shared services may be better exposed to relying parties via the AWS PrivateLink service; this can help you avoid having to peer across VPCs or having to use the AWS Transit Gateway service. This architecture has also separated security logs into their own dedicated account. This approach allows us to use the Service Control Policies[106] (SCP) feature of AWS Organizations to limit the actions of the root user within the logs account, i.e. we can use SCPs to prevent even the root user from being able to tamper with the security log information stored within the account.

Now, pre-approved configurable environments are only one element of an overall DevSecOps approach. It is fairly traditional to represent the DevSecOps approach in the form of an infinity diagram, and I see no need to break that

---

[105] *www.wired.com/story/notpetya-cyberattack-ukraine-russia-code-crashed-the-world/*.

[106] *https://docs.aws.amazon.com/organizations/latest/userguide/orgs_m anage_policies_scp.html*.

tradition. Figure 21 illustrates the overall DevSecOps approach.

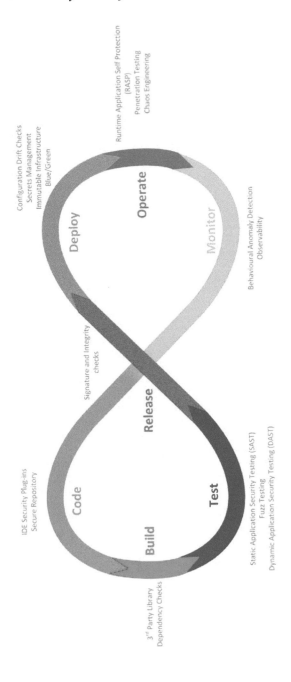

Figure 21: The DevSecOps approach

Let's describe each element of the approach in turn, beginning with 'code'. An Integrated Development Environment (IDE), such as Eclipse or Visual Studio, is used by developers to code their applications. IDEs will typically include code editors (with code completion and syntax checking) and debuggers and they allow the inclusion of a variety of other plug-ins. These plug-ins can, and should, include plug-ins relating to security functionality. Examples may include plug-ins that natively identify known programming weaknesses or that call out to the code analysis tools available in the 'deploy' and 'test' elements of the cycle. Thinking back to the SRM (Figure 7), the code element of the cycle needs to consider the *coding standards*, *code review* and *repository* security services. It is imperative that organisations do not forget to secure their code repository; as we move towards infrastructure-as-code, it is apparent that a compromise of the code repository is equivalent to a compromise of the infrastructure that code describes. In an ideal world the code repository will be located in an environment at least as secure as the relevant application and infrastructure for which it stores information. Cloud-based code repositories, such as those offered by GitHub and BitBucket, can be adequately secured; however, organisations should make sure that they enforce multi-factor authentication: no organisation should find itself in the position of being only the compromise of a single username/password combination away from losing their entire infrastructure.

Once a developer is ready to commit and build their application, we can move on to the 'build' phase of the cycle (and of the SRM). The build phase will see the various components of the application being linked, or incorporated, into an executable, which will likely include a variety of third-party code libraries. Organisations should ensure that these third-party code libraries do not include any nasty surprises such as known security vulnerabilities or unwanted licence conditions. Tools such as those offered by Black Duck[107] and WhiteSource[108] can be used to identify known weaknesses in open source components and to highlight associated licence concerns.

Once the code is built, the developer can run a series of security tests prior to pushing the code through to deployment. This test stage is very important in the DevSecOps approach which often lacks the capability to provide a full penetration test of every release prior to go-live. Tests should include the use of both static code analysis tools (whereby the application code is checked without executing the application itself) and dynamic code analysis tools (which check the application whilst it is running).Organisations may also wish to consider making use of fuzzing tools. Fuzzing tools, such as American Fuzzy Lop (AFL), mutate application inputs to check that the application handles these inputs appropriately. Fuzzing tools are particularly recommended for those applications accepting input from outside a trusted environment.

Third-party dependency checkers, SAST, fuzzers and DAST tools can all be incorporated into automated CI/CD (continuous integration/continuous delivery) pipelines; this ensures that if they highlight high priority issues, the CI/CD tool (e.g. Jenkins) will fail the build and send the findings back to the developer for remediation.

---

107 *www.blackducksoftware.com/*.

108 *www.whitesourcesoftware.com/*.

Once any security issues have been remediated, the process moves on to the 'release' stage. In this stage, it is necessary to check that the code about to be deployed is actually the code that the developer believes it to be! These checks can take the form of digital signature or simple hash-based integrity checks of the code about to be deployed. If those checks complete successfully, the code can be deployed.

The 'deploy' stage of the cycle includes a consideration of the SRM's *secrets management* service. Applications and infrastructure components will often need to authenticate themselves to other elements of the overall environment. A good example may be the need for an application to authenticate itself to a back-end database, possibly in the form of a SQL connection string. It is extremely bad security practice to embed such security credentials in the application code because compromise of the code would also see the database itself compromised. Instead, developers should use a secrets management tool as a secure vault for application secrets; these can then be retrieved at run-time or deployment, depending on the nature of the secret. There are a variety of options available for secrets management; these depend on the IaaS in use and on third-party tooling that can be used across a variety of IaaS services. HashiCorp's Vault[109] is a particularly popular third-party secrets management tool, whilst those working with Azure will typically make use of Azure Key Vault[110] for the storage of secrets. AWS offers a variety of secrets management approaches for use in different circumstances, including

---

[109] *www.vaultproject.io/.*

[110] *https://azure.microsoft.com/en-gb/services/key-vault/.*

Secrets Manager[111] and Systems Manager Parameter Store.[112] Users of the Google Cloud Platform will typically need to adopt a more manual process via the use of encryption services provided by Cloud Key Management Service (KMS).[113]

The remaining elements of the DevSecOps cycle will be described as we get to the appropriate elements of the SRM as they are not solely applicable to secure development and DevSecOps.

Integration

The *integration* set of services exists to support working across a diverse Cloud environment, commonly referred to as a 'multi-Cloud' environment. As described earlier, it is commonly the case that organisations select discrete Cloud services to deliver discrete types of workloads rather than looking for true portability of workloads across Cloud services. However, there are some organisations that do seek to deliver such portability of workloads across Cloud providers, usually when driven by strict regulatory requirements relating to business continuity and exit planning. If such portability is deemed to be a requirement, this will often be implemented through the use of containerisation, e.g. through the use of Docker, Kubernetes, OpenShift and related technologies which essentially abstract away the underlying hosting environment. In theory, this approach allows organisations to move containerised

---

[111] *https://aws.amazon.com/secrets-manager/.*

[112] *https://docs.aws.amazon.com/systems-manager/latest/userguide/systems-manager-parameter-store.html.*

[113] *https://cloud.google.com/secret-manager/docs/overview.*

workloads between, for example, Kubernetes environments hosted on-premises and Kubernetes environments hosted on AWS, Azure or GCP. A downside of this approach is the additional complexity – which is the perpetual enemy of security – and the loss of access to the Cloud-native capabilities. Organisations find themselves essentially working primarily in Kubernetes environments rather than in Cloud environments. It is the *API* service within the *integrity* set of services that allows workloads to be moved via calls to the relevant APIs within both the Cloud provider and the containerised environment.

Cloud Access Security Brokers (CASBs) are described fully in chapter 11 but, in essence, they can be used as a form of proxy between Cloud users and the Cloud services that they access, providing a consistent point of control and monitoring across the Cloud environment.

Cloud Workload Protection Platforms (CWPPs) allow Cloud consumers to apply consistent security controls to their Cloud-hosted workloads; they typically provide controls at the Cloud control plane, network, operating system and container level. CWPPs offer two main advantages:

1. They allow controls to be applied across on-premises and a variety of CSPs via a single user interface; and
2. They help to enable portability of workloads through the CWPP abstraction layer.[114]

However, as with previous discussions of Cloud portability, the use of tools like CWPPs also abstracts away some of the ability to directly use the tooling available within the Cloud

---

[114] This is why CWPP sits within the Integration element of the SRM.

platforms. Even so, those organisations implementing multiple services across multiple Clouds in a hybrid environment can benefit from the ability to consistently enforce microsegmentation via CWPP tooling. A few examples of such tooling are provided below:

- Guardicore (*www.guardicore.com/*)
- Twistlock (*www.twistlock.com/*)
- Aqua (*www.aquasec.com/*)

Integrity

In SRM terms, the *integrity* service grouping is all about maintaining trust in the systems and data used to implement an application. The *non-repudiation* service is designed to ensure that actions can be attributed to the correct individual, organisation or process; it works to maintain trust in the provenance of the application or data. The *content check* service is there to ensure that the information object to be processed does not contain any nasty surprises such as corruption, unauthorised modification or inclusion of malware. The *snapshot* service is there to enable (almost) instant backup to a known good image. The *snapshot* service can also be used to capture the contents of a virtual machine image thought to be compromised in order to perform a forensic analysis.

The *non-repudiation* service would typically be delivered using a combination of services defined elsewhere within the SRM. For example, *identity management* services would provide identity information, *monitoring* services would provide event information and the *non-repudiation* services would provide the binding between the user and the event. The *non-repudiation* services could then make use of the cryptographic services to provide true non-repudiation, or simply rely on the strength of the auditing if true, legally binding, non-repudiation is not required. Why might *non-repudiation* be an important service for those working with Cloud services? Consider the pay-as-you-go nature of Cloud services. You really want to be quite certain of who fired up the virtual servers for which you've just been billed. Consumers should ensure that their providers offer appropriate audit trails; as a minimum, these should indicate the users that have requested new or additional resources. Similarly, consumers should ensure that there is an adequate audit trail of the release of resources, e.g. to ensure that a basic denial of service attack of simply shutting down a virtual infrastructure can also be captured.

The *content check* service grouping describes a vital collection of security capabilities. It encompasses traditional antivirus mechanisms and file integrity mechanisms, together with higher-level mechanisms, to ensure that application level traffic does not contain malicious content. In order to make this a little more real, consider the situation whereby our application in the Cloud processes significant amounts of XML-encoded data. How can you ensure that this XML-encoded data is safe to store and process and does not in fact include any malicious embedded content or include any entities containing SQL injection or cross-site scripting attacks? I have come across systems in the past whereby attackers could supply XML that was stored in a back-end database and then later passed from the database to a web browser. Stored cross-site scripting can be fun. What is specific about *content check* and IaaS though? Not an awful lot; in general, many of the best practices associated with traditional application deployments still apply:

- Do not trust user-supplied input;

- Do not trust information sourced from outside of your trusted domain;
- Do not assume that information has not been modified since it was created or last accessed; and
- Do not allow code to run unless you know what it's going to do.

Many of the tools used on a traditional deployment are equally suitable[115] for use on an IaaS deployment; your antimalware system of choice, for example, can be used to protect your IaaS-hosted application (subject to licensing).

As one option, Cloud consumers may wish to consider using Cloud-based *content check* services, e.g. web application firewalls (WAFs) with associated malware-checking/sandboxing capabilities such as those offered by Akamai Kona or Imperva Incapsula. Figure 22 shows how this approach can be used to isolate an organisation's Cloud environment from the hostile Internet.

---

[115] Although some security products have undergone more transformation towards becoming Cloud-native than others.

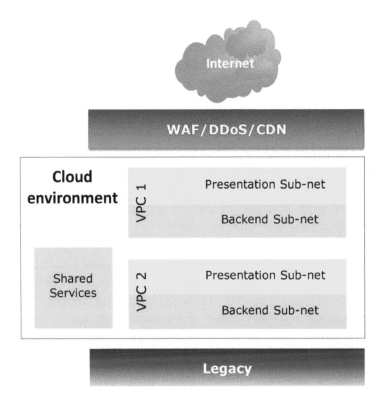

Figure 22: Cloud WAF

Another advantage of the approach illustrated in Figure 22 is that, in some circumstances, it allows you to limit your secure environment's inbound traffic to the source addresses of your Cloud-based WAF service, substantially reducing your overall attack surface.

The move to Cloud is often associated with a move to more loosely coupled service-oriented applications (aka microservices) and away from monolithic applications. This will typically involve exposing a number of service interfaces – each of which will (ideally) require some form of validation of the input passed to them. There are a number of third-party security tools that can be used to perform such security validation/content checking, for example:

- Axway AMPLIFY (*www.axway.com/en/products/api-management*)
- CA API Gateway (*www.ca.com/gb/products/ca-api-gateway.html*)
- Forum Systems (*www.forumsys.com*)

I should note that such products typically call out to an external antivirus engine to perform traditional checks for malware. These tools are necessary if you need to parse the XML being passed between your applications and your users and ensure that this XML does not include malicious content. If you can't parse the XML, you can't check the content. The requirements and risks underlying your security architecture will dictate whether such tools are necessary or whether you can rely upon the schema validation capabilities of more standard XML parsers. The Cloud providers themselves also offer API management/gateway capabilities, e.g. AWS API Gateway, Azure API Management and Google Apigee. These Cloud-native capabilities are often not as fully featured as the dedicated third-party API security products but they will likely be suitable for some less sensitive workloads.

Cloud consumers also have a number of choices when it comes to the provision of traditional anti-malware capabilities for use on their IaaS environments. Consumers of Azure have access to Microsoft Antimalware for

Azure[116](built on the same platform as Windows Defender) as part of the Azure suite of services. Users of other major IaaS vendors will need to look to third-party tooling to provide anti-malware capability. One of the more popular options is TrendMicro's Deep Security tool which offers a variety of end point protection capabilities (e.g. file system integrity monitoring and host IPS) in addition to traditional anti-malware protection. Deep Security, and other similar tools designed for deployment on the Cloud, tend to be API-driven; this means that they can be configured and articulated as code just like the rest of the Cloud infrastructure.

In addition to this traditional mechanism of checking content for malware and then removing it if identified, a more recent innovation is the approach of content re-writing. Using this approach, content such as a Word document or a PDF document is analysed and then re-rendered in a new document. This approach strips out any macros or other potentially malicious code and the new, re-rendered document is known to be clean. This capability can be delivered using tools from vendors such as Deep Secure[117] or Menlo Security[118].

Another driver for an increased awareness of content checking within IaaS deployments is that the data to be stored and processed on your application is likely to be stored within shared storage systems. Depending on the level of trust you have in those shared storage mechanisms, and the level of risk that you are willing to accept, you may wish to

---

[116] *https://docs.microsoft.com/en-gb/azure/security/fundamentals/antimalware*.

[117] *www.deep-secure.com/*.

[118] *www.menlosecurity.com/weaponized-documents*.

perform some level of integrity checking prior to processing any information objects retrieved from such storage. For example, one of the classes of information objects stored in an IaaS environment will include virtual machine images – you really would not want to fire up a Trojaned image.

Now, this is where the security requirements underlying the *snapshot* service become apparent. There is a need to capture a snapshot of an information object at a specific point in time and then be able to verify that the information object matches the snapshot when it is next accessed. The conceptual snapshot service within the SRM would typically require the use of cryptographic services to provide a signed hash of the information object in an actual implementation. There would also need to be technical services to generate the snapshot to validate the signed hash. These capabilities are typically offered natively by the Cloud platform. Such services would reside within the *encryption* conceptual service grouping of the SRM.

Availability

One of the perceived strengths of the Cloud model is the ability to deploy highly available systems without the need to invest in multiple data centres complete with fully replicated technology stacks, diverse communications links and data mirroring.

However, CSPs are not immune to availability issues themselves and, being high profile, outages of Cloud services such as Office 365 and Amazon EC2 are well publicised. The downdetector[119] website provides an

---

[119] *https://downdetector.com/*.

independent service for tracking the issues of specific Cloud providers, which is useful if you do not wish to place complete trust in the availability status pages of the Cloud providers themselves. The status pages of the main IaaS Cloud providers are listed below:

- AWS: *https://status.aws.amazon.com/*
- Azure: *https://status.azure.com/en-us/status*
- GCP: *https://status.cloud.google.com/*
- Digital Ocean: *https://status.digitalocean.com/*
- UKCloud: *https://status.ukcloud.com/*

The major Cloud providers tend to be very transparent in their write-ups of any incidents because they recognise the importance of trust: Cloud consumers will not place the well-being of their business in the care of an IaaS provider that they cannot trust to meet their availability requirements.

In terms of maintaining the availability of a hosted service, you should consider whether your CSP has multiple data centres and whether these data centres are appropriately isolated from each other. If so, then you could consider hosting your services across the CSPs data centres so as to provide redundancy or resilience (or both) depending upon your architecture.[120] You should, however, bear in mind that any replication traffic between the two data centres may entail having to pay for the traffic to leave one data centre, traverse the Internet Cloud and then enter the other data centre –such replication does not always go over the Cloud

---

[120] The Azure Site Recovery service can be used to automate the cross-region (or on-premises to cloud) failover of virtual machines, *https://docs.microsoft.com/en-gb/azure/site-recovery/site-recovery-overview*.

provider's own wide area network. Given that most CSPs charge to transfer data into their Clouds and/or out of their Clouds (usually more for the latter) replication of data between data centres is usually viewed as two independent data transfers and charged accordingly. Consumers looking to implement their application using the IaaS model could consider hosting their services on two or more different IaaS platforms to provide their redundant service rather than just using two data centres from the same provider. Some Cloud consumers may face regulatory pressures to demonstrate this level of multi-Cloud business continuity in the event of Cloud service provider failure or contract exit, particularly in the financial services sector. This can lead to Cloud consumers looking to achieve levels of workload portability that may adversely impact their ability to make use of native Cloud provider functionality due to a need to avoid lock-in. For example, a number of financial services organisations have been driven towards building their own containerised microservices architectures that may allow workloads to move across the major Cloud providers. This level of cross-provider failover may help to address regulatory concerns but it comes at the cost of increased complexity. Added complexity may also adversely affect the overall availability goals and it will definitely abstract the consumer away from the benefits offered by rapidly evolving Cloud provider native capabilities.

Another issue related to the inconvenience of working across Cloud providers is the necessity of mastering the intricacies of the management tooling and APIs of each Cloud provider; even though using containers can make workload portability more straightforward, it is still necessary to design, provision and operate the hosting infrastructure. The pain of having to deal with two sets of management APIs could be mitigated through the use of tools such as Rightscale (*www.rightscale.com*), which enable the management of multiple Clouds from a single interface or through contractually handing that pain over to a third-party to manage via a Cloud service brokering arrangement. Consumers do have options for moving their workloads across Clouds in the event of a failure at their main provider; however, in most circumstances, it is uncertain whether the resulting increase in complexity provides more benefits than a reliance upon the resilience available within a single Cloud provider.

Cloud providers do tend to build resilience, including geographic separation, into their offers. Amazon, for example, host separate instances of their services in different regions, based on their geographical locations. Example regions include US East, US West, EU (Ireland), EU (London), Asia-Pacific (Tokyo) and South America (São Paulo). Each region is then split into separate Availability Zones. Availability Zones are designed to be insulated from failure within other Availability Zones. For example, should Amazon's Simple Storage Service (S3) fail in one Availability Zone, clients using other Availability Zones in the same region should not be affected. At least that was the theory. Unfortunately an incident in 2011 showed that the levels of isolation between Availability Zones were not sufficient to prevent an incident in one Availability Zone spilling over into an effect on the wider region. To their credit, Amazon provided an extensive review of the incident that led to this outage (essentially a configuration management error during a scheduled upgrade which rapidly snowballed into a major outage). This review can be found at:

https://aws.amazon.com/message/65648/.

There is an interesting related blog entry from Don MacAskill of SmugMug (customer of AWS) at:

https://don.blogs.smugmug.com/2011/04/24/how-smugmug-survived-the-amazonpocalypse/.

This blog entry provides an interesting perspective on how the AWS outage referred to above looked to a customer who was able to keep their service running, and provides some insight into how they were able to stay up whilst others were not.

There have, of course, been other outages since 2011. The S3 outage of 27 February 2017 not only took out Amazon's US-East-1 Region, it also adversely affected a number of well-known web services that rely upon S3 for back-end storage, including Netflix, Reddit and The Associated Press. This latter incident was found to be due to simple human error; it occurred when an operator mistakenly removed too many S3 servers from the available pool as part of a business as usual hardware refresh.[121] The number of websites affected by this incident shows how the major Cloud providers are becoming a systemic risk to our digital way of life; it also partly explains the wariness of financial services regulatory bodies when it comes to maintaining the stability of the wider financial environment.

I should point out that Amazon have taken steps to resolve the process and technology issues that led to these outages. The use of Availability Zones should not, therefore, be discounted to provide a certain amount of resilience. For true resilience however, consumers of AWS should consider running their service across different Regions rather than

---

[121] *https://aws.amazon.com/message/41926/.*

relying upon Availability Zones. As noted earlier in this section, this would have cost implications, particularly if you need to transfer significant quantities of data between regions. The link below provides further information on AWS regions and Availability Zones:

https://docs.aws.amazon.com/AWSEC2/latest/UserGuide/us ing-regions-availability-zones.html.

Amazon are not the only IaaS CSP able to provide discrete Cloud services hosted within different data centres. Azure recently implemented their own version of availability zones, functioning very similarly to those of AWS with a minimum of three such zones within each region offering the capability. Further detail on the Azure version of availability zones can be found here:

https://docs.microsoft.com/en-us/azure/availability-zones/az-overview.

The Google Cloud Platform also offers zones to deliver the same kind of fault and update domain separation as documented here:

https://cloud.google.com/compute/docs/regions-zones/.

The implementation of availability zones is one feature that significantly differentiates the hyper scale Cloud providers, such as Azure, GCP and AWS, from the smaller players. Whilst UKCloud does have a concept of zones, they are not as discrete or isolated as the equivalent functionality offered by the Big 3; for example, the different zones within UKCloud may share network infrastructure and power[122] and

---

[122] *https://docs.ukcloud.com/articles/other/other-ref-sites-regions-zones.html?q=availability%20zone#introduction.*

offer increased resilience but they are not true isolated fault domains. At the time of writing, Digital Ocean do not offer functionality akin to the availability zones described in this section.

Regardless of the mechanisms that you decide are the most appropriate for your application, e.g. hosting across multiple CSP data centres, hosting across multiple CSPs or hosting across on-premise and the Cloud, you must still test that the failover mechanisms work as anticipated. There's very little worse than only finding out that your business continuity and disaster recovery plans are worthless at the time they are invoked. Better to test them regularly and fine-tune them such that, in the event of a serious incident, you are able to continue to serve your users.

As an aside, remember to adopt some of the traditional best practices around resilience and redundancy from the on-premises world when designing your virtual infrastructure. Avoid single points of failure. Build in resilience where necessary. Design to handle the failure of individual components gracefully. As with your business continuity plans (BCPs) and disaster recovery plans (DRPs), test your infrastructure to ensure that failures are handled as expected. It is important to remember that even if you do make the wise decision to split your applications across availability zones, this does not happen automatically; consumers still need to design and build in the necessary capability, e.g. through implementation of Elastic Load Balancers (ELBs) to split load across zones.

Technical failure at a CSP data centre aside, the other major potential availability issue facing Cloud consumers is a commercial one. What happens if your CSP goes out of business? Or is acquired by a competitor who then closes down the service? This is not an unprecedented situation; Coghead were a PaaS provider who closed down in 2009 with their intellectual property being acquired by SAP. Coghead customers had a matter of weeks to make alternative provision for the operation of their services; a task made even more problematic as services designed to run on the Coghead platform could not be easily ported to a different platform. There is currently a significant amount of consolidation in the Cloud and security industry, e.g. the purchase of Duo Security by Cisco in 2018, or the acquisition of Skyhigh Networks by McAfee in 2017. Whilst I do not expect either of those products or services to be adversely impacted by their acquisitions, it is not uncommon for enterprises to have their own 'bogeymen' vendors that they refuse to do business with, either because of a past commercial dispute or a simple dislike. The acquisition of an organisation's favoured Cloud-based service by such a 'bogeyman' vendor creates an uncomfortable situation. Cloud consumers must ensure that financial stability and the potential for acquisition factor into their due diligence of prospective Cloud providers.

The latest iteration of the SRM introduces two services that merit further discussion: *evergreen* and *reliability & chaos.*

Evergreen

In this context, Evergreen refers to a mechanism for keeping your Cloud-based workloads up to date with the latest security patches without the pain of deploying such patches into a live environment. This approach goes by a number of other names, notably 'blue/green' (as noted earlier) and 'red/black'; the latter term is used in the context of Netflix and Netflix-related Cloud deployment tooling such as

Spinnaker.[123] The concepts remain similar regardless of terminology.

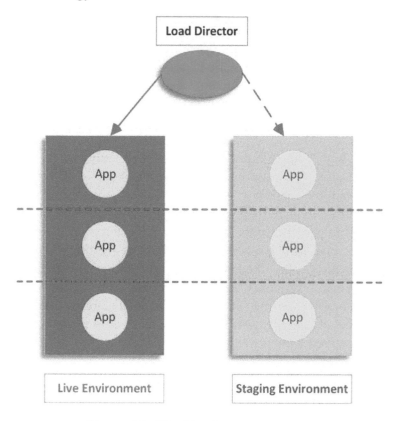

Figure 23: The blue/green approach

Figure 23 illustrates the concept of blue/green deployments at a high level. A Cloud consumer can deploy two application stacks, one which is currently used for production (live environment/blue) and one which is

---

[123] *www.spinnaker.io/.*

continually refreshed with security patches and the latest releases from the application stack (staging environment/ green). At their chosen frequency, the Cloud consumer can switch traffic/load from the blue environment to the green environment via the 'load director' component. The load director is a conceptual service but it can be delivered in a number of ways, including load balancers, proxies and DNS. Once the load has switched, the formerly blue environment becomes green and is continually refreshed. This approach offers a number of advantages:

- Servers and code do not need to be updated in the live environment, which reduces the risk of service outage and of requiring downtime in which to apply patches;
- The blue stack can be made immutable once in production, which reduces the risk of human error; and
- A simple rollback to the old blue is possible in the event of issues during deployment.

The dashed lines in Figure 23 demonstrate that organisations do not have to do blue/green in monolithic chunks: different elements of the stack could be deployed as individual components in a blue/green manner.

Whilst blue/green can offer a number of operational advantages, as described above, there are some complexities that also need to be considered. For example, the handling of information and live databases can be problematic in terms of the synchronisation across blue/green, particularly during switch-over. Similarly, the implementation of the load director component can be problematic; for example, when using DNS there may be a period in which load is being directed to both blue and green prior to the expiry of previously cached DNS entries. As with most matters of architecture and design, blue/green comes with trade-offs between risks and benefits.

Reliability & chaos

One of the major developments in the Cloud world over the last decade or so has been the emergence of chaos engineering approaches and the wider field of Site Reliability Engineering (SRE). SRE is a wide topic and worthy of a book in its own right – fortunately Google have produced just such a book and have made it available for free download. Those interested in how to architect, deliver and operate reliable systems at scale are strongly encouraged to read Google's thinking, available from:

https://landing.google.com/sre/sre-book/toc/index.html.

Chaos engineering is a discipline that has been both helped and hindered by its nomenclature. The use of the term 'chaos' has certainly garnered a lot of interest amongst technical staff, but it also raises concerns among business stakeholders when such approaches are discussed. The idea behind chaos engineering is to introduce deliberate errors within systems to ensure that they can recover and maintain service. One of the first manifestations of this approach was the Chaos Monkey tool published by Netflix as part of their wider, now retired, Simian Army[124] tool-set. The Simian Army tools enabled organisations to purposefully introduce errors into AWS environments, from the deliberate removal of EC2 instances through to the emulation of an entire AWS Region failure. The aim of this being to engineer the overall service to survive any such outage.

---

[124] *https://github.com/Netflix/SimianArmy*.

The key point, which sometimes gets missed in discussions of chaos engineering, is the absolute imperative of agreeing on the failure domain, the scope of testing and the rollback plan. Whilst the introduced failures may be 'random' within the agreed scope, organisations must be able to limit the blast radius associated with the testing via appropriate containment and recovery/rollback approaches. Organisations should on no account begin applying chaos approaches to production systems without a view as to how to prevent any leakage outside the agreed test scope.

So, given the dangers, why would any organisation consider chaos approaches? The clear answer relates to a need to be able to support always-on digital services. Netflix developed the Simian Army tool-set because its business model depends on it being able to deliver content on demand. The introduction of random failures identifies potential failure conditions that may not have been considered during architecture and design meetings and, as a result, encourages the incorporation of additional self-healing or failover capabilities. On which note, organisations should certainly hold desk-based chaos assessments of their architectures and designs prior to conducting such activities on live services. There is less risk associated with breaking and fixing designs than production systems, even if only from a career management perspective.

Chaos engineering is clearly more suited to some organisations than others. It definitely has great potential benefits for those offering digital services targeted at the consumer market; it is, however, unlikely to be an approach suitable for ICS environments where errors have potential real-world consequences that cannot be reverted.

Cryptography

In terms of cryptography, IaaS consumers have the flexibility to build in (within reason) whatever levels of cryptographic protection they feel their application merits. This can be a benefit, or simply an extra development and/or implementation overhead, depending upon your perspective. PaaS providers may well offer their own cryptographic services within their platform. SaaS providers will either offer encryption of data at rest or they will not; SaaS consumers have little room for manoeuvre.

The hyperscale Cloud providers have adopted similar mechanisms to enable encryption within their platforms – both AWS and GCP have key management systems (KMS), whilst Azure offers similar capabilities through the Azure Key Vault, which makes it possible to generate, store, rotate, revoke and present cryptographic keys for consumption by other services. The keys produced by KMS services are used by Cloud provider native services, e.g. for encrypting data at rest in services like AWS S3, GCP Cloud Storage or Azure Storage (both GCP and Azure Storage are encrypted by default, and S3 buckets can be configured to become encrypted by default). The keys produced by KMS services can also be used by applications hosted on the Cloud provider systems – Cloud consumers do not have to implement their own key management services and, indeed, they should not attempt to unless they have a very high level of implementation abilities. Cryptographic systems are notoriously difficult to implement without introducing weaknesses, and organisations are well-advised to avoid 'rolling their own'.

There is one important difference between on-premises and in-Cloud when it comes to cryptographic services: the issue of trust. If your Cloud provider is responsible for the generation and management of the cryptographic keys, then CSP staff are, in theory, capable of decrypting consumer data encrypted using those keys. Cloud consumers that are uncomfortable placing such trust in their Cloud providers have options available to them. The hyperscale Cloud providers also offer tamper-proof hardware-based key storage capabilities, e.g. AWS CloudHSM, Google CloudHSM or Azure Dedicated HSM; these use hardware security modules to secure key storage under the control of the Cloud consumer. However, whilst using HSMs does provide more assurances concerning the security of cryptographic keys, it does not necessarily address the core question of trust. Consumers must still place a degree of trust in the Cloud provider and HSM vendor that these Cloud-based services function as claimed, even if they are within the scope of independent assurance activities such as ISO 27001 certification.

Those Cloud consumers with an extremely low appetite for risk are able to implement their own HSMs on-premises for the purposes of key management. Such consumers can then either encrypt all data prior to upload to Cloud services or else, if they are slightly more trusting, import the generated keys into the appropriate Cloud-based KMS for use by their Cloud-hosted services (commonly referred to as bring your own key (BYOK)). BYOK scenarios do introduce a degree of risk: consumers are responsible for key generation, rotation and revocation and must bear responsibility for the availability of those keys, including for backup and archive purposes. A loss of encryption keys will result in a loss of access to data and, consequently, to service.

Now, one of the major categories of IaaS provision is Storage as a Service – either as a service in its own right or as part of wider provision, e.g. S3. With Storage as a Service, consumers trust the CSPs with the secure storage of their data. Typical use cases for Storage as a Service include data storage for the purposes of archive, backup and disaster recovery. More generic IaaS implementations will also require the use of persistent storage mechanisms; for example, these may be required to store virtual machine images or to function as the back-end storage for database systems. In both cases, when the consumer is sending sensitive data to the Cloud, it is likely that this data will need to be encrypted, both in transit and at rest.

Encryption in transit is a fairly easily solved problem: most CSPs will support the upload of data via TLS encrypted communications. In addition, the hyperscale CSPs all support dedicated links between a consumer's on-premises data centre and their Cloud environments. Each provider has a different name for this service: AWS calls it Direct Connect, Azure calls it ExpressRoute and GCP calls it Dedicated Interconnect. Dedicated connections can reduce the number of encryption requirements when the data requiring transfer is no longer traversing the Internet. Consumers can, therefore, send their data into the Cloud relatively safely via TLS (always bearing in mind the increasingly shaky foundations of the trust infrastructure underlying the protocol), or other VPN link or dedicated connection. As noted earlier, once on the Cloud, the hyperscale CSPs will typically enable encryption of that data by default. Consumers of other, smaller Cloud providers, must assure themselves of the data-at-rest encryption capabilities of their chosen providers as they may not offer the same levels of protection.

There is an approach that can enable you to store your sensitive data in the Cloud without needing to trust your

Cloud providers; on-premises encryption using your own encryption keys. If you perform your encryption on-premises, and only transfer the encrypted data, then you will never be sending your sensitive data out of your secure environment in the clear. This approach is suitable for the archiving and off-site storage for backup and disaster recovery use cases. It is less suitable for more transactional systems whereby you want to actually process the data once it is in the Cloud. Later in this book, we will touch upon tokenisation and order-preserving encryption approaches, and using these to enable SaaS services to process sensitive data (see chapter 11).

In summary, if you are performing encryption activities and view CSP staff as a threat actor, then perform as much of your data encryption (including key management) on-premises as you possibly can. However, the encryption and key management facilities offered by the major Cloud providers should be viewed as sufficient for all but the most sensitive use cases.

Access management

The SRM includes a significant number of services relating to *access management* (AM):

- *Identity management (IdM)*
  - o *Registration*
  - o *Provisioning*
  - o *Privilege management*
  - o *Directory*
- *Validate*
  - o *Authenticate*
  - o *Authorise*

- *Federate*
- *Reputation*
- *Policy*
- *Filter*

These services are shown in Figure 24, which is an extract from the SRM.

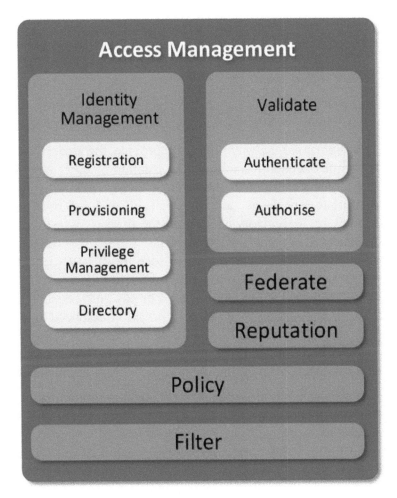

Figure 24: Access management

The SRM is primarily there to guide us in the development of services relating to a hosted application; however, it would be remiss if we did not use the same conceptual services to secure the administration of the infrastructure hosting the application. I will, therefore, talk a little about the *identity management* services offered by some example IaaS providers in addition to those relevant to hosted applications.

Identity management

The *identity management* grouping includes the *registration, provisioning, privilege management* and *directory* services.

The *identity management* services provide the underlying capabilities needed to facilitate the creation of users within your application, and to then assign those users with the appropriate privileges and store all of this information securely in a directory. Some of these services will be implemented outside of your organisation if you are following a federated approach to identity management. I will expand upon this more fully when I talk about the *federate* service later in this chapter. For now, just remember that your application needs users, users will often need to be able to perform tasks according to their levels of authorisation, and that you need a mechanism to manage these users and tasks during the lifetime of your application.

How are such services impacted by hosting an application within a public IaaS Cloud? The procedures governing registration are likely to be independent of whether an application is being hosted on-premises or in the Cloud. The requirements for the amount of proof a new user needs to provide to confirm their identity and then gain access your application will typically be driven from compliance requirements. Registration requirements can vary from practically zero (provision of an email address for example), to more invasive information requests (name, address, date of birth, credit card details, etc.) all the way through to a requirement to conduct a physical inspection of official documentation such as passports. Whilst the requirements regarding registration are independent of delivery model, you must remember any compliance requirements dictating where you may store any personal data obtained during the registration procedure. This is particularly relevant where you are dealing with information relating to EU citizens or PCI-compliant data.

The *provisioning* service relates to the creation, amendment and deletion of user accounts within the application, together with the mechanisms used to distribute credentials to the end users. The *provisioning* service can be viewed as the next step in the process of granting users access to your application, once you are content that they have provided sufficient proof of their identify via the *registration* service. How you provision users is very dependent upon your application and the underlying technologies that you choose to provide the *directory* services (e.g. an on-premises Windows Active Directory, the Cloud-based Azure Active Directory or perhaps a managed directory service). I am not going to detail the processes for creating, amending and deleting users across these different products as that's a level of detail too low for me to hope to cover in this book. However, I will comment upon the credential distribution aspect.

Clouds tend to be viewed as being quite insubstantial. You don't need your own physical data centre or physical hardware, rather everything takes place in a virtualised environment in a CSP data centre. However, if your application requires strong authentication, it is possible that you will have to distribute physical tokens such as those offered by RSA SecurID or Gemalto. These tokens tend to generate random sequences of numbers either upon request (usually after entry of a Personal Identification Number (PIN)) or at set intervals (e.g. every 60 seconds). These random sequences must then be entered as part of the process of authenticating to an application – this form of authentication represents the classic two-factor authentication (2FA) model, i.e. something you know (the PIN and the password associated with the account) and something you hold (the physical token generating the random number sequences). A consequence of implementing token-based authentication is that, even if the application itself is hosted in a CSP data centre, you must still have the facilities to store, configure and then distribute the tokens used to authenticate users to your application.

However, there are alternative approaches. The use of hardware tokens outside of the most sensitive environments is declining in favour of soft token technologies based on the Time-based One-Time Password (TOTP)[125] and FIDO U2F (Universal 2nd Factor) schemes.[126] Soft tokens are implemented in software rather than hardware so they can be installed on mobile devices, effectively turning the mobile device into a second factor. The Google Authenticator application is a popular implementation of a TOTP-based authentication provider – it is also the default second factor authentication provider for a variety of Cloud-based service providers, such as Service Now.

There are a number of companies offering Identity as a Service, for example Okta (*https://www.okta.com/*), as well as authorisation and Authentication as a Service (AaaS) providers like Duo Security (*https://duo.com/*), which was acquired by Cisco in 2018. Such providers offer a number of

---

[125] *https://tools.ietf.org/html/rfc6238*.

[126] Now rebranded as CTAP1 (Client-to-Authenticator Protocol) *https://fidoalliance.org/specifications/*.

different authentication mechanisms including token-based (hard and soft), SMS-token (whereby the random number sequence is sent to a mobile device via SMS) and simple password-based authentication (which is not recommended). The major Cloud providers also offer multi-factor authentication services that can be consumed by hosted services, e.g. AWS Cognito or Azure MFA. Such authentication services can then be integrated into a Cloud consumer's application using established protocols and standards such as OpenID Connect or SAML. There are two obvious advantages to using an AaaS provider:

1. You no longer need to concern yourself with the problems of implementing your own provisioning or directory services for the application; and
2. You no longer need to worry about storing, configuring and distributing physical access tokens.

The obvious disadvantage of using an AaaS provider is that you are now entrusting the task of controlling access to your application to a third party. The capability for trusting third parties is dependent upon organisational culture; the purpose of this book is to provide you with options for securing your Cloud applications; the choice of which option to adopt for your application depends upon your particular situation.

I have outlined some of the options available for the logical elaboration and physical implementation of the conceptual *identity management* services for a hosted application; but what options are available to provide *identity management* services at the IaaS management plane level? Valid concerns could be raised that the effort expended to implement strong authentication for an application could be undermined by weak authentication to the hosting infrastructure.

AWS and identity

Let us begin with Amazon Web Services. Amazon offers a number of mature mechanisms for managing identity and access entitlements; these are centred on the AWS Identity and Access Management (IAM) service. The AWS IAM service (*https://aws.amazon.com/iam/*) enables their customers to provision multiple users, each with their own unique password, and to then define the AWS APIs and resources they can access. AWS consumers can also choose to continue to manage their users and their entitlements by using an existing Windows Active Directory via the AD Connect tool. AWS IAM enables customers to group their users according to their access needs and to add conditional aspects to their access, e.g. by providing the option to restrict the times of day that they can access the services. AWS customers can, therefore, implement segregation of duties, for example by having one group of users able to manage the virtual compute resources hosted upon AWS EC2 whilst having another group of users responsible for managing the storage services hosted upon S3.[127] Best practice however is to make use of IAM Roles rather than groups, with users assuming the role with the access rights that they need at time of use. AWS IAM policies generally use the AWS Account as the default security boundary, though customers can choose to trust identities in other accounts. Furthermore, AWS introduced the concept of AWS Organizations in 2017 to enable cross-account policy management, and this led to the introduction of the Service Control Policy (SCP)

---

[127] In reality, some users will likely require access to both EC2 and S3 in order to configure persistent storage for EC2 services.

capability.[128] SCPs can be applied to limit what users can do within accounts, e.g. an SCP could be applied to prevent the root user within an account being able to delete an S3 bucket containing security logs. SCPs are useful for enforcing dual control in secure environments.

As well as AWS IAM, Amazon also offer the capability to implement two-factor authentication (2FA) via the AWS Multi-Factor Authentication service, AWS MFA (https://aws.amazon.com/iam/features/mfa). AWS MFA supports 2FA via either physical tokens, in the form of Gemalto hardware tokens or Yubikey U2F tokens, or via software installed on to a physical device such as a smartphone or tablet which can also generate one-time passwords. This effectively makes the smartphone or tablet the equivalent of the physical token. Each user defined using AWS IAM can be allocated their own authentication token using AWS MFA. MFA can be used to secure both AWS Management Console users and AWS API users.

Azure and identity

Users of Microsoft Azure can manage their identities via Azure Active Directory (AAD).[129] Microsoft uses the 'tenant' concept to refer to a dedicated AAD instance. A tenant can be used by multiple Azure subscriptions, but each subscription can only trust one tenant. In summary, a consuming organisation will have an account (for billing), at least one tenant and one or more subscriptions. Subscriptions act as a security boundary but do rely on AAD for identity

---

[128] https://docs.aws.amazon.com/organizations/latest/userguide/orgs_manage_policies_scp.html.

[129] https://azure.microsoft.com/en-gb/services/active-directory/.

services. Where AWS has Organizations and SCPs, Azure offers similar capabilities through Management Groups[130] and Azure Policy[131]. Subscriptions can be added to Management Groups, with Azure Policy then being used to enforce consistent controls/policy guardrails across the Management Group hierarchy.

AAD borrows a lot of the concepts and terminology associated with Microsoft's traditional, on-premises Active Directory; however, there are some fundamental differences:

- **The available authentication mechanisms:** AAD supports web-friendly mechanisms such as SAML, OAuth, OpenID and WS-Federation, but not traditional AD mechanisms such as Kerberos and NTLM.

- **There are no Group Policies and Group Policy Objects (GPOs) in AAD:** it focuses on user identity rather than machine management (although limited capability to managed Windows 10 devices via AAD Join is available). AAD Domain Services (AAD DS) must be used if an organisation has a requirement for traditional domain joins and management by GPO.

- **It is flat in structure:** there are no domains, Organisational Units (OUs) or 'forests' in AAD, and organisations would need to look to AAD DS to maintain more familiar structures.

Users can be created directly within AAD or via synchronisation with existing identity repositories. The AD

---

[130] *https://azure.microsoft.com/en-gb/features/management-groups/*.

[131] *https://azure.microsoft.com/en-gb/services/azure-policy/*.

Connect tool offers a variety of options for synchronising AAD identities with on-premises identities. Once within AAD, users can be allocated the access rights that they require via groups. It should be noted that the synchronisation of identities between on-premises AD and AAD stores a hash of the AD password hash within AAD and not the actual password hash, i.e. compromise of the AAD hash would not support pass the hash[132] attacks targeting on-premises resources. However, having the authentication hashes within AAD would provide Azure consumers with a backup authentication mechanism if they are currently using on-premises AD as their authentication provider. Indeed, the NCSC goes further and recommends the use of Cloud-native authentication via AAD over the use of ADFS, including password synchronisation, for hybrid environments, as documented here (albeit in the context of Office 365):

www.ncsc.gov.uk/blog-post/securing-office-365-with-better-configuration.

As with AWS, Azure supports Multi-Factor Authentication (MFA) as part of its wider conditional access capability. Azure offers a variety of MFA options including SMS tokens, other forms of soft tokens and OATH[133] hardware tokens (in preview at the time of writing). Conditional access[134] enables organisations to move towards 'zero trust' approaches; it does this by supplementing authentication

---

[132] *https://attack.mitre.org/techniques/T1075/.*

[133] *https://openauthentication.org/.*

[134] *https://docs.microsoft.com/en-gb/azure/active-directory/conditional-access/concept-conditional-access-conditions.*

decisions with additional considerations, including the nature and location of the device from which the user is requesting access.

AAD offers some advanced capabilities relating to the management of machine identities including managed identities.[135] Managed identities abstract away the problem of having to create and manage identities for Azure resources (e.g. virtual machines) by automatically creating such identities within AAD alongside the associated credentials. The managed identities service takes away the pain associated with creating and managing credentials for nonhuman actors, but the consumer must be willing to place complete trust in the strength of the identities and passwords created for those identities by the Azure platform.

AAD also offers other identity services for Business to Consumer (B2C) and Business to Business (B2B) purposes that make use of the underlying AAD technology; AAD can, therefore, also offer identity management services for your hosted applications.

Google Cloud platform and identity

GCP uses Google Accounts as the main identity store to provide user identities to those developing for, or operating on, the GCP. The Google accounts for an organisation's users are then added to their GCP Organization via the Google Cloud Identity service.

---

[135] *https://docs.microsoft.com/en-us/azure/active-directory/managed-identities-azure-resources/overview.*

Identities can be synchronised from an existing identity repository through the use of the Google Cloud Directory Synchronisation (GCDS) capability.[136]

Cloud IAM[137] is the mechanism used to manage the access of those Google Accounts granted access to the relevant GCP resources via Cloud IAM policies. Cloud IAM allows policies to be applied at all levels of the GCP hierarchy: 'organisations', 'folders', 'projects' and 'resources'.

GCP supports a variety of multi-factor authentications via the Cloud Identity service, including U2F hardware security keys, the Google technology-focused Titan Security Key and the Google Authenticator application. If a GCP consumer decides to use a third-party identity provider service, the authentication mechanism will be determined by the authentication mechanisms supported by that identity provider. It should be noticed that the Cloud Identity service can also be used to manage end user identities, i.e. the identities of those using an application hosted on the GCP.

This section has highlighted that the identity management capabilities offered by the hyperscale IaaS providers are mature and that they offer flexible, configurable approaches towards the provisioning and management of user identities relating to both the Cloud platforms themselves and their use by the applications hosted on those platforms.

Validate

The *validate* service grouping is responsible for checking that a user's claim to be able to access a service is legitimate.

---

[136] *https://support.google.com/a/answer/106368*.

[137] *https://cloud.google.com/iam/docs/overview*.

The *validate* service grouping contains two conceptual services: *authenticate* and *authorise*. The *authenticate* service validates that the user credentials presented in an access request (e.g. a password or a token-generated number sequence) matches the credentials associated with the user. The *authorise* service validates that a user has been granted permission to access the resource (e.g. data, system or function) that the user is attempting to access. So, authentication is focussed on validating the user whereas authorisation is focussed on validating their access.

Authenticate

When it comes to the application that you are choosing to host on an IaaS service, you have free rein to decide upon the most appropriate authentication mechanism. Example mechanisms could include traditional username/password authentication, certificate-based authentication, token-based authentication, or the use of federated identity management techniques such as OpenID. I provide more detail about OpenID in the section describing the *federate* service.

However, from a security purist perspective, you could question the true merit of implementing an application-level authentication mechanism that is stronger than the authentication mechanism protecting the operating system and underlying infrastructure. If you lose trust in the underlying infrastructure, then you can have little faith in the operating systems and applications it hosts.

So, from an authentication perspective, you have a number of areas to address: authentication to the Cloud platform (covered in the previous section), authentication to the operating system on the virtual machines on that platform and, finally, authentication to the application and/or APIs that you have built upon this stack.

Concerning the operating system, there is little to prevent you from implementing whatever strength of authentication control you require; for example, you could choose single factor, multi-factor or SSH authentication mechanisms. This is one of the strengths of the IaaS model: consumers can choose what they need based on their own appetite for risk and compliance requirements. However, one risk that must be considered is the unfortunate tendency of IaaS consumers to embed security credentials within their virtual machine images, particularly where those machine images include processes that need to communicate with other services. This can become a major issue if an IaaS consumer decides to share a machine image with other Cloud platform users. Do not embed your security credentials within your machine images; instead, make use of secret management solutions like those previously described in the *secure development* section.

Authorise

The *authorise* service is responsible for authorising access to a resource. In the context of a hosted application, the *authorise* service dictates the requirements for authorisation to data or functionality. In the context of the underlying IaaS, the *authorise* service dictates the requirements for authorisation to add, delete or modify IaaS resources (compute, storage, etc.) or users.

In order to perform authorisation, you would normally require:

- A set of resources that will be protected;

- A set of authorised users to whom access will be granted;
- A *directory* in which to store users and their access privileges;
- A policy that dictates who can access resources and what levels of access will be granted, e.g. create, read, update and delete (CRUD); and
- A *filter* service to enforce that policy.

I've used the conceptual services from the SRM in the above bullets. From a logical service perspective, you would expect to use more common industry terms associated with identity and access management such as policy information points, policy decision points and policy enforcement points.

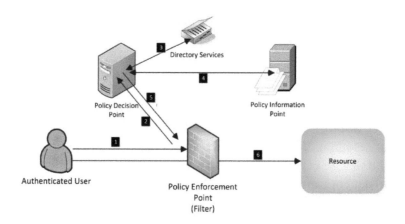

Figure 25: Authorisation flow

Figure 25 shows a typical authorisation sequence. The steps shown in this example sequence are:

1. An authenticated user requests access to an information resource and the request is intercepted by a policy enforcement point (PEP).
2. The PEP queries a policy decision point (PDP) as to whether the access request is authorised.
3. The PDP queries a directory service to obtain details of the authenticated user, such as group membership, access privileges et cetera.
4. The PDP queries a policy information point (PIP) to request information on the access policy to the resource concerned (for example, to obtain the list of groups allowed to access the resource, any time-based or IP-address constraints etc.).
5. The PDP applies the policy based on the information it has obtained and informs the PEP of the access decision.
6. The PEP now allows the user to access the resource (or not if the request has not been authorised).

From a technology perspective, these interactions would likely involve a number of different HTTP(S) requests transporting SAML tokens backwards and forwards. I am not going to go into further detail of the technologies providing authorisation capabilities – there are enough textbooks dedicated to identity and access management that I could not possibly do the topic justice in one short section.

However, there is a Cloud-specific element to the authorisation process described in Figure 25. Whilst it is not necessary to host each of the PEP, PDP, PIP, et cetera on separate servers, hosting certain on separate servers can provide Cloud consumers with additional flexibility. For example, if you have concerns about hosting the personal data contained within a directory on a Cloud server, then you could host the directory, PIP and PDP on-premises. In this scenario only the PEP and the resource itself are hosted within the Cloud – and they may not require knowledge of the sensitive personal data that you are keeping on-premises.

Similarly, you could host the directory, PIP, and PDP services on one Cloud and then manage access to all your other Cloud services from this single (although I would suggest replicated) authorisation Cloud. There are a number of Cloud-based security as a service offers that could deliver this logical capability, e.g. Okta.

Another option for delivering authorisation services would be to adopt a federated approach, e.g. through the use of protocols such as OAuth.

Federate

Federation has already been mentioned a number of times in this chapter, primarily relating to authentication and authorisation, but without much detail of what it means. Federated identity management is a trust-based approach to identity management whereby an organisation trusts the authentication and/or authorisation decisions made by another organisation. Federation can be useful to prevent users constantly having to re-enter their credentials every time they begin to interact with a new service. Similarly, federation can be useful to enable smoother interaction across services. For example, to provide one service with access to information held by a separate service.

When talking about federated authentication, two terms that commonly occur are 'identity provider (IdP)' and 'relying party (RP)'. Relying parties are sometimes known as 'service providers' (SPs). The relying party is the application or service to which a user is attempting to authenticate. If the service incorporates a federated authentication scheme then, at this point, the RP will ask its IdP whether or not the user is authenticated. If so, the RP will now provide the user with access. If not, the user will typically be prompted to authenticate using the RP's own authentication mechanisms.

Federation can be used to deliver a number of benefits in addition to providing single sign-on (SSO) across services. Consider the case of a community Cloud hosting a shared application. One approach to delivering identity management for such an application would be to have a centralised directory containing accounts for each user from the community requiring access to the service. However, this approach has some negative implications:

- The community needs to find someone to administer this directory;
- The users now have yet another set of credentials to either remember or, in the case of a physical token, keep safe; and
- Access management processes will be laborious, requiring authorisation from within the source organisation and then actioning (possibly via another authorisation step) at the centre.

An alternative would be to adopt a federated approach, whereby the shared application trusts the authentication decisions made at each of the organisations that comprise the community. So, the shared application becomes an RP and each member of the community becomes an IdP. This approach has a number of advantages:

- Authentication decisions are made by each community organisation;
- There is no central user directory — each community organisation controls the user information it allows to leave its secure domain; and
- Access management processes occur at a faster rate— accounts can be created at the IdP and then replicated to the RP using, for example, SPML[138] or SCIM.[139]

Of course, there are some compromises associated with this approach; e.g. members of the community must trust that the other members implement appropriately strong authentication mechanisms. There can also be a degree of pain involved in the implementation of the cryptographic services needed to establish the technical trust between the different parties. Finally, significant effort needs to be expended to establish the governance structures needed to establish the trust infrastructure, e.g. to set appropriate standards for authentication. However, overall I prefer this federated approach to the more centralised model due to the greater flexibility it offers to the users and the ability of the community organisations to retain control of their own information.

Two commonly implemented federation technologies in the web space are OpenID[140] (which provides federated

---

[138] *www.oasis-open.org/committees/tc_home.php?wg_abbrev=provision.*

[139] *https://tools.ietf.org/html/rfc7644.*

[140] *https://openid.net/.*

Figure 26: Google account

From Figure 26, you can see that I have allowed both Epson iPrint and Disqus to use Google as an identity provider, i.e. they will allow me access provided I am currently logged into my Google account.

Figure 27 outlines this process from the perspective of a web service that relies upon Google for account sign-up and authentication (in this case Disqus).

Figure 27: Disqus

From the login/sign-up screen, if the user clicks on the 'G' button (for Google), they will be presented with the following screen (Figure 28); from there, the user must choose which of their Google accounts they wish to use (there may be multiple options).

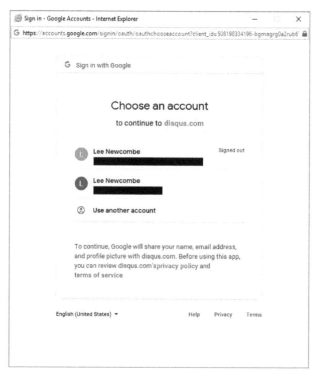

Figure 28: Selecting a sign-in account

Once an account has been selected, the user is required to authenticate to Google prior to the services being linked for authentication services as shown in Figure 29.

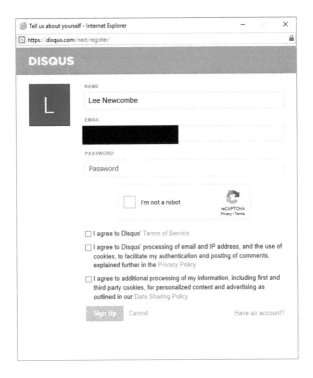

Figure 29: Creation of Disqus account

At this point, Disqus sends an email to the selected Google email account with a confirmation link that must be accessed to finalise the process. The Disqus account is now created, and the linkage between Disqus and the selected identity providers is available within the account settings, as shown in Figure 30.

Figure 30: Disqus "Connected Accounts"

OAuth 2.0 allows users to share access to specific information and functionality at their own discretion; this is a benefit for users and, potentially, for their application providers if they are subject to privacy regulations that require the demonstration and management of user consent.

Currently, OpenID is probably the most widely implemented federated authentication solution, but it is not the only solution.

Okta – mentioned earlier in the section on authentication service – is able to act as an IdP through its support for security assertion markup language (SAML).[143] Consumers can, therefore, implement multi-factor authentication by using federation across all of their applications via a Cloud-based service. Okta is not the only service space of this kind, and competition is heating up as enterprises look to adopt approaches based on zero trust networking; in this model,

---

[143] *www.oasis-open.org/committees/tc_home.php?wg_abbrev=security.*

access to services is based on the identity of the user and their access device rather than on the network from which the access is being requested. The Google BeyondCorp whitepapers[144] arguably set the standard for zero trust networking (building on the Jericho Forum principles relating to de-perimeterisation), and the GCP is able to support this approach via Google Identity and the Google Identity Aware Proxy. Other implementations of the zero trust networking approach towards authentication and authorisation are also available from the likes of Duo Security[145] and Ping Identity.[146]

Cloud consumers can also implement federated authentication solutions to allow their users to authenticate to Cloud-based services using an on-premises identity provider. In this scenario the Cloud-based applications are the relying parties. This can enable Cloud consumers to make use of existing investments in authentication and identity management technologies. At the same time, such an approach also enables Cloud consumers to present their users with transparent access to services, whether they are hosted on-premises or on-Cloud. Furthermore, by hosting the IdP on-premises, organisations are effectively keeping the keys to their Cloud-based applications and data within their secure domain (although this protection could be bypassed should the underlying Cloud infrastructure suffer from a weakness lower down the technology stack, e.g. in the hypervisor). This approach to federated identity management is most common when implementing SaaS delivery models,

---

[144] *https://cloud.google.com/beyondcorp/#researchPapers*.

[145] *https://duo.com/docs/beyond-overview*.

[146] *www.pingidentity.com/en/platform/platform-overview.html*.

particularly if the consumer makes use of multiple SaaS providers. An increasingly popular option for those organisations moving towards an Azure-based future is to make use of Azure AD as the main identity repository and then control access to SaaS services via Cloud App Security (other Cloud Access Security Brokers can also be used) and to on-premises applications via the AAD App Proxy.

So far I have written about how the *federation* service may be implemented within an application that you may wish to host on an IaaS Cloud. Some IaaS providers also support federated identity management such that you can manage your virtual infrastructures whilst authenticated via federation. Amazon allow you to create temporary security credentials that you can then distribute to users that have been authenticated via your existing authentication service. Once your users are in possession of these temporary security credentials, they can then access the AWS Management Console directly without being prompted for a password. The lifetime of the temporary security credentials are defined at the time of creation. The link below describes how to create temporary security credentials using the Amazon Security Token Service (STS):

https://docs.aws.amazon.com/IAM/latest/UserGuide/id_cre dentials_temp.html.

Once you have understood the nature of AWS temporary security credentials (and also the AWS services that support such credentials), you can consider using this approach to secure access to AWS resources, including via the AWS Command Line Interface (CLI) and APIs. The link below provides a description of this approach:

https://docs.aws.amazon.com/IAM/latest/UserGuide/id_cre dentials_temp_use-resources.html.

As Amazon themselves note, just because the security credentials are temporary it does not mean that the actions of those with such credentials will not be permanent. For example, should a user with temporary credentials, e.g. via assuming a privileged IAM Role, start a new Amazon Machine Image, this virtual server will continue to run (and be charged) even after the temporary credentials of the user have expired.

Similar temporary credential approaches can be used on the GCP,[147] whilst Azure adopts a different route and allows temporary access via the Just in Time access controls offered by the Azure Privileged Identity Management (PIM) service.[148]

Policy

The *policy* service (within the *access management* grouping) of the SRM is responsible for the setting of policy for access management decisions. Policies are required to dictate which users (individuals, application accounts, service accounts, etc.) are allowed access to an information resource (data, function, server, etc.) and what privileges they are allowed to that resource (e.g. create, read, update and delete, etc.). PIP were mentioned during the section on authorisation which explained their role in the authorisation process. At the logical and physical levels, policy may be stored centrally on a PIP; however, in many cases policies will be physically

---

[147] *https://cloud.google.com/iam/docs/creating-short-lived-service-account-credentials*.

[148] *https://docs.microsoft.com/en-us/microsoft-identity-manager/pam/privileged-identity-management-for-active-directory-domain-services*.

implemented at a more local level. For example, firewall policies are more than likely (and recommended) to be stored separately to access management policies at the application level.

There is little more to be said about *policy* in this context – your policies for access to information resources must be dictated by your business requirements. The business requirements must indicate which types of users require access to which information resources and at what level this access should be granted.

The *policy* service interacts with a number of other SRM services, notably *authentication, authorisation* and *filter* to perform many of the tasks commonly associated with information security, i.e. preventing unauthorised access to information, or, in a positive light, enabling authorised access to information.

Filter

The *filter* service within the SRM serves as a good illustration of what is meant by a conceptual service. The *filter* service enforces the policy requirements. As it's a conceptual service, it does not dictate how filters should be delivered at the logical or physical level. Why is it a good illustration? Because the *filter* service tells you what you need to do – deny or allow access – but does not tell you how to do it, or how to enforce it. Although it may not look it at first sight, this is a good thing. Consider the many different areas where you need to control access, e.g.:

- Data centre
- Storage
- Data
- Operating system

- Database
- Application
- Container
- API
- Cloud service
- Network
- Hypervisor

Each of these aspects will require their own physical set of filtering technologies. At the lowest level, data centres will require suitable mechanisms to prevent unauthorised access to the equipment that they host. With a public Cloud this is an issue for the CSP; with community and private Clouds this issue may be one for the Cloud consumer. Similarly, physical and administrative access to the low-level storage devices is typically within the purview of the CSP in the context of a public Cloud.

When you get to the data level, e.g. which users (including applications) are allowed access to which data, things start to become more complicated. For example, Amazon offers a number of different storage services including the Simple Storage Service (S3) and Elastic Block Storage (EBS). Access to data stored within the AWS S3 storage can be secured in a number of ways as highlighted at:

https://docs.aws.amazon.com/AmazonS3/latest/dev/access-control-overview.html.

In summary, access can be controlled at an S3 bucket level or at an object level basis and these controls can be applied in a number of ways to enable sharing either just within your AWS account or across different AWS accounts. In response to the number of reported incidents in which consumers have accidentally opened access to their S3 buckets up to the

Internet, AWS has also implemented some specific options to block public access to S3 buckets.[149] AWS released Access Analyzer[150] at re:Invent 2019, a tool that enables AWS users to more easily identify those with access to S3 buckets and to then remediate any excessive or unexpected access.

The key point here is that the enforcement point is still within the realm of the CSP (in this case, AWS). The consumer gets to decide which users can access the device (via the *policy*), but the enforcement of that access control (via the *filter*) sits with the CSP.

Now, Cloud consumers also require logical and physical *filter* services at levels other than those concerning data. What about the network? The majority of the network access controls in the IaaS environment are provided by the CSP. The CSP infrastructure is directly connected to the Internet; it is the responsibility of the CSP to ensure that Internet-based attackers cannot compromise the underlying infrastructure. They must implement appropriate firewalling and intrusion prevention technologies.

However, what about your virtual servers? Once you have your Cloud server instance, you may be placed directly onto the Internet. If you do not have a host-based firewall then you are now at the mercy of whatever network-based controls the CSP may have implemented. From an AWS EC2 perspective, this is a relatively safe position to be in as the AWS firewall capability offered as part of the standard AWS

---

[149] *https://docs.aws.amazon.com/AmazonS3/latest/dev/access-control-block-public-access.html.*

[150] *https://docs.aws.amazon.com/AmazonS3/latest/user-guide/access-analyzer.html.*

service adopts a default deny position, i.e. all network traffic to the instance will be dropped. This means that it is the responsibility of the consumer to open up access to the network ports required to run their service.

Azure Virtual Machines are in a similar position as the default Network Security Groups (NSGs) block inbound Internet traffic; however, implementors should be aware that all outbound traffic is allowed by default. GCP takes a somewhat different approach, and the pre-populated firewall rules associated with the default network of new virtual machines allow inbound access for both SSH and RDP to all instances by default. GCP users should look to tighten up these default rules during implementation. GCP does offer other mechanisms for enforcing a perimeter around Cloud-hosted resources via VPC Service Controls[151] functionality, and this complements the controls offered by their more identity-centred IAM capabilities. Once again though, this question of network access control is really a policy question, with the *filter* aspect being implemented by the relevant CSP(s).

Once you reach the level of the operating system (OS), the responsibility for implementation of *filter* services sits firmly with any consumer working with IaaS Clouds. Consumers can implement host-based firewalls, host-based intrusion prevention systems, operating system ACLs on file system objects and any other traditional operating system-level access control mechanism. Given that the servers are operating within the Cloud, it is worth considering what controls are available over and above those that would be

---

[151] *https://cloud.google.com/vpc-service-controls/.*

installed in an on-premises environment. A good example may be the potential to implement your own virtual private Cloud using a tool such as Cohesive Networks VNS3.[152] VNS3 enables a Cloud consumer to implement an SSL-encrypted overlay network that effectively prevents CSP staff from being able to access or view the consumer's data whilst it is within the encrypted overlay. CSP staff would still have the ability to close down instances should they wish, and to see data entering and leaving the overlay, be that to and from the Internet or to and from the underlying storage devices, although they would not have access to the traffic flowing across the overlay network itself. Such tools can be a useful *filter* with regard to CSP staff who are otherwise fairly impervious to the controls available to Cloud consumers. VNS3 could be viewed as a form of a Cloud Workload Protection Platform (CWPP).

At the application level, you can consider the use of a WAF to provide a *filter* if you are using an IaaS Cloud to host a web service. There is little difference here between applications hosted on-premises and those hosted within a Cloud; at the application level, the WAF is there to filter out malicious traffic lurking within the HTTP(S) communications. Figure 22 illustrated the potential of using a Cloud-based WAF service to protect your IaaS-hosted web applications. Cloud consumers can, of course, choose to implement their own WAFs as virtualised network appliances within their IaaS environments; alternatively, they can consider using any WAF capabilities offered by the Cloud platforms themselves, such as AWS WAF[153] or Azure

---

[152] *www.cohesive.net/products/vns3net.*

[153] *https://aws.amazon.com/waf/.*

Application Gateway.[154] The benefit of using the services offered by the Cloud provider is that the consumer no longer needs to concern themselves with building and operating their own redundant, resilient WAF solutions; the downside is that the CSP offers may not be as fully featured as the best-in-breed WAF solutions.

One of the issues to bear in mind when considering the logical elaboration, and subsequent physical implementation, of the conceptual *filter* service is that any such controls must be appropriate to the task at hand. Consider a traditional firewall. Most firewalls are very good at controlling the network communications that traverse them; dictating allowed sources, the allowed destinations, the allowed types of traffic between the sources and destinations and, often, ensuring that the traffic adheres to the relevant protocol specifications. Unfortunately, this is often insufficient for today's complex applications. Consider a web application processing XML-encoded information transported via SSL/TLS encrypted communications. A traditional firewall will be blind to the nature of the traffic flowing over the encrypted channel; even if it could see the XML on the network, it most likely would not be able to parse the XML so as to understand whether the traffic was malicious. A more appropriate choice for a *filter* service would be an XML firewall that is designed to parse XML, perform basic checks (such as schema validation) and to spot more elaborate attacks, such as embedded malicious binaries. XML firewalls are particularly relevant where a Cloud consumer is building a web services based information system. I mentioned a number of such XML

---

[154] *https://azure.microsoft.com/en-us/services/application-gateway/.*

firewalls products in the section on the integrity service earlier in this chapter, namely:

- Axway AMPLIFY (*www.axway.com/en/products/api-management*)
- CA API Gateway (*www.ca.com/gb/products/ca-api-gateway.html*)
- Forum Systems (*www.forumsys.com*)

At the database level, consumers should consider the use of specific database security products. Such products are able to understand the queries and commands being passed back and forth between the database server, application servers and administrators. The database firewall – also known as database activity monitoring (DAM) – market is now mature, with many of the early market leaders having been acquired by more established entities. Examples include:

- Guardium (purchased by IBM: *https://www.ibm.com/security/data-security/guardium*);
- Secerno (purchased by Oracle: *www.oracle.com/us/products/database/security/index.html*); and
- Sentrigo (purchased by McAfee: *www.mcafee.com/us/products/database-security/index.aspx*).

Where you have a need to monitor the activities of your database administrators, or you wish to lock down the database access available to application accounts, then you should be looking towards database activity monitoring products as part of your *filter* service. As with other potential realisations of the *filter* service, the major CSPs are now also starting to deliver some basic DAM capabilities within their Cloud services, e.g. Azure SQL Database Threat Detection[155] and the more manual approach that AWS Aurora offers via integration with CloudWatch for monitoring.[156]

One of the major differences between a physical deployment and a virtual deployment is the addition of a new attack surface – the hypervisor. In a public Cloud environment the security of the hypervisor is firmly within the realm of the CSP. In a private or community Cloud, the consumer is in the position to be able to specify the security controls protecting the hypervisor and controlling the inter virtual machine traffic flowing across it. In a VMware environment, there are a number of different options for providing this capability, e.g.:

- VMware vSphere Platinum and AppDefense (*www.vmware.com/uk/products/appdefense.html*)
- Trend Micro Deep Security (*www.trendmicro.co.uk/products/deep-security/index.html*)
- HyTrust (*www.hytrust.com*)

Understandably, the VMware AppDefence and software-defined security products only work with the VMware hypervisor. These products make use of the visibility available within the hypervisor to identify known good

---

[155] *https://docs.microsoft.com/en-us/azure/sql-database/sql-database-threat-detection.*

[156] *https://aws.amazon.com/about-aws/whats-new/2017/09/amazon-aurora-enables-database-activity-monitoring-with-cloudwatch-logs/.*

application traffic and, subsequently, to flag and/or block traffic that falls outside of its baseline. Neither Deep Security nor Hytrust actually sit within the hypervisor so their available visibility is quite limited when compared with that available to VMware tooling.

In essence, the VMware tooling sits beside the hypervisor, monitoring and controlling the traffic flows between the hosted virtual machines and can also be used to control the network to and from the hypervisor, protecting the hypervisor itself. These products typically allow you to group virtual machines into zones (or application stacks) and then control the network traffic between these zones (although they also work on an individual virtual machine basis). This approach allows you to mimic a more traditional n-tier architecture by using different zones rather than different physically separate network segments. Concerns have been raised by some, including the UK government's National Technical Authority for Information Assurance (NCSC), that little assurance should be placed in these products. The primary reason for such concerns relates to the fact that compromise of the hypervisor itself would render these controls worthless; they could be bypassed through reconfiguration at the hypervisor level. As such, NCSC and others would not recommend using these tools to provide a security barrier between domains at different levels of trust, but that they may be used within a security domain.

Another valid concern is that, whilst with a traditional n-tier architecture you may consider implementing different firewall products at the different tiers, with a virtualised environment you will be limited to one selected product. Figures 31 and 32 below illustrate the differences between a traditional n-tier application architecture and a virtualised alternative making use of a hypervisor-based firewall.

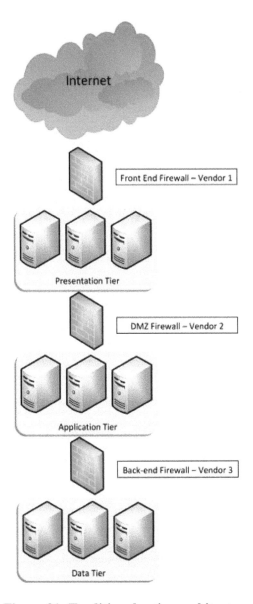

Figure 31: Traditional n-tier architecture

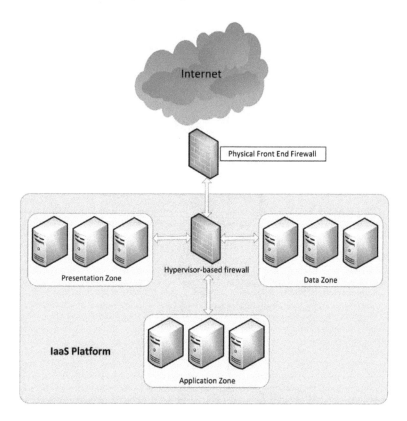

Figure 32: A zoning approach

Figure 31 shows that the traditional approach makes use of three different firewall products (to guard against the failure of a single product) and that it has the ability to control traffic across each tier boundary. Figure 32 shows that, instead of physically separate firewalls and servers, we now have a set of virtualised servers grouped into different zones with the separation (*filter*) being provided by hypervisor-based firewalls.

My guidance is to consider your levels of risk and act accordingly – do you believe that the assets within your virtual environment are valuable enough to merit an attacker 'giving away' a valuable zero day (i.e. unpublished) hypervisor exploit? If so, then you need to invest in suitable levels of physical separation within your application (e.g. implement a physically separate demilitarised zone). If not, then you may be willing to rely upon the *filter* services that hypervisor-based technologies can deliver.

Similar considerations exist within the public Cloud world. Cloud consumers can choose to rely upon the CSP-provided firewalling and network segmentation capabilities that are equivalent to VMware protections (e.g. Security Groups and VPCs in the AWS world, or Network Security Groups and VNets in the Azure world) or else look to implement their own virtualised network appliances (VNAs) such as firewalls. There are a number of trade-offs to be considered regarding this choice between Cloud-native capability and VNAs. The two main considerations are:

1. **Complexity:** relying upon the CSP-native capabilities can lead to a complex mesh of security groups that require ongoing maintenance; consequently, organisations may view the relative simplicity of a VNA within a transit VPC/VNet as a more straightforward proposition from a management perspective. This may be particularly true if that firewall is API-enabled because this means that the rule-base and policy can be articulated as code as easily as the CSP-native controls.

2. **Defence in depth:** implementing a separate VNA on top of the Cloud provider native capability could be viewed as providing an extra level of security (although, in reality, should the inter-virtual private Cloud

networking be compromised, it is questionable whether the VNA would provide any extra defence in practice).

Either way, the Cloud consumer has a number of options regarding the realisation of the *filter* service for controlling access into and out of their IaaS-hosted application.

Security governance

With the IaaS service model, the primary delivery responsibility for security governance remains with the Cloud consumer. The Cloud consumer retains primary delivery responsibility for the *security management*, *risk management* and *coordinate* services. The *personnel security* service is a joint delivery responsibility, reflecting that CSP staff have access to the infrastructure whilst consumer personnel have access to the virtualised environment. The *security governance* services from the SRM are shown in Figure 33.

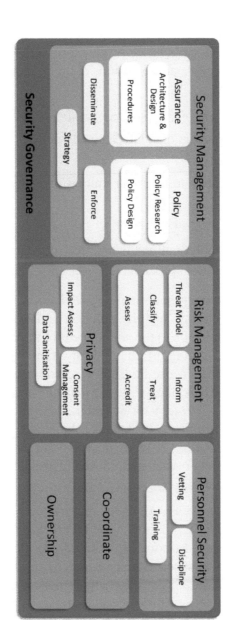

Figure 33: Security governance services

Security management

The *security management* service provides many of the traditional concepts and functions of an IT security practice. These include:

- Determining overall security strategy;
- Conducting the mandated privacy activities that impact upon policy;
- Setting policy to meet the strategy and privacy needs;
- Disseminating policy;
- Enforcing policy; and
- Assuring policy implementation within technical design and operational procedures.

The SRM's *strategy* service is key to determining the wider shape of the overall security solution and for aligning the shape of that solution to the wider needs of the business. This includes the shaping of the security function itself, e.g. deciding whether to use traditional centralisation or a more distributed and delegated structure that suits more agile ways of working. The *strategy* service interacts with the *ownership* service to ensure that ownership of the strategy is allocated and that the residual risks associated with the strategy are also appropriately owned and tracked by stakeholders within the wider business.

The *privacy* services relate to the requirements of the GDPR and other similar regulations. The GDPR has a requirement for organisations to consider "privacy by design", i.e. to consider privacy issues at the very start of application design in order to guide the development of that application. The output of a privacy impact assessment[157] will provide a set of high priority requirements relating to strategy and policy for a Cloud-hosted application.

The SRM's *policy* service has two aspects: *policy research* and *policy design*. The *policy research* service provides the capability to research recent developments regarding compliance (including any outputs from the *privacy* services), technology and evolving business requirements concerning any application that will be hosted on an IaaS Cloud. The output from the research capability can then be passed to the *policy design* service which outputs security policies relevant to the application. Policy design is likely to be something of an iterative process. For example, an initial security policy may help to dictate which IaaS providers are suitable to host your application, perhaps based on their geographical locations. The next iteration of the application security policy may then incorporate some specific aspects relating to the CSP, e.g. which of the individual offerings of the CSP are approved for implementation, which are not judged suitable, et cetera. These security policies can then be used to drive more technical policies such as those required for access management purposes, personnel security vetting, encryption standards, et cetera.

Unfortunately, one of the areas where information security often fails is in the translation from information security policy through to actual implementation. The SRM includes two services aimed at ensuring that all relevant individuals are aware of the policy requirements (*disseminate*) and that the policy requirements are enforced (*enforce*). Dissemination can be achieved via security awareness

---

[157] Also commonly referred to as a Data Protection Impact Assessment.

training (for consumer personnel) and via provision of appropriate guidance documentation. The goal of the *dissemination* service is to ensure that everyone understands their security obligations and, as importantly, to try and convince them that following the policy is in their own best interests. The enforcement capability is necessary to shepherd those elements of the organisation (or user community) that may not buy into the message that is promulgated via the *disseminate* service. Enforcement can be achieved centrally or through the deployment of local security champions to the business units and project teams implementing on Cloud services. Placing security champions within agile scrum teams can be a very effective way of embedding security into the products near the beginning of the development lifecycle. The enforcement capability must have appropriate links to personnel functions, in particular the *discipline* service, to ensure that adequate and proportional sanctions are in place for those that may choose not to adhere to policy. The enforcement function also requires explicit support from authoritative figures within the consumer to provide policy implementation with the necessary impetus.

The final capability provided by the *security management* service grouping is that of *assurance*. From a security management perspective, assurance refers to assuring that the requirements of the relevant security policies have been adopted within the technical design of the application and the associated operating procedures. Wider security assurance testing activities are covered elsewhere (e.g. *compliance* and *vulnerability management*). The assurance capabilities require sufficient expertise in the Cloud technologies in question in order to be effective. The staff involved must be able to understand whether a proposed technical architecture meets the policy requirements. A lack of understanding will likely equate to failure to meet policy and so increase the possibility of a security or compliance breach. Whilst I am of the view that Cloud computing is an evolution rather than a revolution, the security impacts of this evolution on underlying technical delivery, service-oriented design and global compliance requirements are significant. Organisations should consider the training requirements of any existing assurance function. An 'old-school' security assurance function could de-rail any number of Cloud deployments based on misunderstanding of the underlying technologies or an overly risk averse approach. The cost of training and up-skilling of security personnel should be outweighed by the benefits of enabling a risk-managed (rather than risk-averse) approach to adopting Cloud services.

Risk management

I do not intend to write reams of text describing the *risk management* service grouping. Most organisations should have adopted a preferred approach to risk management and there is little reason why such approaches should not be extended to the Cloud. At a high level, a risk management approach should consist of the following steps:

1. Threat model

Identify the threat sources and threat actors looking to compromise the application and/or data. Document the threats (competitors, hackers, governments, employees, CSP staff, journalists, environmental threats, accidental threats, etc.) to your assets. A number of different threat actor catalogues are available including the IRAM v2 Common Threat List and the Intel Threat Agent Library.

2. *Classify*

Classify your assets in terms of their value to the business. Value could be measured in terms of confidentiality, integrity and availability for example. Value could also be measured in monetary terms.

3. *Inform*

Involve the relevant organisation personnel. Asset owners should be involved in assessing and agreeing the classifications associated with their assets. Suitable safeguards should be built into the process to ensure that the human tendency to overvalue your own assets is adequately managed (e.g. through involving higher levels of management with sight across the assets concerned).

4. *Assess*

Assess the attack surface of your application. Consider which potential vulnerabilities could realistically be exploited by each previously identified threat. Consider the business impacts of a vulnerability being exploited by a threat actor. Bear in mind that the business impact may be dependent upon the threat actor concerned. For example, a well-meaning customer may identify a potential vulnerability in your application and inform you through a published notification process. A black-hat hacker may identify the same vulnerability and post an exploit on the Internet. The same asset, the same vulnerability but the impact is different because of the actions of the threat actor. Document your risks (e.g. asset, vulnerabilities, threats, impacts) in an accessible manner. There are a number of published risk analysis methodologies such as IRAM2[158], FAIR[159] and OCTAVE.[160]

5. *Treat*

Using the risk register produced by the *assess* service, treat each risk in turn appropriately. Standard treatments would include accept, transfer, mitigate or avoid. It is perfectly acceptable to simply accept risks that fall within the tolerance of your organisation. Not every risk must be mitigated or avoided. Document the proposed treatment of each risk in a risk treatment plan – ensure that any mitigations are explained to a level of detail sufficient to allow the overall risk owner to judge the suitability of the mitigation.

6. *Accredit*

An appropriate figure within the organisation should review the risk analysis and associated risk treatment plan and confirm that they are content that all relevant risks have been identified and appropriately treated. This final sign-off effectively provides a security accreditation for the application. Some organisations may wish to extend this process such that formal accreditation is only offered after penetration testing has been completed and the necessary remediation undertaken.

---

[158] *www.securityforum.org/tool/information-risk-assessment-methodology-iram2/.*

[159] *www.fairinstitute.org/.*

[160] *www.cert.org/octave.*

This type of formal accreditation is unlikely to be effective in a digital (Mode 2) environment. A more appropriate mechanism in this environment would be to develop a pre-approved set of templates (e.g. machine images, AWS Landing Zones et cetera) – perhaps made available within a mandated service catalogue[161] – and a development pipeline (e.g. code analysis tools); projects should be allowed to progress as long as they operate within the pre-approved security guardrails. In this model, the accreditation process is much more of a 'trust, but verify' function – should any subsequent audits or penetration tests indicate that the pre-approved processes were avoided or ignored, then appropriate action should be taken; however, the default posture is one of trusting your teams to do the right thing. Spot checks should, of course, be conducted to verify that the authorised processes are being followed and indeed, such checks may well be mandated by other compliance requirements.

Personnel security

Within the SRM, I have marked *personnel security* as being a joint delivery responsibility when considering the IaaS service model. This reflects the fact that CSPs must hire, manage and release staff in a manner that does not place the security of their customers' data or service at undue risk. By the same token, IaaS consumers must also ensure that their users, application developers, system administrators, database administrators, et cetera are also appropriately managed.

---

[161] For example, *https://aws.amazon.com/servicecatalog/* or *https://azure.microsoft.com/en-gb/services/managed-applications/*.

I suggested three main services within the SRM:
1. *Vetting*;
2. *Discipline*; and
3. *Training*.

The *vetting* service (in combination with *compliance* and other services via associated service contracts) dictates the levels of background checking needed prior to employing personnel or moving personnel from a less sensitive role to a more sensitive role. The UK Centre for the Protection of National Infrastructure offers some useful guidance on pre-employment checks (at *www.cpni.gov.uk/content/security-pre-screening*), whilst there is a British Standard on security vetting (BS 7858:2012); the latter was originally targeted for those organisations working in the security industry but is, in fact, more widely applicable.[162] Background checks can vary in intrusiveness from simple identity verification through to extensive interviews with acquaintances of the individual concerned together with financial and criminal record checks.

From a consumer perspective, vetting processes for their users accessing Cloud-based resources should be no different to those used elsewhere within their organisation. Consumers must, however, content themselves that the vetting processes adopted by the IaaS providers match the levels of rigour that they themselves require, or else accept a known residual risk.

The *discipline* service ensures that appropriate sanctions can be enforced against users and/or employees who fail to meet

---

[162] *https://shop.bsigroup.com/ProductDetail/?pid=000000000030237324*.

their security obligations. As with the vetting process, consumers should simply adopt their existing disciplinary processes when implementing services in the Cloud.

The final *personnel security* service within the SRM relates to *training*. As noted earlier in this chapter, it is vital that your users receive appropriate training in order to make the best use of the new ways of working offered by Cloud computing. This is as true for security professionals as it is true for other IT professionals. Developers should receive training on the implications of working with their chosen IaaS provider, e.g. how they should secure Cloud storage, the appropriate forms of API authentication and authorisation, which form of database service is the most appropriate for their current needs, et cetera. If you do not train your developers on the security implications of working in a multi-tenant environment, do not be surprised if they leave your application, and so your organisation, exposed.

Security operations

The *security operations* service grouping is the last of the major elements of the SRM to be considered. Figure 34 shows the security operations section of the SRM.

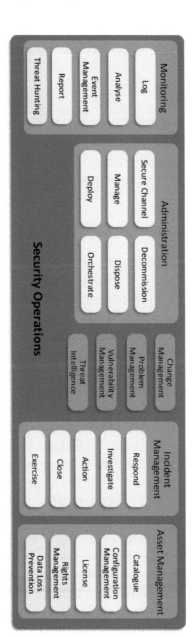

Figure 34: Security operations

As can be seen from Figure 34, the security operations grouping includes a number of different capabilities:

- *Monitoring*
- *Administration*
- *Incident management*
- *Threat intelligence*
- *Asset management*
- *Vulnerability management*
- *Change management*
- *Problem management*

Within the IaaS SRM, *monitoring* is assigned to be a joint delivery responsibility. Whilst the consumer is responsible for security monitoring of everything from the operating system upwards, the CSP is responsible for security monitoring of the underlying physical infrastructure. The *monitoring* service grouping includes a number of different services to provide a cohesive approach to security monitoring. The *log* service is conceptually responsible for capturing the information required to identify (and then investigate) any security incident or to meet compliance-driven auditing requirements. Information must be captured at all relevant levels; this includes those areas within the control of the CSP such as that relating to the physical infrastructure (firewalls, network IPS, storage, etc.) and those areas that are the responsibility of the consumer (cloud provider API use, operating system, host-based IPS and firewalls, database, application, etc.). Historically, Cloud providers have limited the ability of their consumers to log network traffic, with consumers usually only able to capture packet headers of network traffic using tools such as VPC Flowlogs and Azure Network Security Group flow logs.

The providers have recognised that some consumers require more insight into the network traffic, including full packet capture, and now offer capabilities to support such packet capture namely:

- AWS VPC Traffic Mirroring[163]
- Azure Virtual Network TAP[164]
- GCP Packet Mirroring[165]

Consumers can now use these capabilities to copy network to traditional network intrusion detection solutions should they wish. I would recommend that consumers try to ascertain the levels of logging undertaken by their CSPs so that the entirety of the logging capabilities of a cloud solution is understood– the most likely source for this information is the ISO 27001 statement of applicability, output from a SOC2 Type II assessment, a CSA STAR entry or a 'trust' artefact produced by the CSP themselves.

Logging is only the beginning of a true security monitoring capability, the logged information must then also be securely stored[166] in a forensically sound manner where possible (in case it must later be relied upon in court). The *analyse* service is responsible for identifying events of interest within the logged information. This is likely to involve the collection, normalisation and correlation of the logs from the

---

[163] *https://aws.amazon.com/blogs/aws/new-vpc-traffic-mirroring/*.

[164] *https://docs.microsoft.com/en-us/azure/virtual-network/virtual-network-tap-overview*.

[165] *https://cloud.google.com/vpc/docs/packet-mirroring*.

[166] The storage service resides within the hosting service grouping in the SRM.

different sources mentioned in the preceding paragraph. One advantage of the IaaS model, compared to the PaaS and SaaS models, is that consumers can often use the same security monitoring agents within their Cloud-based virtualised environment as they use within their own data centres. Depending on your willingness to accept security event information coming from outside of your trusted domain, you could also simply reuse existing collation and analysis points within your on-premises security architecture. If your posture is more risk averse, a separate collation point for information sourced from Cloud systems could be implemented, either on-premise or on-Cloud. To reduce costs, it may be prudent to implement a single collation and analysis point (subject to scalability) that is able to monitor events across all of your Cloud-based services. This logging and analysis point should be separated from your secure, trusted domain.

One of the challenges of Cloud monitoring relates to noise and data egress costs: the major CSPs charge for the transfer of data outside of their environments, and consumers can find themselves paying to export a lot of worthless data from their IaaS environments. This is leading some of the traditional security information and event management (SIEM) vendors to adopt more distributed and delegated approaches towards security monitoring; consequently, in many cases, local agents installed on the monitored IaaS environments only pass on a subset of the total information generated to the central stations. Cloud consumers now have the choice between more fully centralised logging and monitoring solutions and distributed solutions that are potentially more cost-effective.

Once the information has been collated, whether centrally or in a more distributed manner, it will usually need to be normalised in a common form to enable more effective correlation and analysis. The *analyse* service must then examine the logged and normalised information and highlight any events of interest – be these potential security incidents or other preconfigured events. The *analyse* service is increasingly making use of machine learning approaches whereby activity on the monitored environments is baselined, and anomalies from that baseline are identified as potentially malicious activities. Behavioural anomaly detection is a growing market and may be the most effective way of monitoring security in large Cloud-based environments. The major CSPs offer a degree of behavioural anomaly based detection and threat intelligence capabilities natively (e.g. AWS GuardDuty and Azure Advanced Threat Protection); these can then be aggregated into wider reporting solutions, such as AWS Security Hub or Azure Sentinel and the Azure Security Centre.

Once an anomaly, or other suspicious event, has been identified then the *event management* services should kick in. The purpose of the *event management* service is to recognise the next point of escalation for an event; this could be a case of no action required or escalation to either the *incident management* (for security issues) or *problem management* services. The final service within this pipeline is the *report* service and this service is as simple as it sounds – enable reports to be produced from the *monitoring* service. Both the raw log information and the output from the *analyse* service should be able to be securely produced and exported from the *monitoring* service via *report*. *Threat hunting* is also incorporated in the *monitoring* set of services. *Threat hunting* refers to the more advanced approach of identifying indicators of compromise (IOCs) for potential compromises and then looking for those IOCs within the collected log information; working on this basis of assumed compromise allows for an earlier detection of threats within your environments than is possible with more reactive approaches. AWS Detective, Azure Sentinel and GCP Backstory are useful sources of information for *threat hunting* purposes.

There are some IaaS-specific elements to the *monitoring* service grouping that consumers should consider:

- Communication channels must be available both to and from the CSP in the event of a security incident requiring one party to notify the other;
- Tools such as VMware AppDefense and others can be used to log and monitor the information flows across the hypervisor in private Cloud approaches;
- Traditional security agents(e.g. anti-malware), can also be configured and reused in the IaaS environment;
- Consumers need to investigate the logging options available within the specific Cloud services that they are adopting. Log information may be available beneath the operating system level. For example, whilst consumers cannot install physical network taps into Cloud provider environments, logging capabilities similar to these technologies may be available as outlined earlier, e.g. Azure virtual network TAP. For those consumers that do not require full packet capture, other capabilities are available to monitor traffic flows – both AWS and GCP offer a capability known as VPC Flow Logs, whilst Azure has the NSG Flow Logs option within the Network Watcher tool, and all of these monitor traffic

flows. Separate logging information may also be available from the other 'as a Service' elements of the IaaS platform as well, e.g. storage. IaaS consumers should not consider themselves limited to the monitoring capabilities that they implement themselves at the operating system level.

Security monitoring is a vital part of any security regime. I view it as even more important where the services and data are hosted outside of your secure, trusted, domain.

Administration

The *administration* service grouping includes those activities typically associated with system administration roles – deploying new services, managing those services whilst in operation and then decommissioning and disposing of the relevant kit when the service reaches end of life. As the SRM reflects an application security architecture, the majority of these administrative tasks remain the primary delivery responsibility of the consumer in an SRM context. Whilst CSP staff are responsible for the physical deployment and management of the physical hardware, the consumer retains responsibility for the management and deployment from the operating system upwards (including their virtual networking). The *administration* service grouping includes the following services:

Secure channel

The *secure channel* service provides a secure communications path between the relevant system administrator and the server, database or application that they manage. In many cases, with IaaS services access to the console will likely be physically implemented via SSH. Some providers will also provide the ability to rent dedicated virtual private network connections into their virtualised environments, e.g. Azure ExpressRoute. From the operating system upwards it is the responsibility of the consumer to implement suitable secure communication channels for their administrators; I recommend the use of TLS or SSH encryption as a minimum for such activities. In many circumstances, Cloud consumers do not actually need to expose their administration ports, such as SSH and RDP, to the Internet. The AWS Systems Manager capability allows administrators to run operating system commands via the Systems Management Agent[167]; alternatively, Azure Security Centre's just-in-time[168] administration feature can be used to automatically open up network access to the necessary management ports, following a request from an authenticated user who holds the necessary roles. The ability to remove Internet-facing SSH and RDP management ports significantly reduces the attack surface of IaaS-hosted virtual machines.

Manage

The *manage* service delivers the capabilities for the day-to-day administration activities, e.g. patching, with regard to operating systems, applications, et cetera. Consumers should consider how they wish to manage their Cloud-based services; do they wish to simply extend their existing

---

[167] *https://docs.aws.amazon.com/systems-manager/latest/userguide/execute-remote-commands.html*.

[168] *https://docs.microsoft.com/en-us/azure/security-center/security-center-just-in-time*.

processes or do they wish to adopt some more tailored services for operating with IaaS-based servers? I strongly advise against the simple lifting and shifting of tooling and processes from on-premises data centres into the Cloud; this can severely limit the ability of Cloud consumers to move towards DevSecOps approaches. Instead, consumers should consider automated Cloud management approaches, e.g. the use of AWS Config and Lambda to identify and automatically remediate configuration drift.

Deploy

The *deploy* service, much like the *manage* service, requires a number of underlying logical services to deliver the conceptual functionality of deploying new services on to a Cloud service. Many of these services would be drawn from other areas of the SRM including the *risk management*, *testing*, *configuration management* and *architecture* services. In addition to the deployment of virtual machine images, the *deploy* service would also be responsible for the deployment of application code on to the Cloud. This entails the usual processes around release management so as to ensure a smooth migration to a new or updated version of code.

Orchestrate

The *orchestrate* service relates to the need to coordinate change across different elements when operating on Cloud environments, particularly when moving towards automated deployment approaches through the use of an appropriate balance of Cloud-native capabilities and third-party tooling, such as Terraform, Puppet, Chef, Ansible, Packer, Spinnaker and Jenkins.

Given the ease with which virtual servers can be initiated, great care must be taken to manage the proliferation of unnecessary running images. This is similar to the well-known issue of image sprawl in virtualised environments. The difference in the Cloud environment is that unnecessary images will all be charged back to the consumer – pay-as-you-go is only advantageous if you are actually using the resources you have active.

Decommission

The *decommission* service is the polar opposite of the *deploy* service. Once an application or server has reached the end of its usefulness it should be decommissioned. The increased ease of releasing resources like storage and compute is one of the strengths of the Cloud model (and of other virtualisation models) over physical environments. However, decommissioning is a joint delivery responsibility. Consumers need to ensure that they have implemented formal procedures governing the decommissioning of Cloud-based applications and virtual servers. Given the simplicity of shutting down virtual servers in an IaaS environment it is easy to mistakenly take down a virtual environment which is still in use, either through accident or through misunderstanding of other applications making use of the same virtual infrastructure. *Decommission* is a joint delivery responsibility as it is only the CSP that can ensure that virtualised resources are released cleanly and that no information will leak from the releasing consumer to the next consumer making use of the same physical resources.

Consumers should content themselves with the statements provided by their CSPs regarding how they prevent information leakage when resources are released or when consumers decide to terminate their relationship with the

CSP. If Cloud consumers are unwilling to simply trust the decommissioning approach of their CSP, then they can adopt the technique of 'cryptoshredding'. Cryptoshredding refers to the encryption of data prior to its deletion, with the encryption key then being destroyed. Cryptoshredding mitigates the risk of the consumer's data being inadvertently made available to other tenants; as even if their data is not adequately destroyed, it is still unavailable to any other tenant due to its encrypted status.

Dispose

The *dispose* service is firmly within the domain of the CSP. In a private Cloud environment, the CSP and consumer may be one and the same. The purpose of the *dispose* service is to securely dispose of hardware or media when necessary, e.g. upon failure or reaching end of life. Consumers should be comfortable that their data will not risk entry into the public domain when, for example, their CSP disposes of, or recycles, their storage devices.

Change management

The *change management* service, at both the consumer and CSP levels, should follow normal established best practice as documented within ITIL®[169] and elsewhere for more static Cloud-based environments. However, given the potentially volatile nature of Cloud services, e.g. rapid provisioning and subsequent release of resources, consumers adopting Cloud services must have *change management* processes that are capable of reacting to such change requests efficiently and effectively. The need to manage change does not disappear

---

[169] *www.axelos.com/best-practice-solutions/itil/what-is-itil.*

when moving to the Cloud; the challenge becomes managing change at a speed that does not compromise the flexibility and agility that the Cloud model offers. This necessity is one of the factors driving organisations towards the SecDevOps processes described in the *secure development* section of this chapter.

Problem management

As with *change management*, Cloud consumers and CSPs should adopt accepted best practices with regard to *problem management*. It is vital that appropriate communications mechanisms are in place to enable the appropriate allocation of responsibilities in the event of a problem. For example, many CSPs maintain web pages and Twitter feeds dedicated to the status of their services (as described in the section on *availability*).

Such information feeds enable their consumers to identify when a problem is within their remit to fix or when the problem is wider, affecting the IaaS as a whole. CSPs must also offer adequate support contacts to enable their consumers to raise new problems as and when they occur.

Vulnerability management

The *vulnerability management* service is responsible for delivering a cohesive and comprehensive approach to managing the vulnerabilities associated with a Cloud-based application. In terms of the remediation activities that may result from *vulnerability management* processes, such activities will be passed to the relevant risk management and then *change management* services elsewhere within the SRM. The *vulnerability management* service in the SRM is primarily targeted at identifying appropriate *vulnerability management* approaches and then implementing such approaches to actively identify vulnerabilities.

The potential for embedding some of your vulnerability assessment activities into the development lifecycle was explored within the *secure development* lifecycle. It should be noted that the Cloud providers also offer tooling that can help to inform the *vulnerability management* process; for example, the AWS Inspector[170] service allows virtual machine images to be instrumented to report configuration issues, whilst the GCP Security Scanner[171] can detect common web application security issues in applications hosted on the App Engine, Compute Engine or Kubernetes Engine. Azure Secure Score allows similar vulnerabilities in configuration to be identified in the Azure environment, whilst Azure Compliance Manager[172] will identify deviations from set compliance standards (e.g. ISO 27001, CIS benchmarks or NIST 800-53) from both the provider and consumer perspectives.

It is also possible to run traditional vulnerability assessment tools, such as those from Tenable and Qualys, across the Cloud-hosted environment. Using this established tooling has the advantage that it also tends to integrate with the Cloud provider security consoles such as Security Hub, Security Center and Command Center.[173]

---

[170]*https://docs.aws.amazon.com/inspector/latest/userguide/inspector_introduction.html*.

[171] *https://cloud.google.com/security-scanner/*.

[172]*https://servicetrust.microsoft.com/ComplianceManager/V3*.

[173] *https://docs.microsoft.com/en-us/azure/security-center/security-center-secure-score*.

At a high level, similar *vulnerability management* strategies should be adopted whether an application is being hosted on-premises or on the Cloud. Ideally, applications should be tested during development, prior to entering production and then again at regular intervals (depending upon criticality of the application) and after any major changes to the application or underlying components, such as databases or operating systems. The problem with this approach when working with public Cloud providers is the potential need to obtain specific permission to conduct vulnerability assessments, or more intrusive penetration testing, of your application. This may delay your ability to conduct testing depending on how slick the penetration authorisation process is at your CSP.

The CSPs are gradually relaxing requirements concerning the pre-approval of penetration testing activities; however, this is definitely an area in which Cloud consumers need to check the latest guidance prior to commencing any such testing. The latest guidance for the major CSPs can be found at the links below:

- AWS: *https://aws.amazon.com/security/penetration-testing/*
- Azure: *www.microsoft.com/en-us/msrc/pentest-rules-of-engagement*

Google take a more relaxed approached to penetration testing by their clients:

If you plan to evaluate the security of your Cloud Platform infrastructure with penetration testing, you are not required to contact us. You will have to abide by the Cloud Platform Acceptable Use Policy and Terms of

Service, and ensure that your tests only affect your projects (and not other customers' applications). If a vulnerability is found, please report it via the Vulnerability Reward Program.[174]

If organisations are more interested in simple configuration checks (e.g. checking for missing patches and common misconfigurations, both of the Cloud platform and the hosted operating systems), such checks could be performed via Cloud-specific tooling to avoid having to notify the CSP. For example, the major CASB vendors offer the capability to check Cloud platform configurations against the relevant CIS benchmarks.[175] There are a variety of other open-source Cloud-specific vulnerability assessment tools available to supplement more traditional tooling; these include: Azucar,[176] for testing Azure environments;

- Prowler[177] and Scout2,[178] for testing AWS environments; and
- CloudCustodian[179] for checking against all three main providers.

---

[174] *https://support.google.com/cloud/answer/6262505?hl=en*.

[175] *www.cisecurity.org/cis-benchmarks/*.

[176] *www.nccgroup.trust/uk/about-us/newsroom-and-events/blogs/2018/april/introducing-azucar/*.

[177] *https://github.com/toniblyx/prowler*.

[178] *https://github.com/nccgroup/Scout2*.

[179] *https://cloudcustodian.io/*.

The major Cloud providers all offer native solutions to perform checks against the relevant CIS benchmarks, namely:

- AWS Security Hub[180];
- Azure Security Center Regulatory Compliance; Dashboard[181]; and
- GCP Security Health Analytics[182].

Once vulnerabilities have been identified, the *vulnerability management* must then route these vulnerabilities, via the *coordinate* service, to those other services in the SRM that are able to decide on the most appropriate course of action.

Incident management

Consumer *incident management* services for Cloud-based applications should follow traditional processes. Within the SRM, I have defined five services relating to *incident management*:

1. Respond
2. Investigate
3. Action
4. Close
5. Exercise

The *respond* service represents the initial triage aspect of incident response. The *event management* service identifies

---

[180] *https://aws.amazon.com/security-hub/.*

[181] *https://azure.microsoft.com/en-gb/updates/regulatory-compliance-dashboard-in-azure-security-center-now-generally-available/.*

[182] *https://cloud.google.com/security-command-center/docs/how-to-manage-security-health-analytics.*

events of interest, and, if they are suspected of indicating a security incident, these are passed on to the *incident response* service. The *incident response* service should also take feeds from CSP status updates and wider industry alerts (e.g. widespread virus or worm activity) and respond appropriately. The *respond* service must, therefore, incorporate an appropriate communications mechanism to receive and obtain notifications, pass these notifications on to the relevant staff and initiate the creation of an incident log.

The other main responsibility of the *respond* service is the establishment of an appropriate group of incident response personnel drawn from the relevant technical areas (e.g. operating system, database and application) and an appropriate business stakeholder authorised to make decisions on behalf of the business. Any decision regarding closing down an affected service, or leaving it running pending an investigation, must be made with full knowledge of any business impacts; these decisions should be at the discretion of the business and not the technology function. In the DevSecOps world, it may be possible to automate certain incident response activities based on predefined runbooks. This automation could be performed via SOC Orchestration and Automated Response (SOAR) tooling, such as IBM Resilient[183] and Demisto,[184] or through more bespoke automation via AWS Lambda or Cloud Functions. In the latter approach, certain event types could trigger an automated response function that could, in turn, alter API-enabled security tooling; for example, a function could

---

[183] *www.ibm.com/security/intelligent-orchestration/resilient.*

[184] *www.demisto.com/.*

automatically add an IP address to a block list within a DDoS prevention tool or firewall. This situation also serves as a good example of why automation needs to be applied in an informed manner: no organisation would want to accidentally blacklist all their customers because of an overactive incident response function.

The *investigate* service forms the main part of the overall *incident response* service in which automation is not deemed to be an appropriate response. The initial tasks of the *investigate* service are to contain the incident and then gather sufficient evidence to enable an informed investigation to take place. In order to contain an incident you must have thorough knowledge of the application at hand and the systems with which the application interacts – each of which may also have been compromised. How can you obtain such knowledge? Examine logs for indications of unusual activity; conduct passive (i.e. non-interactive) investigations where you can (e.g. output from network monitoring tools or native tooling such as AWS Detective) so as not to tip-off an attacker that their activities have been detected. All aspects of this initial investigation must be recorded in the incident log. Once you have an idea of the likely scope of the compromise, you can make a more informed decision as to how the incident should be contained. For example, whether or not the service should be taken down, whether certain communication lines should be cut to prevent further contamination or whether everything should be left as-is to enable further monitoring of the activities of the attacker. Once you have decided upon your containment approach it is time to begin a more thorough investigation.

Where possible, evidence should be obtained in a forensically sound manner; this may not be possible in an IaaS environment without extensive cooperation from your

CSP. Whilst working in an IaaS environment may make obtaining forensically sound evidence more problematic, there is a definite advantage to being able to snapshot a virtual machine image that is suspected of being compromised and then analysing the captured image. As ever with incident response you need to be aware of the consequences of your activities: keep an eye out for a change in behaviour from the attacker that may indicate a realisation that they have been detected. A deeply embedded attacker may be quite destructive in their attempts to cover their tracks if they believe they have been spotted which could lead to a longer down-time and more drawn-out investigation. Ensure that you capture all of your activities in the incident log – such logs are vital evidence should you wish to pursue criminal charges against the attacker. The purpose of the *analyse* phase is to identify exactly which information assets have been affected, the attack vector(s) used to infiltrate the service and then to identify how to remediate the exploited vulnerabilities to enable clean-up to begin without fear of the service being immediately re-hacked when it is brought back online. This is where the benefit of the virtual image snapshot really comes into its own. The snapshot should contain volatile aspects, e.g. process address spaces in memory that can be difficult to obtain in a physical server without destroying the evidence. Once you are content that you have obtained all of the information you need about the compromise, then it is time to pass the relevant information across to the *action* service.

The *action* service is responsible for implementing the activities needed to recover from an incident. This will include working with other services within the SRM, e.g. *problem* and *change management, vulnerability management*, and others, to make the necessary changes in a managed manner. Likely activities will include the restoration of data from backups known to be good (i.e. dating from before the compromise), application of security patches to operating systems or vulnerable applications and the conducting of some penetration testing to ensure that the system is no longer vulnerable to the identified attack vector(s). In an IaaS scenario, those recovering from an incident may have other options available to them; for example, if it was running a blue/green model, an organisation could switch to the stack it believed to be clean.

Similarly, organisations could simply decide to close down an infected environment and bring up an entirely new stack using fresh images. Cloud-based organisations also have the option to regularly tear down and rebuild their IaaS environments as a precautionary measure: attackers do not like having their operations continually disrupted.

The *close* service is responsible for ensuring that the incident log has been completed satisfactorily and storing the log in a secure manner. Furthermore, the *close* service must also capture any lessons learned during the incident response process; this helps to avoid making the same mistakes twice, but also helps to spread good practice where certain activities have been shown to work well.

The *exercise* service provides organisations with the opportunity to practice their incident response preparedness. Exercises can range from tabletop discussions of the plans through to intense full-on real-time incident simulations. When running incident simulations, it is essential to involve all of the stakeholders required in a genuine incident response; such response teams may range from a service desk user all the way to the CEO and include external support from legal services and public relations experts, depending on the nature of the incident. These incident simulations work best when the required stakeholders are unaware of what is happening until they are brought into the simulated response.

However, it is critical that such responses are contained; respondents should not take actions on live systems, and no news of the simulated incident should end up in the media. The Cloud does offer an opportunity for a very realistic incident simulation; it has the ability to spin up a replica of the production environment, and a cyber test range can be established within this for running such exercises. These test ranges can be short to contain costs but they can provide much better insight into the capabilities available to incident responders and, even more importantly, insight into the gaps in those capabilities.

Asset management

The *asset management* service grouping reflects the need for a consumer to account for its information assets, even where those assets reside in an IaaS Cloud.

The first aspect of the *asset management* service grouping is the *catalogue* service. The purpose of the *catalogue* service is to establish an asset register containing the information assets relevant to the application; this register should include references to the relevant virtual machine images, relevant storage locations, relevant software images, et cetera. Identifying Cloud-based assets can be a challenge if Shadow IT has been allowed to flourish within an organisation and it may be necessary to use tools like Cloudmapper[185] to obtain

---

[185] *https://duo.com/blog/introducing-cloudmapper-an-aws-visualization-tool*.

better visibility of your Cloud-based environment. Cloud provider native tools, such as AWS Trusted Advisor[186] and Azure Advisor,[187] can also help consuming organisations obtain better visibility of their Cloud-based assets and, subsequently, to optimise associated costs, usage and security.

A variety of enterprise asset management tools now include cloud provider plug-ins and/or connectors to enable asset discovery within cloud environments, e.g. both ServiceNow and JIRA Service Desk (via the Insight plug-in) can identify and catalogue cloud assets.

The next aspect of the *asset management* is the *license* service – many software vendors offer specific licensing terms for implementation in Cloud services. Consumers must ensure that they have the correct licenses for operating their software in a virtualised Cloud environment. Consumers should carefully investigate the terms and conditions of software that they plan to implement to examine whether or not the license terms are appropriate for a Cloud implementation. For example, how do the terms and conditions account for the elasticity inherent in the Cloud? Do your vendors charge for maximum peak usage or on a pay-as-you-go basis? Do your vendors charge on a per virtual machine or virtual core basis? Do your vendors even support implementation in a Cloud environment?

Configuration management is as important in an IaaS (or other virtualised) environment as it is when dealing with

---

[186] *https://aws.amazon.com/premiumsupport/technology/trusted-advisor/.*

[187] *https://azure.microsoft.com/en-gb/services/advisor/.*

physical hardware. One aspect that must not be forgotten when dealing with IaaS Clouds is that of patching of currently redundant images. Given the elastic nature of Cloud services it may be that machine images are de-activated and then stored for future use after a spike in usage. Alternatively, those using Cloud services for development and test purposes may not require their images to be constantly active. The issue here is that these currently inactive images could present a security risk to your virtualised infrastructure when they are activated if they contain unpatched vulnerabilities. From this configuration management perspective, the adoption of blue/green style approaches may help because, in these methods, patches are continually applied and tested and the environments are only switched over when stability has been proven.

However, configuration management is not just about patching. It is important to know the overall state and usage of your IaaS services not only from a security perspective but also from a billing reconciliation perspective. Cloud is normally charged on a pay per use basis, consumers should check every so often that these charges are accurate.

Information Rights Management (IRM) and *Data Loss Prevention (DLP)* are different but closely related services. IRM enables providers to control what users can do with the information that they are entitled to access; for example, IRM could be used to prevent the printing of documents or the opening of documents on certain classes of devices. DLP enables providers to prevent data leaking out of the selected environment. IRM can form an element of an overall DLP solution. One example of an IRM is the Azure Information

Protection (AIP)[188] solution which is a Cloud-native way of delivering information rights. AIP allows organisations to scan their information assets and, if they hold the correct licence (currently E5), to automatically apply a classification to the scanned information. Controls of usage, such as the prevention of distribution via email, can then be applied to that information to provide a completely Cloud-based IRM solution.[189]

Conclusion

This chapter has provided some practical advice with respect to the implementation of the security services described within the SRM in an IaaS environment. In addition to the guidance provided in this book, consumers should also consider the guidance provided by the CSPs themselves. Most CSPs now offer whitepapers or sections of their website describing their security capabilities, for example:

- *https://aws.amazon.com/security/*
- *https://azure.microsoft.com/en-gb/resources/whitepapers/search/?term=security&type=WhitePaperResource*
- *https://cloud.google.com/security/overview/whitepaper*

I recommend that those considering the use of a CSP closely examine the information that they provide on their security processes and that they take advantage of any offers to provide further detail, even if they are under an NDA.

---

[188] *https://azure.microsoft.com/en-gb/services/information-protection/*.

[189] An on-premises component is available to extend AIP to legacy data centres.

CHAPTER 10: SECURITY AND PLATFORM AS A SERVICE

This chapter describes how the security services defined within the SRM shown in Figure 7 may be delivered by consumers implementing an application upon a PaaS Cloud.

Whilst I may occasionally provide examples of the security services offered by PaaS providers it is not my intention to provide a comprehensive overview of any particular PaaS platform. Similarly, I am not attempting to provide an exhaustive catalogue of available PaaS solutions. As with the rest of this book, my aim is to help you to adopt a way of working that enables you to find the most appropriate solution to your own particular set of requirements rather than to specify how security *must* be delivered. As we move up the stack from IaaS through PaaS towards SaaS (via FaaS), the diversity of Cloud solutions increase, and, consequently, security solutions must become increasingly tailored to each specific situation.

PaaS is a broad category, and the boundary between PaaS and SaaS is somewhat blurry. In this section, I differentiate between PaaS and SaaS according to the degree of customisation available to the user alongside the ability to run scripts or code of the consumer's own choosing. When the CSP offers the consumer the ability to heavily customise functionality and/or run their own code or scripts, I view its services as PaaS rather than SaaS.

Examples of different types of PaaS offers are shown below.

Database; examples include:

- Amazon Relational Database Service (*https://aws.amazon.com/rds/*)
- Azure SQL (*https://azure.microsoft.com/en-us/services/sql-database/*)
- IBM Cloudant (*www.Cloudant.com*)
- Google Spanner (*https://cloud.google.com/spanner/*)

Data warehouse and big data; examples include:

- Azure Data Lake Store (*https://azure.microsoft.com/en-gb/solutions/data-lake/*)
- AWS RedShift (*https://aws.amazon.com/redshift/*)
- GCP BigQuery (*https://cloud.google.com/bigquery/*)

Integration; examples include:

- Apigee (*https://cloud.google.com/apigee/*)
- Boomi (*https://boomi.com/*)
- OpenText AppWorks (*www.opentext.com/products-and-solutions/products/digital-process-automation/appworks-platform/bpm-in-the-Cloud*)
- Oracle Integration (*www.oracle.com/middleware/application-integration/*)
- ServiceNow (*www.servicenow.com/*)

Machine learning (ML) and artificial intelligence (AI); examples include:

- AWS SageMaker (*https://aws.amazon.com/sagemaker/*)
- Google Machine Learning Engine (*https://cloud.google.com/ai-platform*)
- Azure Machine Learning (*https://azure.microsoft.com/en-gb/services/machine-learning/*)

Internet of Things (IoT); examples include:

- AWS IoT Core (*https://aws.amazon.com/iot-core/*)
- Azure IoT Hub (*https://azure.microsoft.com/en-gb/services/iot-hub/*)
- Google IoT Core (*https://cloud.google.com/iot-core/*)

General purpose; examples include:

- SalesForce Lightning (*www.salesforce.com/products/platform/overview/*)
- Google App Engine (*https://cloud.google.com/appengine/*)
- Azure App Service (*https://docs.microsoft.com/en-gb/azure/app-service/overview*)
- Heroku (*www.heroku.com*)
- AWS Elastic Beanstalk (*https://aws.amazon.com/elasticbeanstalk/*)
- Cloud Foundry (*www.Cloudfoundry.org/*)

I will focus upon the latter category in this book – those CSPs that provide one or more run-times within which consumers can deploy applications.

PaaS and the SRM

The rest of this chapter is dedicated to explaining how the services described within the SRM can be delivered when deploying services on a PaaS Cloud. As discussed in chapter 7, PaaS can be the most complex of the Cloud service models to secure due to the amount of cross-over and the number of interfaces between the CSP and the consumer for the provision of security services. Consumers must make sure that they are aware of, and address, potential gaps between the aspects of security services delivered by the CSP and the aspects delivered by the consumer.

Secure development

With the PaaS service model, the *secure development* services are very much a joint delivery responsibility. Whilst Cloud consumers are directly responsible for the security of the code that they develop to run within a PaaS run-time, the CSPs are directly responsible for the security of the code underpinning the run-time together with the code delivering any PaaS-specific APIs. What does this mean in practice? No matter how secure the code that a consumer develops, the application could still be vulnerable to application-level exploits targeting problems with the code of the PaaS provider. However, this is a risk that many organisations currently face in more traditional deployments; most major systems will include a few proprietary closed-source applications within their technology stack. Any issues with these applications could also place the overall system at risk. So, whilst the use of code provided by PaaS services may represent a risk, it is only an extension of risks that organisations are used to managing rather than something completely new.

In terms of general good practice regarding the implementation of a secure development lifecycle (SDL), I recommend investigating the variety of SDL documentation made available by Microsoft at:

www.microsoft.com/en-us/securityengineering/sdl/.

There are a number of useful tools that can be accessed via links on the main SDL page, including a Threat Modelling tool and an Attack Surface Analyzer:

- *www.microsoft.com/en-us/securityengineering/sdl/threatmodeling*
- *https://GitHub.com/microsoft/attacksurfaceanalyzer*

The SDL and its supporting tools are effective additions to the DevSecOps processes and tooling described in the previous chapter.

The SDL processes adopted by Microsoft helped to rehabilitate the company's reputation from a security perspective. Many years ago the security of Microsoft products was often the butt of jokes amongst the security research community; this is no longer the case. The efforts that Microsoft have made to develop their software more securely, and also respond to vulnerabilities more cooperatively when they are discovered, have led to Microsoft now being viewed as something of an exemplar amongst their peers.

Coding standards

Since platforms such as Azure, Heroku and the Google App Engine support standard languages such as Java, Ruby, Python and C#, you should be able to use many of the standard secure development processes associated with the relevant languages. Life may be more difficult for those adopting PaaS services using proprietary languages, such as the Apex language[190] offered by Salesforce.com, where a whole new set of coding standards will need to be created (albeit Apex uses Java-like syntax). In either situation, you should standardise which PaaS-provided APIs you adopt (e.g. access control and cryptographic APIs) and where you code, or otherwise implement, your own equivalent functionality.

For the sake of clarity, I shall emphasise that Salesforce.com originally began as a vanilla SaaS offer; however, it has evolved over the years into a PaaS via its 'Lightning' platform (and, prior to that, via its Force.com platform). In fact, the Salesforce.com SaaS application is hosted on the same platform that the organisation makes available to its PaaS consumers, so its consumers have access to services of proven scale and utility. Salesforce.com have made significant quantities of documentation available for developers via their website and their 'Trailhead' online learning platform.[191]

---

[190] *https://trailhead.salesforce.com/en/content/learn/modules/apex_data base*.

[191] *https://trailhead.salesforce.com/en/home*.

The main website section devoted to security and relevant security learning for the Lightning platform can be found at:

https://developer.salesforce.com/docs/atlas.en-us.securityImplGuide.meta/securityImplGuide/salesforce_s ecurity_guide.htm

and

https://trailhead.salesforce.com/en/content/learn/modules/s ecurity-for-lightning-components.

Salesforce.com have also issued some specific secure coding guidelines, available at the link below:

https://developer.salesforce.com/docs/atlas.en-us.secure_coding_guide.meta/secure_coding_guide/secure _coding_guidelines.htm.

These secure coding guidelines offer developers advice and guidance on how to avoid common security weaknesses, such as SQL injection, cross-site scripting and cross-site request forgery. The Lightning platform itself offers protection against some of these common attack vectors – again highlighting that the interface between consumer code and platform capabilities needs to be fully documented and understood.

The Microsoft Azure platform boasts a number of platform-specific security features, e.g. an authentication and authorisation module that can be reused within consumer-developed applications:

https://docs.microsoft.com/en-us/azure/app-service/overview-authentication-authorization.

Developers can also make use of the wider Azure RBAC capability via Azure Active Directory. Microsoft retired their Access Control Services (ACS) capability in November

2018; this retirement serves as a good reminder of both the need to keep track of CSP product roadmaps and of the control that consumers must give up when operating on Cloud services.

Microsoft have produced guidance that describes the security services offered by the Azure platform and provides useful information on the development of secure applications on the Azure PaaS. This document links to guidance for both bespoke applications delivered via App Services and those making use of PaaS services, such as SQL Database and SQL Datawarehouse. This guidance is available from:

https://docs.microsoft.com/en-gb/azure/security/fundamentals/paas-deployments.

Users of PaaS providers like Heroku, Elastic Beanstalk and Google App Engine should adopt typical best practices for the languages they use; however, they must also consider any peculiarities that their chosen delivery platform may have in terms of data storage, concurrency, et cetera.

Many of the principles of the DevSecOps approach outlined earlier in relation to IaaS remain equally applicable to PaaS, e.g. the need for secure code repositories and automated security testing. Certain PaaS features make the deployment of DevSecOps approaches more straightforward, particularly with respect to build, automation, the use of techniques like canary deployments[192] and the running of blue/green approaches. The use of Azure App Services Deployment Slots to deliver these capabilities will be explored further in the deploy element of this chapter.

---

[192] Canary deployments allow organisations to test new functionality on a subset of users or servers prior to general release.

Integrity

As with the vast majority of service groupings within the SRM in the context of PaaS, the *integrity* service grouping is a joint delivery responsibility, split between the CSP and the consumer. The CSP must ensure that it has sufficient controls in place to provide sufficient levels of *non-repudiation* with regard to activities affecting the platform. For example, CSPs should maintain strict audit and process controls when making changes to the systems underlying their platform. Similarly, CSPs should ensure that sufficient content checking is in place to prevent their systems (including management systems) becoming infected with malware.

Consumers of PaaS services must also build in their own *non-repudiation* services where these services are required by their application. As we are currently considering applications hosted on PaaS Clouds, the consumer still has the opportunity to code whatever *non-repudiation* controls are required. This may vary from simple logging and auditing of user activities through to the use of digital signatures provided via cryptographic services.

Content checking is more complicated within a PaaS environment than within an IaaS environment. Whereas standard antivirus packages may be implemented within virtualised servers on an IaaS Cloud (subject to licensing), this is not the case with PaaS. However, this does not mean that consumers are unable to implement content checking for their PaaS-hosted applications.

There are two main options. In the first approach, the PaaS-hosted application could redirect all content import (and, perhaps, export, depending on business requirements) to an on-premises or IaaS-hosted standard content checking application. This could be achieved by building a form of 'sandpit' within another part of the hosting Cloud, e.g. via EC2 (for Elastic Beanstalk) or via Virtual Machines (for Azure). Depending on the use case, it may be wise to use hosted content rewriting capabilities, such as those offered by the Deep Secure[193] tooling, in conjunction with standard anti-malware.

The second approach would be to make use of a SaaS antivirus provider such as Scanii[194] or Virustotal.[195] In this second scenario the files to be checked are provided to the antivirus SaaS and an answer is returned indicating whether the file is clean or infected. Obviously, this does not emulate a fully featured antivirus solution (e.g. there is no intrinsic eradication capability); however, it does enable consumers to detect malicious content before it is acted upon or stored within 'trusted' datastores. The Scanii service adopts a REST-based approach and enables consumers to direct Scanii to pull content from REST-based storage services such as AWS S3 rather than requiring the relevant content to always be pushed for checking. Using something like a Lambda function can enable the consumer to call out to Scanii whenever new content is posted to an S3 bucket (Scanii would then use a pre-signed URL/query string authentication[196] to fetch the content for checking); such functions can even give consumers the ability to delete such

---

[193] *www.deep-secure.com/.*

[194] *https://scanii.com/.*

[195] *www.virustotal.com/faq/.*

[196] *https://docs.aws.amazon.com/AmazonS3/latest/API/sigv4-query-string-auth.html.*

content should Scanii return a result indicating the presence of malware.

The *snapshot* service is interesting in the PaaS environment given the potential distributions of data and application code. For example, your data may be stored using the platform's own storage mechanisms, kept on-premises or perhaps hosted using a different storage as a service provider (e.g. Amazon S3). Similarly, your application code may be stored on the platform or elsewhere. The executable code itself must exist on the PaaS in order for your application to run.

Consumers must consider whereabouts each element of their service is located and then derive appropriate mechanisms to obtain snapshots where required. As an example, the Microsoft Azure Blob storage facility offers the capability to take a read-only snapshot of a blob.[197] This capability can be valuable as Azure virtual hard drives are stored as blobs – you can, therefore, use blob snapshots to take a snapshot of the state of the virtual hard drives.

With respect to application source code, I recommend that consumers secure their source code repositories and take verified snapshots/copies of their codebase for backup and recovery purposes. Application code should also be signed and verified as part of the CI/CD pipeline to ensure that the code being deployed is identical to that which passed through the various test phases. Where such code is compiled on-premises and, subsequently, launched in the Cloud, I would also recommend storing a copy of the compiled executable. This can be more troublesome in platforms like the Heroku

---

[197] *https://docs.microsoft.com/en-us/rest/api/storageservices/Creating-a-Snapshot-of-a-Blob.*

platform where executables (slugs in the Heroku context[198]) are compiled within the PaaS. This is potentially troublesome as it means that consumers hand over responsibility for the traceability of the integrity of their code at an earlier stage of deployment then in an on-premises or IaaS deployment, in which consumers can trace an executable directly back to the source.

Availability

The *availability* grouping of the SRM consists of services relating to *business continuity (BC)*, *disaster recovery (DR)*, *backup* and *failover*.

There are fewer options for providing (relatively) seamless *business continuity* and *disaster recovery* capabilities with PaaS than there are for IaaS. Whereas it is feasible to switch compute workloads across IaaS providers in the event of an incident (as described in chapter 9) it is not feasible to perform a similar failover between PaaS providers. For example, consider those making use of the Lightning platform in which consumers may implement applications in the proprietary Apex language. Other Cloud providers may have an abundance of compute and storage resources but they do not have the ability to execute applications written in Apex. Consumers cannot, therefore, simply 'lift and shift' their application and data from the Salesforce.com platform to a competing PaaS in the event of a major outage. Consumers of the Salesforce.com PaaS and most other PaaS consumers, are heavily reliant upon the resilience of the services offered by their providers.

---

[198] *https://devcenter.heroku.com/articles/slug-compiler*.

In the interests of fairness, I should note that Salesforce.com maintains high levels of availability (above 99.9%). It is those consumers who are concerned about the remaining 0.1% of unplanned downtime, or those using less reliable PaaS providers, that need to manage the residual risk. One approach may be to maintain a copy of the underlying business data within another CSP, alongside a cut-down application providing bare-bones business capabilities sufficient to keep your business operational whilst either your main CSP recovers, or you find a more permanent solution. This approach would obviously incur costs with respect to the development of such a bare-bones application and possible transformation of data into non-proprietary formats. There would also be recurring costs with regard to ongoing storage requirements. Enterprises need to consider these costs in the context of the unavailability of their application over a variety of timeframes. For example, such an approach may be overkill if a service was only unavailable for a matter of minutes. Would this still be overkill if the PaaS-hosted application was unavailable for a matter of hours, days or perhaps even longer? Consider the potential business impact and the likelihood of the event and use this analysis to drive your approach towards business continuity and disaster recovery.

Now, although PaaS providers do not tend to offer 99.999% uptime service level agreements, they do tend to provide their consumers with managed run-times that aim to maintain availability of the applications that they host. For example, the Heroku model involves running processes (dynos) within the Common Runtime (one per Region[199]), supervised by the Dyno Manager. The Dyno Manager restarts crashed processes without requiring intervention from the consumer and they can move dynos to new locations automatically should there be a failure in the underlying hardware.[200] Such capabilities can be expensive to implement in an on-premises environment.

Of course, one of the perceived advantages of the Cloud model is the ability to dynamically scale resources to meet spikes in processing requirements. This ability enables organisations to maintain the availability of their applications in the face of increased demand or, potentially, to cope with denial of service attacks. Heroku enables their consumers to scale their application up (and down) via the ps:scale command as documented at:

https://devcenter.heroku.com/articles/scaling.

Scaling is automatic within the Google App Engine, subject to quota limits as explained at:

https://cloud.google.com/appengine/quotas?csw=1.

Whilst the Google App Engine approach is desirable from an overhead perspective, it can cause problems should you breach your quota. At this point the service becomes unavailable. Fortunately, the Google quotas are generous; however, if you find that the default quotas are insufficient, they can be increased by submitting a request via the 'quotas' page in the GCP console. The App Engine also includes an

---

[199] Private Spaces are an alternative approach for those wanting more isolation: *www.heroku.com/dynos/private-spaces*.

[200] *https://devcenter.heroku.com/articles/erosion-resistance*.

anti-Denial of Service (DoS) capability; this enables their consumers to blacklist IP addresses and subnets, which then drop requests before they are processed. This capability is explained further at the link below:

https://cloud.google.com/appengine/docs/standard/java/con fig/dos?csw=1.

This form of anti-DoS capability is being deprecated by Google in favour of its App Engine Firewall[201] and Cloud Armor.[202] (It should be mentioned that Cloud Armor currently does not support Google App Engine due to its interdependency with the global HTTPS load balancing capability, which does not support App Engine.)

It should be noted that the Cloud model does introduce a new form of denial of service vulnerability. Whereas traditional Distributed DoS attacks tend to rely on the exhaustion of resources such as network or compute resources, DDoS on the Cloud can focus on economic exhaustion. Cloud is pay-as-you-go; by forcing their victims to use more Cloud-based resources attackers can rapidly increase the costs associated with those resources. Where there are set budget limits this can lead to a denial of service once the budget has been exceeded. This type of attack is known as an economic denial of service.

Consumers can automatically scale the resources that they consume on the Azure platform via use of the Autoscale

---

[201] *https://cloud.google.com/appengine/docs/standard/python/creating-firewalls*.

[202] *http://cloud.google.com/armor/*.

capability.[203] The Autoscale capability allows consumers to configure a set of rules and constraints to govern the resources allocated to their applications. As an example, Azure consumers can allocate additional resources during set periods of time to cope with regular peaks in activity, e.g. specific days of the week. This type of configurable functionality enables consumers to deliver the elasticity and cost-savings that Cloud has always promised.

Another advantage over on-premises deployments that PaaS services tend to share with IaaS services is the ease of data replication across multiple data centres. For example, Azure Storage offers a number of different data resilience options from simple Local Redundancy within a zone through to Geo-Redundant storage across geographic regions.[204] These storage options are also available to other Azure PaaS services, e.g. Azure Data Lake Store (Gen 2 only). GCP also offers a similar range of choices between local storage within a single region and multi-regional storage for extra redundancy.[205] AWS S3 stores multiple copies of data across devices within a region by default, and consumers can choose to store across different regions if they prefer. Such features are designed from a resilience and durability perspective rather than a data backup perspective. PaaS consumers must continue to maintain separate (off-platform) data backups where required. From an availability and backup solution, you must ensure that you understand the

[203] https://docs.microsoft.com/en-gb/azure/azure-monitor/platform/autoscale-get-started.

[204] https://docs.microsoft.com/en-us/azure/storage/common/storage-redundancy.

[205] https://cloud.google.com/storage.

underlying data storage mechanisms and choose the ones most appropriate to your requirements.

There is one final point I will make in consideration of *availability* and the PaaS approach. Although PaaS consumers are typically unaware of the underlying virtual machines, the availability of the platform is intrinsically dependent upon the availability of such virtual machines and the underlying infrastructure. As an example, the Heroku PaaS is both hosted by and built upon Amazon Web Services. The availability of the Heroku PaaS is, therefore, dependent on the availability of the underlying Amazon Web Services. This is a good example of where consumers need to be aware of the overall supply chain. Consumers should extend their due diligence activities to any underlying Cloud services in addition to their investigation of the front-end Cloud service.

Cryptography

As with the other Cloud service models, if you see Cloud service provider staff as posing a threat to the confidentiality of your data then you must consider encrypting your data before it enters the Cloud. Encryption of data once it enters the Cloud leaves a window of opportunity whereby your data is in the clear prior to encryption. Furthermore, encrypting data in the Cloud means that your encryption key is also in the Cloud. If you are using symmetric encryption (where the encryption and decryption key is one and the same) then this means that a compromise of the Cloud service may provide access to both your encrypted data and the decryption key. However, the issue with encrypting your data on-premises is that it leaves your data in a state where it is difficult to work with from an application perspective unless the application has access to the appropriate decryption key. This issue removes the security advantage of encrypting on-premises.

Certain PaaS providers have sought to achieve compromise positions; for example, ServiceNow offers Edge Proxy[206] which allows a variety of forms of field-level encryption to be applied to information being transferred to ServiceNow. Consumers can choose to use either standard encryption, equality preserving or order preserving encryption; this choice dictates what functionality remains available within the ServiceNow application. Standard encryption will allow users to use any kind of filtering, sorting or comparison operation on the uploaded data.

Order preserving encryption allows sorting and equality operations to be performed and enables the ServiceNow PaaS to offer more benefits to end users. The ServiceNow Edge Proxy also supports tokenisation and can act as a cut-down CASB. (CASBs and tokenisation will be discussed more widely in the next chapter.)

Consumers should consider how their data will be used by their application or end users and then secure the data appropriately, either by encryption on-premises, encryption on-Cloud or some other mechanism, such as tokenisation.

Now, the selling point of the PaaS service model is that it abstracts away the infrastructure issues whilst still providing consumers with the flexibility to build and deploy applications of their own choosing or design. In an IaaS environment, consumers have complete freedom to

---

[206] *www.servicenow.com/content/dam/servicenow-assets/public/en-us/doc-type/resource-center/data-sheet/ds-edge-encryption.pdf.*

incorporate whatever standard encryption libraries[207] they like into their Cloud-based application. In a PaaS environment, the choice of cryptographic libraries available to the on-PaaS application is limited to the cryptographic libraries provided by the PaaS or by the languages supported by the PaaS. Fortunately, many PaaS providers have recognised the importance of encryption and provide access to cryptographic functionality.

The Salesforce.com platform has the Apex Crypto class which provides applications with the capability to encrypt and decrypt information, generate hash values, create digital signatures and generate signed hash values (message authentication codes). The Crypto class supports a number of different hashing algorithms including MD5[208], SHA-1, SHA-256 and SHA-512. AES-128, AES-192 and AES-256 are available for data encryption. More information on the Salesforce.com Apex Crypto class can be found at:

https://developer.salesforce.com/docs/atlas.en-us.apexcode.meta/apexcode/apex_classes_restful_crypto.htm.

Consumers of Microsoft Azure have access to the Cryptographic Service Providers built into the Microsoft .NET framework. Similarly, consumers of other PaaS services can make use of the crypto libraries that they are using.

A critical aspect of the use of cryptographic libraries in the Cloud is to secure the keys appropriately, usually through the

---

[207] It is generally a security anti-pattern to implement your own cryptographic libraries.

[208] SHA-256 and SHA-512 are the recommended options.

use of secure storage capabilities, such as Azure Key Vault, AWS KMS, Cloud KMS or the use of Protected Custom Settings or Protected Custom Metadata Types[209] in the Salesorce.com platform. Consumers should ensure that they meet the requirements dictated for the conceptual *key management* service in the SRM.

So far I have only spoken about the data encryption aspects of cryptography. The other common encryption aspect related to Cloud-hosted application is the encryption of data in transit, typically through the use of TLS. Given that one of the common use cases for PaaS is the hosting of customer-facing web applications, PaaS providers have made it fairly straightforward to implement TLS support within an application. The links below refer to relevant guidance with respect to the implementation of TLS for a number of PaaS providers:

- *https://docs.microsoft.com/en-gb/azure/app-service/configure-ssl-bindings#enforce-tls-1112*
- *https://docs.aws.amazon.com/elasticbeanstalk/latest/dg/configuring-https.html*
- *https://help.salesforce.com/articleView?id=security_keys_about.htm&type=5*
- *https://devcenter.heroku.com/articles/ssl*
- *https://cloud.google.com/appengine/docs/standard/python/securing-custom-domains-with-ssl*

As ever with TLS (or other network encryption in general) be aware of the impact of encryption on the capability of

---

[209] *https://developer.salesforce.com/page/Secure_Coding_Storing_Secrets*.

your (and your CSP's) network security tools such as firewalls and intrusion prevention systems. If the traffic is encrypted then it cannot be inspected. Consumers should consider where in their architectures they break TLS connections to ensure that the traffic entering their domain can be inspected prior to processing. For example, TLS traffic could terminate in a specific front-end application that then forwards the traffic to the main application which would allow inspection of the plain text traffic (via the *content checking* service) prior to processing.

Access management

An extract from the SRM showing the *access management* service grouping and indicating the primary delivery responsibility for each service is shown in Figure 35.

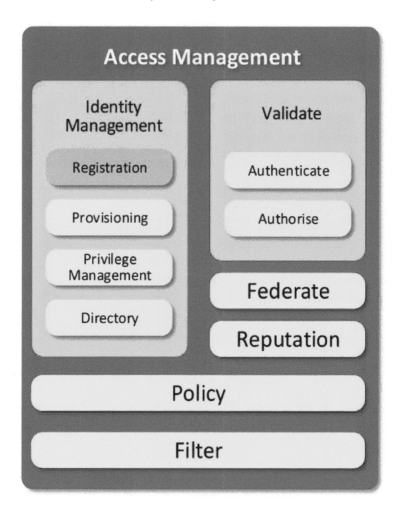

Figure 35: PaaS access management

Figure 35 indicates that the majority of the *access control* services are jointly delivered. The *validate* services are noted as being the primary delivery responsibility of the CSP. This is based on the assumption that the consumer is making use of authentication and authorisation services provided by the platform. The primary delivery responsibility would shift towards the consumer should this not be the case.

I will not repeat content that I previously presented in chapter 9; for example, I shall not repeat the overviews of OAuth 2.0 or OpenID Connect. However, both OAuth and OpenID can be relevant to applications hosted on PaaS services.

Before I expand upon the individual *access management* services, I will provide references to CSP documents that describe the access control capabilities of their platforms.

Microsoft Azure App Services includes a set of authentication and authorisation capabilities as described in the links below:

- *https://docs.microsoft.com/en-us/azure/app-service/overview-authentication-authorization*
- *https://docs.microsoft.com/en-us/azure/app-service/app-service-authentication-how-to*

These services allow application developers to make use of the App Services module to:

- Authenticate users via specified authentication providers;
- Validate, store and refresh access tokens; and
- Perform session management.

These App Services-specific capabilities supplement the wider Azure Platform access control capabilities offered by Azure Active Directory.

Users building upon AWS Elastic Beanstalk can use whichever form of identity and access management provision they choose; however, the AWS platform does offer a specific end user identity and access management service in the form of AWS Cognito,[210] which allows developers to support federation and authentication. The standard AWS IAM service can be used to control access to AWS resources by Elastic Beanstalk-hosted applications.

The Salesforce.com App platform provides identity management capabilities via Salesforce Identity:

https://developer.salesforce.com/docs/atlas.en-us.identityImplGuide.meta/identityImplGuide/identity_over view.htm.

Salesforce Identity provides user federation, authentication and directory services, supporting integration with third-party applications via OAuth 2.0 and OpenID Connect.

Salesforce offers a different set of capabilities to control access to information and capabilities within the platform itself:

https://developer.salesforce.com/page/Enforcing_CRUD_a nd_FLS.

The guidance available via the second link explains the data-centric access controls; these are the mechanisms available to control user access to data within the platform, i.e. CRUD access alongside Field Level Security (FLS).

For those platforms that support Java, e.g. Google App Engine and Heroku, consumers should consider the use of Spring Security to provide their authentication and authorisation services – the links below provide more information on Spring Security:

- *https://spring.io/projects/spring-security*

---

[210] *https://aws.amazon.com/cognito/.*

- *https://spring.io/guides/topicals/spring-security-architecture*

Let's explore the individual areas of *access management* in a little more detail.

Identity management

The *identity management* services of the SRM include:

- *Registration*
- *Provisioning*
- *Privilege management*
- *Directory*

As described within chapter 9, user *registration* processes should be independent of the IT delivery mechanisms; the proof of identity required to access your systems is related to the value of your data and the impact of compromise.

The *provisioning* mechanisms available to your application differ with each PaaS provider; they range from direct creation via the console (e.g. Salesforce.com *https://help.salesforce.com/articleView?id=users_mgmt_ov erview.htm&type=5*) or via API to synchronisation with other identity repositories such as Active Directory.

Similarly, the *privilege management* and *directory* aspects of PaaS solutions depend upon the platform chosen and the aspects of that platform that you choose to incorporate within your application.

In terms of *privilege management* and access to the PaaS management capabilities, there are also differences in the levels of control available (e.g. the use of role-based access controls). The Google App Engine (GAE) supports Cloud

IAM and offers three different categories for its roles: 'primitive', 'predefined' and 'custom'. The primitive roles include the 'owner', 'editor' and 'viewer' roles used within GAE prior to the introduction of Cloud IAM; predefined roles are provided and managed by Google; whilst custom roles are configured and managed by the Cloud consumer. Google offers a number of predefined roles specifically for GAE; further information can be accessed via this link:

https://cloud.google.com/iam/docs/understanding-roles.

These predefined roles range from full access via the appengine.appAdmin role through to read-only access via the appengine.appViewer and appengine.codeViewer roles; appengine.appViewer permits viewing of the application configuration but does not grant access to source code, whilst appengine.codeViewer does permit access to the deployed source code. If a consumer requires more granular access controls, this can be supported through the creation of *custom* roles in Cloud IAM. This role-based access control is vital for those organisations subject to the segregation of duties requirements.

Salesforce.com offers a privilege model based on the use of profiles, permission sets and sharing rules. Profiles control what users can see and do within the platform. Sharing rules enable administrators to restrict or enlarge the data records available to a user – organisation-wide rules set the default levels of access available to users, and sharing rules are subsequently used to open up further access where required.[211] The Salesforce.com platform controls access to

---

[211] *https://trailhead.salesforce.com/content/learn/modules/lex_implemen tation_user_setup_mgmt/lex_implementation_user_setup_mgmt_config ure_user_access*.

data using a combination of privilege and data-centric mechanisms. Users can be granted create, read, update and delete permissions for standard or custom objects. These CRUD permissions are applied at the profile level to control what activities users can undertake. Organisations requiring more granular control can make use of field level security (FLS) that enables similar CRUD permissions to be enforced on the individual fields within an object. CRUD and FLS controls are explained in more detail at the link below:

https://developer.salesforce.com/page/Enforcing_CRUD_a nd_FLS.

In terms of the provisioning of administrator users, most PaaS platforms will allow you to sign up to access their services with a simple email address (for example, Heroku) or using an existing account with a separate service (e.g. using a Google account to access Google App Engine). This does raise an important consideration from an enterprise perspective; you should not allow your enterprise PaaS administrators to sign up to Cloud services using their own personal email addresses. If you do, you could find yourself in an uncomfortable position should one of your administrators choose to find alternative employment; i.e. locked out of your PaaS-hosted applications. You should instead create specific email addresses, owned by the enterprise, to be used to register for PaaS services.

Validate

The *validate* services of the SRM provide the ability to *authenticate* and then *authorise* user (including service users) access to your Cloud-based application. In the PaaS model, the CSPs bear primary delivery responsibility for the delivery of the *validate* services where the application relies upon the authentication and authorisation services provided by the CSP.

Authenticate

As with applications hosted within IaaS Clouds (discussed in chapter 9), organisations have a number of options for delivering the *authenticate* service. PaaS consumers develop their own applications and so can choose how they authenticate their users – from simple username and password through to more complicated mechanisms such as certificate-based authentication or federated authentication.

The Salesforce.com platform supports username/password authentication by default but can also support delegated and federated authentication. When using delegated authentication[212], users enter their credentials on the Salesforce.com login page but the platform then transmits those credentials to an end point configured by the consumer which then validates the presented credentials. Whilst this approach enables consumers to retain control of their users credentials (i.e. they are not stored within the Salesforce.com platform), it still requires user credentials to be transmitted across the Internet, albeit over an encrypted web service call. Another issue with the delegated authentication approach is the requirement for the consumer to develop an appropriate end point (with access to an identity store and the Internet) to perform the username/password validation. One benefit of this delegated authentication approach is that the consumer is now in full control of password policies and they can also choose to implement token-based authentication using their

---

[212] *https://help.salesforce.com/articleView?id=sso_delauthentication.ht m&type=5.*

own implementation. Delegated authentication is controlled at the permissions level (via the "Is Single Sign-On Enabled" permission) rather than at the organisation level, so consumers have the capability to use delegated authentication as a way to enforce 'step up authentication' for more privileged users should they so choose.

Federated authentication via SAML is a more flexible approach, particularly where a consumer has a requirement to use multi-factor authentication. In this latter scenario, a consumer can make use of an authentication and identity provider like Okta to provide multi-factor authentication to secure their Salesforce.com application.

With respect to the Azure platform, authentication is primarily driven from Azure Active Directory (AAD). AAD offers a number of different approaches to support a variety of scenarios; for example, AAD B2B provides identity and authentication capabilities in a 'business to business' scenario, whilst AAD B2C provides the same in a 'business to consumer' scenario – both support federation, so Cloud consumers can select their preferred method of authentication. Consumers can also use the built-in authentication and authorisation capabilities to control access to their hosted applications (as described earlier in the *access management* section).

The Google App Engine platform supports multiple authentication mechanisms including[213]:

- Firebase Authentication
- Google Sign-In

---

[213] *https://cloud.google.com/appengine/docs/standard/python/oauth/?cs w=1.*

- OAuth 2.0 and OpenID Connect
- Users API

Firebase authentication lets Cloud consumers incorporate social login via the GCP Firebase service, whilst consumers can also choose to incorporate such functionality themselves via the OAuth 2.0 and Open ID Connect capability. The Google Sign-In option provides the capability to authenticate application users via their Google accounts (individual or G-Suite), whilst the Users API offers capabilities to detect if users are already authenticated and to redirect them to a sign-in page if they are not.

Authorise

The *authorise* service grouping controls what an authenticated user may do within the application, e.g. what data and functions they may access. The authorisation process described within Figure 25 for IaaS-based applications is equally applicable to PaaS-based applications.

Organisations looking to build on top of PaaS platforms must choose between using inbuilt capabilities, such as those offered by Azure Active Directory, or building their own authorisation processes, e.g. using Spring Security. I highlighted some of the predefined roles and access management capabilities using example PaaS offers earlier in this chapter.

Federate

Rather than repeat generic *federation* content from chapter 9, I shall limit the below discussion of federation technologies to those relevant to PaaS services.

The Azure platform provides extensive support for federated authentication and authorisation via Azure Active Directory, AAD B2C and claims-based security. Claims-based security refers to the granting of access to an application based upon a specific claim presented by a user request. For example, a simple request could contain a claim that the user originates from a specific geographic region and so is authorised to access content specific to that region. In order to function, such claims must be issued by a trusted entity and then validated by the receiving application. Within AAD, such claims will be issued in the form of JSON Web Tokens.[214] In general, a claims-based process would typically proceed as described below:

1. A user wishes to access an application.
2. The user contacts a security token service (STS) able to create a token containing a relevant claim (e.g. a geographic location claim).
3. The STS verifies that the user meets the criteria to validate their claim, which may just be a case of the STS trusting information provided by an identity provider.
4. If the claim is valid, the STS issues a security token containing the validated claim.
5. The user passes their security token to the desired application alongside their request for access.
6. The application extracts any relevant claims from the security token.

---

[214] *https://docs.microsoft.com/en-us/azure/active-directory/develop/id-tokens.*

7. The application passes the claims across to a policy decision point (PDP) to decide whether the claim is sufficient to authorise access.

8. The application grants or denies access based on the response from the PDP.

Claims-based access control is similar to the authorisation process illustrated in Figure 25, e.g. in the abstraction of policy decisions from the application. The Azure AD B2C service supports the following identity providers out of the box: Amazon, AAD, Microsoft, Facebook, GitHub, Google, LinkedIn, OIDC and Twitter.

The GCP App Engine offers the Identity Platform which includes the ability to incorporate SAML, OIDC and custom claims into hosted applications. More details on the incorporation of SAML-based authentication and authorisation into App Engine hosted applications can be found here:

https://cloud.google.com/identity-platform/docs/how-to-enable-application-for-saml.

The Salesforce.com platform also supports federated authentication via the use of SAML. Any identity provider able to produce SAML or OpenID tokens (e.g. Microsoft's AAD) can be used to authenticate Salesforce.com users.[215]

A more complete guide to the implementation of single sign-on for Salesforce.com applications can be found at:

http://resources.docs.salesforce.com/218/19/en-us/sfdc/pdf/salesforce_single_sign_on.pdf.

---

[215] *https://developer.salesforce.com/docs/atlas.en-us.sso.meta/sso_about.htm.*

As well as OpenID and SAML, Salesforce.com also supports OAuth v2.0 to allow for the federated authorisation of access to Salesforce.com resources.

Details of the OAuth support can be found at:

https://help.salesforce.com/articleView?id=remoteaccess_a uthenticate_overview.htm.

The Heroku Identity Federation capability enables Heroku users to federate authentication and authorisation but it is not directly applicable to hosted applications. If they require them, consumers must incorporate support for federated authentication and authorisation themselves. The Spring Security framework incorporates support for OpenID Connect and OAuth 2.0 so it may be a good basis for those PaaS consumers coding in Java.

Policy

Within the SRM's *access management* service grouping, the *policy* service delivers information required by other services, including the *authenticate*, *authorise* and *filter* services. The *policy* service dictates the access available to the relevant information resources. The *authenticate*, *authorise* and *filter* services then use this information to determine whether or not to provide access.

The *access management policy* service should be informed by the *policy* service within the *security management* grouping (taking, in turn, a feed from the *compliance* service), in order to ensure that access management decisions are taken in line with the business requirements.

In terms of Azure, for example, consumers need to develop a *policy* service that is capable of processing the claims contained within the security tokens presented by their IdP (e.g. Azure AD) and deciding whether or not these claims are sufficient for access to be provided. At the logical level, *policy* services would typically comprise a policy information point (containing the policy information) and a policy decision point (which makes the access decision based upon the information within the PIP and the presented claims).

At the PaaS level, consumers have fewer policy decisions to worry about (or control, depending on your perspective) than at the IaaS level. PaaS consumers do not have the freedom to implement their own host-based or network-based commercial off-the-shelf (COTS) security products, such as firewalls, intrusion prevention systems, database firewalls, et cetera; consequently, they are reliant upon the *policy* decisions made by their PaaS provider.[216]

Filter

The *filter* service is responsible for enforcing the access decisions made elsewhere, e.g. the *authorisation* service. The *filter* service becomes more straightforward as you move through the Cloud service models from IaaS through to SaaS as the number of available logical and physical filters decreases. For example, whilst an IaaS consumer must (or at least should) concern themselves with filters at the network, operating system, database and application level, consumers at the PaaS level need not concern themselves with the implementation of filters below their run-time. At least in theory. In practice, things are a little more complicated.

------

[216] With the exception of the ability to control which IP address ranges (for example) may access their services or other host-based firewalling capabilities exposed by their CSP.

Consider the Azure Service Bus[217] offer, which enables Cloud consumers to easily integrate and orchestrate web services across Cloud and on-premise environments. The Azure Service Bus is a great way to build mash-up applications consisting of capabilities provided by a variety of different web services. Consumers expose their internal web services to the Azure Service Bus whilst the Service Bus then controls access to those exposed web services. Communications between the on-premises web services and the Service Bus are encrypted using TLS. However, consumers are now reliant upon the Cloud-based Service Bus to secure their on-premises web service. A misinformed employee, however well-intentioned, could expose sensitive on-premises web services to the Cloud through encrypted tunnels that are beneath the radar of your security team. This is another example of where consumers should consider implementing content-aware network-level filters on-premises to manage issues relating to Cloud security if operating a hybrid environment.

When it comes to database and application level security filters (e.g. XML gateways, anti-malware services), then PaaS consumers are limited in their options – COTS products providing such functionality cannot be installed in a PaaS Cloud. PaaS consumers are limited to the capabilities offered by their provider (e.g. the Azure API Management service); if these do not meet their needs, they must consider alternative options, such as redirecting incoming requests or content to either an on-premises or SaaS-based content-checking service.

---

[217] https://docs.microsoft.com/en-us/azure/service-bus-messaging/service-bus-messaging-overview.

In Figure 9 (chapter 7), I identified the *filter* service as a joint responsibility in the PaaS delivery model. This is because PaaS consumers are reliant upon the separation mechanisms enforced by their CSPs to isolate their data and services from those of other PaaS consumers. Consumers should content themselves that the level of isolation is adequate to meet their needs. Different PaaS providers offer different levels of isolation depending upon their approach to delivering multi-tenancy.

For example, the Salesforce.com platform approaches multi-tenancy from the perspective of offering a single database and infrastructure stack, and separating organisations using a meta-data driven approach as described below:

https://developer.salesforce.com/page/Multi_Tenant_Archit ecture.

Salesforce has multiple instances of these infrastructure stacks, which are known as points of deployment (PODs) ; with around 10,000 customers operate on each POD. Each POD can be viewed as a single giant application, accompanied by a single giant datastore, with resources set aside for specific clients. The client-specific resources are identified via meta-data stored within the datastore, e.g. the use of the organisation ID (OrgID) to scope which users can access resources specific to that organisation.

Conversely, the Heroku approach is based on the use of Linux Containers[218] to provide resource isolation for dynos and chroot to deliver filesystem isolation, supplemented with host-based firewalls to provide network isolation. Each dyno is, therefore, isolated from all other dynos. Customers

---

[218] *https://linuxcontainers.org/.*

requiring more discrete operating environments can choose to deploy into 'private spaces'.[219] These are run-times dedicated to a specific customer and they take up the entirety of a virtual machine, i.e. they essentially remove the multi-tenancy element.

Microsoft Azure offers isolation controls at the hypervisor and network levels. The Azure hypervisor prevents an Azure role operated by company A from being affected by the activities of an Azure role operated by company B on the same physical hardware. Azure also enforces network level controls to ensure that customers can only access their own Azure roles. Google offers two different environments for their App Engine: 'standard' and 'flexible'. The Google App Engine standard environment runs each application within its own Sandbox[220] which strictly limits the interactions available to the application. For example, applications within the Sandbox cannot write to the local filesystem, open a network connection to another host directly, spawn sub-processes or make system calls.[221] However, Google App Engine customers are utterly reliant upon the strength of the Sandbox protecting their applications; delivery of this sandbox is completely in the domain of the CSP. The App Engine flexible environment blurs the line between PaaS and IaaS as it allows customers to customise the run-time and even the operating system of the hosting virtual machine

---

[219] *www.heroku.com/private-spaces*.

[220] A sandbox is a mechanism for isolating and executing untrusted security programs.

[221]*https://cloud.google.com/appengine/docs/the-appengine-environments?csw=1*.

using Dockerfiles. Customers operating within the flexible environment can even obtain SSH access to the underlying operating systems. In this situation, the isolation is provided by the capabilities of the underlying Google Compute Engine IaaS service.

In summary then, delivery of the *filter* services must be through a combination of services delivered by the CSP and by the consumer. The consumer must understand the *filter* services delivered by the CSP in order to identify any gaps in capabilities that they may need to address or which result in risks that must be managed (or simply accepted based on an analysis of risk versus benefit).

Security governance

The *security governance* services of the SRM, from a PaaS perspective, are shown in Figure 36.

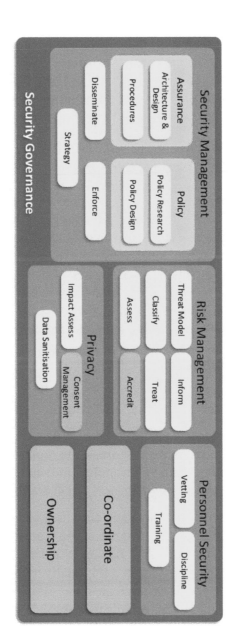

Figure 36: PaaS governance

As you can see in Figure 36, all of the *security governance* services, with the exceptions of the *coordinate, ownership, accredit* and *consent management* services, are now joint delivery responsibilities. The *coordinate* and *ownership* services always remain the responsibility of the *consumer*, regardless of the Cloud delivery model.

The capabilities that the *security governance* services need to deliver are independent of the chosen IT delivery model. However, the delivery responsibility for the services varies per Cloud service model. For example, whilst *architecture* and *design* of a hosted application is primarily a consumer responsibility when deploying on an IaaS Cloud, it is a joint responsibility when deploying on a PaaS Cloud and primarily the responsibility of the CSP when deploying on a SaaS Cloud. The capabilities associated with the individual services are described within chapter 9; I will only briefly describe some PaaS-specific elements below.

Security management

There is a joint responsibility to deliver the security management services of the SRM when working with PaaS.

Assurance, architecture and *design, procedures, policy* and *risk management* activities must be completed by the consumer (with respect to the application) and the CSP (with respect to the underlying platform and shared APIs).

Consumers must trust that such activities take place within their CSPs, preferably evidenced via certification to an international standard that demands such activities take place. The *strategy* service is a joint delivery responsibility; consumers can decide on strategic approaches, but these will also be impacted by strategic decisions made by their CSPs. The retirement of Azure Access Control Services is a good example of how consumers' security strategies can be adversely affected by strategic decisions made by their CSPs. In this case, Azure consumers were required to migrate their applications away from ACS and, in some cases, this required the identification of a new identity provider able to close the functionality gap between the retired ACS and Azure AD.

With regard to services such as *disseminate*, consumers must ensure that they keep a close eye on the latest policy and procedural updates from their CSPs. These updates should then be further disseminated within the consumer to ensure that they feed into the application level considerations. Furthermore, these updates should also be compared against the consumer's underlying compliance and security policy requirements to ensure that the PaaS provider remains in a position to deliver these underlying requirements.

The consumer has an important role in relation to privacy: they are responsible for coding the application that will be hosted on the PaaS service, so they retain responsibility for the delivery of the *consent management* elements of any application processing personal information. The *impact assess* and *data sanitisation* services form a joint responsibility because both parties have a role to play: the CSP with regard to the underlying platform services, and the consumer with regard to the use of those platform services.

Security operations

Security operations are an area in which PaaS consumers can begin to realise some of the cost-savings associated with Cloud. For example, as such consumers have no visibility of the operating system they have no requirement to concern themselves with the patching of operating systems. This is the responsibility of the PaaS provider and delivered as part of the 'S' within Platform as a Service. However, not all security operations are the responsibility of the PaaS provider. In fact, the majority of such services are a joint delivery responsibility in the PaaS model, as shown in Figure 37.

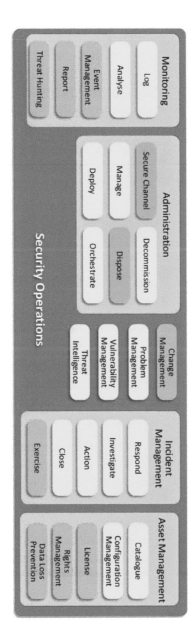

Figure 37: PaaS security operations

It is in the area of *security operations* where the need for joint delivery of security services becomes apparent. It is also the area where gaps are most likely to appear between the capabilities offered by the CSP and the capabilities implemented by the consumer. When I wrote earlier in this book that PaaS is the hardest of the Cloud service models to secure, it is primarily in the area of security operations that my concerns sit. Consumers must ensure that no gaps form between themselves and the CSP in areas such as *monitoring*, *vulnerability management* and *incident response*.

Monitoring

The *monitoring* service grouping of the SRM includes services to *log*, *analyse* and *report* on security events alongside an *event management* service.

In the PaaS environment, it is the responsibility of the CSP to log events at the underlying network infrastructure and operating system level. Consumers must trust their CSPs to provide adequate security monitoring capabilities alongside an event management process that will enable CSPs to inform their consumers of events requiring their attention and, more importantly, action.

It remains the responsibility of the consumer to instrument their application to provide the information required to meet both compliance requirements relating to audit and general security logging requirements. The Azure App Services platform provides a diagnostics capability that can log both web server events and application events.[222] Web server diagnostics include detailed error logging, which retains a

---

[222] *https://docs.microsoft.com/en-us/azure/app-service/troubleshoot-diagnostic-logs.*

maximum of 50 HTML files (one for each request resulting in an HTTP status code of 400 or greater); failed request tracing, which provides one folder per event to contain an IIS trace of the failed event (again, up to a maximum of 50 events); and web server logging, which creates logs using the standard W3C extended log file format. Application diagnostics allows developers to instrument their application to produce required event information. The diagnostics service can be configured to write event information to either local storage (file system) or to an Azure Blob. Event information can be retrieved via FTP/S or through the Azure CLI.

The Heroku PaaS also offers a specific logging capability (the Logplex) which enables consumers to obtain log information from their application, the Heroku platform (e.g. restarting of crashed processes) and information from the Heroku management API (e.g. deployment of new dynos, changes in scaling, etc.). The information held within the Logplex can be retrieved via the command line using the 'Heroku logs' command. More usefully, Heroku can also be configured to push the logs out to 'drains'. Heroku currently supports two types of drains which the consumer defines: syslog and HTTPS. Further information about the logging capabilities of Heroku can be found at:

https://devcenter.heroku.com/articles/logging.

It is important to note that the Heroku Logplex service is hosted in the US, i.e. all Heroku log information will be routed via the US by default. This can be problematic from a compliance perspective. Customers with strict compliance requirements that rule out the transfer of data to the US should look to implement Heroku Private Spaces. When using Private Spaces, customers are able to dictate that their log information stays within a particular region; however, this comes at the cost of losing access to Logplex functionality, including the ability to forward events to multiple log drains and to access information via the Heroku logs command in the CLI or via the Dashboard viewer.[223]

Users of the Google App Engine have access to the Stackdriver[224] logging capability of the Google Cloud Platform. All requests and responses are automatically logged to Stackdriver and can be viewed using the Stackdriver Logs Viewer. The standard App Engine environment produces the following log types by default: request, App and run-time. The App Engine's flexible environment also logs more information from the run-times, which you may expect given its pseudo-IaaS nature. Developers should also instrument their applications to emit other logging information as required. Events can be pushed to either standard output (stdout) or standard error (stderr). If consumers do not wish to rely purely upon the GCP platform capabilities for monitoring, alerting and reporting, they can choose to stream log information to a tool of their choosing via the GCP Cloud Pub/Sub service.

The Salesforce.com offer includes an Event Monitoring Analytics App[225] that consumers can enable to monitor behaviour within their Salesforce.com environments. It comes with a set of pre-built dashboards to enable consuming organisations to identify suspicious behaviour

---

[223] *https://devcenter.heroku.com/articles/private-space-logging.*

[224] *https://cloud.google.com/logging/.*

[225] *https://help.salesforce.com/articleView?id=bi_app_admin_wave.htm &type=5.*

and poor application performance from the outset. Event information can be downloaded using cURL or Python scripts for import into third-party monitoring tooling if required.

With PaaS, the developer of the application has the opportunity (and responsibility) to instrument their application to produce meaningful event information. Their aim should be to provide full observability of the application, i.e. the emitted event information should be sufficient to give the observer complete understanding of the internal state of the application.

Now, given that CSPs tend to charge for storage and for data export per usage, there is a real incentive to ensure that you only log and then store information that is of real relevance. There is now a real cost driver to target your security logging rather than logging everything 'just in case'. Consumers should consider the activities and resources that are of most concern and target their logging at those activities, conscious of the wider driver of 'observability'. Consider the information likely to be of most value to an investigator, don't capture information that is likely to be of no value unless there are compliance requirements demanding the capture of such information.

Logging is only the first part of the security monitoring process. Once the information has been captured it must be analysed. In most cases, I would recommend PaaS consumers to export the log information from the Cloud and then pass the information across to whichever security event management tool you currently use to deliver *analysis* services, via an appropriate check for malicious content. No organisation would wish to see its trusted security operations centre (SOC) compromised via content imported from a semi-trusted Cloud service. However, due to the costs discussed earlier, PaaS consumers may decide to use provider-native functionality rather than importing data into an external service.

Examples of such capabilities include, Event Monitoring Analytics and Login Forensics on Salesforce and the Stackdriver Viewer on GCP. Relying on provider-native tooling may be a particularly attractive choice where consumers have adopted a single Cloud provider and, consequently, have little reason to worry about reconciling events across a diverse supply chain.

Following on from the *analysis* service is the *event management* service. This again exposes a potential gap in delivery between the PaaS CSP and the consumer. Appropriate communication channels, including service level agreements, must be in place to enable consumers and CSPs to exchange event information. Should a consumer identify a potentially suspicious event in the logs sourced from a CSP, they may require input from their CSP to decipher the exact meaning and implications of the audit entry. Failure to maintain an appropriate service level agreement may lead to excessive delays in the consumer obtaining the information that they require to act on a potential security event. Conversely, consumers must sustain an *event management* capability that CSPs can contact in the event of their own monitoring capabilities detecting an incident in progress at the consumer. Such an *event management* capability should also be responsible for monitoring the status of websites and their various CSPs to ensure that consumers maintain awareness of system availability or wider security incidents.

Examples of status update sites in the PaaS arena include:

- *https://status.salesforce.com/*
- *https://status.azure.com/en-us/status*
- *https://status.cloud.google.com/*
- *https://status.heroku.com/*

Where any source, be that from the application logs or from the CSP status updates, indicates a security incident then the *event management* service should initiate the *incident management* processes.

Administration

The SRM's *administration* services are shown below:

- *Secure channel*
- *Decommission*
- *Manage*
- *Dispose*
- *Deploy*
- *Orchestrate*

The *secure channel* and *dispose* services are clearly the primary delivery responsibility of the CSP. They provide the channels enabling management of their platforms (usually via a web portal and an API). CSPs are also responsible for the decommissioning and subsequent disposal of the hardware providing the platform. The consumer maintains some responsibility for the decommissioning aspect relating to the treatment of data associated with an application that is being retired.

The consumer is left with a degree of control over the *manage*, *deploy* and *orchestrate* services. Even in a PaaS environment, consumers have a degree of control over their services, e.g. the number of instances that they require to provide their services, the usage quotas that they require et cetera. Consumers also decide when they deploy their applications to the PaaS platform and how these deployments are orchestrated.

However, within the SRM, these services are marked as a joint delivery responsibility given that the CSP provides the *manage* and *deploy* services with respect to the hardware, platform and shared APIs. Consumers should closely control the ability to manage and deploy their applications; not only could a rogue administrator delete (or stop) applications running in a PaaS environment, they could also attack their employers financially through running up excessive charges. Monitor your employee's management and deployment activities via the logs made available by your CSP.

PaaS is often a great choice for those organisations looking to be developer-focussed, i.e. looking to avoid the pain of operating system administration and wishing to focus more on the production of code and its associated business value. Such organisations will also likely wish to adopt the principles of DevSecOps, from the shifting left available through security controls to the use of blue/green approaches and canary deployments. PaaS services may include native capability to support these new ways of working; for example, the Azure App Service uses the concept of 'deployment slots'.[226] Essentially, a 'deployment slot' is a live application with its own hostname. Azure customers can choose to deploy their application into a deployment slot other than their default production slot. Given that

---

[226] *https://docs.microsoft.com/en-gb/azure/app-service/deploy-staging-slots.*

application content and configuration elements can be swapped between two deployment slots, this presents consumers with relatively straightforward opportunities to implement both blue/green and canary approaches.

From the blue/green perspective, organisations can run their production app in one (blue) deployment slot and their next release in a separate (green) deployment slot until they feel comfortable that it is ready to be released to customers; at that point, they can switch deployment slots to make the latest version of the application live and to free up the previously live slot for use as the new green environment. Since deployment slots host essentially 'live' versions of an application, this approach of switching deployment slots allows organisations to 'warm up' the green environment prior to switching and, consequently, avoids any down time that might otherwise be required as part of spinning up the new environment. It also makes rollback a straightforward issue because the slots can immediately be swapped back in the event of any problems.

Azure also allows organisations to split load between deployment slots. This is particularly useful when organisations wish to test new functionality in the form of canary releases.[227] Those features that users do not appreciate can be removed without ever hitting the main production application, whilst any applications containing canary features that users appreciate can have the entirety of the application load directed towards the relevant deployment slot, thereby becoming the main live application. Features such as deployment slots illustrate why PaaS and

---

[227] https://martinfowler.com/bliki/CanaryRelease.html.

FaaS are particularly natural destinations for those organisations wishing to move towards DevSecOps.

Change management and problem management

In a PaaS environment, the *change* and *problem management* services also form a joint delivery responsibility between the consumer and the CSP. A critical aspect of the *problem management* service is the identification of whether an issue resides with the CSP or with the consumer and then managing that issue through to a successful resolution. As with some of the other SRM services, the success of this approach is dependent upon the consumer having a full understanding of the services provided by the CSP and appropriate communication channels being available.

In general, the consumer will be responsible for managing change and problems associated with their application. Issues can arise where problems are found in the platform APIs that are incorporated into a consumer application. Similarly, consumers must be aware of planned changes to such platform APIs to ensure that they make the necessary changes to their application that is reliant upon the common functionality. Once again, the retirement of the Azure Access Control Services[228] capability is a strong example of the need to track CSP product roadmaps.

The PaaS approach can take care of some of the problems associated with *change management*, i.e. changes to the supporting infrastructure now take place 'under the covers' and are no longer the concern of the consumer. CSPs can also

---

[228] *https://azure.microsoft.com/en-gb/blog/one-month-retirement-notice-access-control-service/*.

introduce new functionality that consumers can adopt in a managed fashion through scheduled change windows.

One downside of the PaaS approach is that change, and other maintenance, windows will occur at the choosing of the CSP rather than any individual consumer. This can be a problem if a consumer has an important event occurring at the same time as the PaaS platform (or elements thereof) becomes unavailable.

Vulnerability management

Vulnerability management responsibilities are clearly split between the CSP and the consumer in the PaaS environment. The CSP must perform regular penetration testing and vulnerability assessments of their platform whilst the consumer is responsible for the security of their application. However, the second part can be difficult to achieve, particularly if the PaaS provider does not allow penetration testing. Consumers should always be aware of their CSP's policy prior to undertaking any penetration testing on a live platform: different Cloud providers have different levels of tolerance for penetration testing of their services,[229] with an increasing number of providers moving away from a need for pre-authorisation.[230]

The area of *vulnerability management* highlights a clear disadvantage of the PaaS approach. With IaaS, consumers can run penetration testing exercises either within the Cloud, by installing the necessary tools within their virtualised

---

[229] For example, see *https://help.salesforce.com/articleView?id=000336416&type=1&mode=1*.

[230] *https://devcenter.heroku.com/articles/pentest-instructions*.

environments, or externally over the Internet; it is not possible to provide the same level of service within most PaaS environments. With SaaS, providers can test their services all the way up to the application level. The situation with PaaS can be more uncomfortable: whilst your CSP may scan and fix their platform on a regular basis (and most do), you will still be in trouble if your own application hosts weaknesses that you are not allowed to identify.

Cloud providers are aware of the overheads that having to complete pre-authorisation forms for penetration testing places on their customers and some are addressing this issue by offering vulnerability assessment tools within their platforms. Some examples are listed below:

- Google Security Scanner:
  https://cloud.google.com/security-scanner/
- Salesforce Code Scanner (code analysis tool, delivered by Checkmarx):
  https://security.secure.force.com/security/tools/forceco m/scanner
- Salesforce Chimera (web application scanner, aimed at Independent Software Vendors (ISVs) rather than customers): *www.crmscience.com/single-post/2017/06/12/The-Chimera-Web-Scanner*

Those Cloud providers that do not offer their own scanning tools will often include the ability to integrate third-party tooling into the overall platform security dashboard, e.g. Azure Security Centre.

Incident management

Incident management in the Cloud is another example of the need for comprehensive and timely communication channels between the CSP and the consumer. I strongly recommend that such communications channels are included in contract terms where there is the flexibility for consumers to negotiate (primarily, private or hybrid environments). Consumers will likely require assistance from their CSPs to manage ongoing incidents (e.g. provision of log information). CSPs should also be able to provide extracts of secure logs that are suitable for use by law enforcement or in criminal trials where necessary.

I provided extensive descriptions of incident response processes in chapter 9 so I will not repeat that content here.

Asset management

Even in a PaaS environment, consumers must maintain a catalogue of the assets that they have in the Cloud. This could relate to their applications in an Azure App Services environment, dynos in a Heroku environment or data stored in any PaaS environment.

Consumers are also responsible for the *configuration management* of their PaaS applications, i.e. traditional source code management and deployment activities or more dynamic DevSecOps and automated approaches.

The issue of *License* Management does not completely disappear in the Cloud as certain services are licensed per user (e.g. Salesforce.com) and so consumers must still ensure that they abide by their licensing agreements.

Similarly, PaaS services also offer application stores where pre-built software applications or third-party tooling for the platform can be purchased. Again, such applications will be subject to their own licensing terms and conditions.

Conclusion

This chapter has described some of the ways in which the SRM services can be delivered and some of the associated issues with regard to working in a PaaS environment.

Many PaaS providers offer extensive documentation on the security of their services, I recommend that would-be consumers take a close look at such documentation prior to adopting such a service. Examples of the security documentation available can be found via the following links:

- *https://developer.salesforce.com/developer-centers/security/*
- *https://docs.microsoft.com/en-us/azure/app-service/overview-security*
- *www.heroku.com/policy/security*
- *https://docs.aws.amazon.com/elasticbeanstalk/latest/dg/using-features.managing.security.html*

CHAPTER 11: SECURITY AND SOFTWARE AS A SERVICE

In this chapter, I describe how the security services defined within the SRM, shown in Figure 7, may be delivered by consumers implementing a service using a SaaS Cloud.

There are countless SaaS services available covering a wide range of capabilities, including:

- Billing
- Customer relationship management (CRM)
- Collaboration
- Content management
- Document management
- Enterprise resource planning (ERP)
- Environmental health and safety
- Financials
- Health and wellness
- Human resources
- IT service management (ITSM)
- Personal productivity
- Project management
- Sales
- Security
- Social networks

Examples of SaaS providers include:

- Salesforce.com (*www.salesforce.com*)

- Sage (*www.sageone.com*)
- Intuit (*www.intuit.com*)
- Netsuite (*www.netsuite.com/portal/home.shtml*)
- SuccessFactors (*www.successfactors.com*)
- Oracle (*www.oracle.com/applications/*)
- Office365 (*www.office.com/*)
- Google Apps (*https://gsuite.google.com/*)
- GitHub (*https://github.com/*)
- Zoom (*https://zoom.us/zoomrooms?zcid=2438*)
- Slack (*https://slack.com/intl/en-gb/*)
- Huddle (*www.huddle.com*)
- Confluence (*www.atlassian.com/software/confluence*)
- Box (*www.box.com*)
- Dropbox (*www.dropbox.com/teams*)
- Qualys (*www.qualys.com*)
- MIMECast (*www.mimecast.com*)
- Okta (*www.okta.com/*)
- AlertLogic (*www.alertlogic.com/solutions/product-overview-and-pricing/*)
- Demisto (*www.demisto.com/*)
- Veracode (*www.veracode.com/*)

The selection of SaaS CSPs given above highlights the real diversity that is present in the SaaS ecosystem. It also highlights the impossibility of providing detailed security guidance that is applicable to all categories of SaaS service provision. The security requirements for a financial reporting system or a HR system are clearly different to those for a system designed to promote collaboration or a service providing security testing. The guidance presented in this chapter will necessarily be generic and aimed at helping organisations secure their use of services whereby they entrust their data (and relying business processes) to SaaS vendors.

Secure development

In a SaaS environment, the primary responsibility for the delivery of a secure application rests with the provider. SaaS providers should be strongly incentivised to provide a secure service; given the competitive nature of the SaaS landscape, a series of security mishaps would not be conducive to a long-term future.

One of the drivers for adopting the SaaS model is to rid yourself of the problem of software development (and, perhaps, integration) and the overhead of supporting the developed software on an expensive infrastructure. However, the more complex the SaaS application the more work is required to tailor it to meet your particular needs. Examples of the work involved can include 'skinning' the application with your own logos and visual style guidelines, configuration of the users and their access rights, transformation of any data to be uploaded to the SaaS provider and integration of the SaaS provider into your wider environment (e.g. implementation of single sign-on).

The decision to adopt a SaaS model does not mean that you can immediately reassign your hands-on technical staff to other roles. You will need to retain some skilled resource to configure and then manage the technical or mundane administrative aspects of your chosen SaaS solution.

From a *secure development* perspective then, whilst there will be little in the way of content, you will still require a limited set of *coding standards* (e.g. configuration guidelines) together with the capability to *code review* and *unit test* any preparatory work (e.g. upload scripts) prior to their usage. However, the vast bulk of the delivery responsibility for such services in relation to the application itself rests with the CSP.

Integrity

With a SaaS approach, you are buying into the integrity of the SaaS application and the underlying datastores. The only aspects of *integrity* that a consumer can influence relate to the integrity of the data provided to the CSP and the integrity of the organisation-specific configuration within the SaaS application. Consumers should also ensure that they maintain the integrity of their on-premises datastores by content checking any information sourced from their SaaS provider prior to it being incorporated into a trusted datastore.

From a *non-repudiation* perspective, SaaS consumers are limited to the audit functionality and non-repudiation capabilities offered by their SaaS provider. User activities on a SaaS application can only be captured by the provider, unless such activities are proxied between the consumer and the SaaS provider. Fortunately, such proxies do exist and they can provide significantly more capability than simple logging of traffic between the on-premises environment and a SaaS provider. This capability, commonly referred to as a Cloud Access Security Broker (CASB), will be explored further in the section on *integration* later in this chapter.

The final service within the *integrity* service grouping is the *snapshot* service. In the IaaS and PaaS discussions the *snapshot* service provides a known-good baseline of data, application or configuration information. In the SaaS environment, the *snapshot* service could be implemented through exports of data at specific points and then securely storing such data on-premises (or with an alternative Cloud provider), e.g. through hashing and/or signing of the data export. SaaS providers may also offer their own equivalent snapshot capability, although consumers would need to be comfortable with the verification of such snapshots (e.g. signed hashing) and where such snapshots would be stored.

Integration

The *integration* set of services comprise *CASB, API* and *CWPP. CWPP* (Cloud workload protection platform) products were discussed in chapter 9. *CWPP* is placed within the *integration* services because it provides consuming organisations with the capability to place security controls around their workloads that are either portable or consistent or both. *CWPP* is not relevant in the SaaS context.

The *API* service relates to the need to provide programmatic access to Cloud services; this capability is as applicable to SaaS as it is to other Cloud models. In the SaaS context, the API could be used for user management, audit event configuration and retrieval, and service control.

The *API* service is intimately related to the final service in this grouping: the *Cloud Access Security Broker (CASB)* service. The *CASB* service provides a mechanism to supplement the security controls offered by Cloud providers, predominantly in the SaaS arena but not solely. For example, access to Cloud management APIs across all types of Cloud providers can be controlled by a broker.

The CASB name refers to a class of real-world products and services that can be used to deliver the conceptual service within the SRM. Examples of CASB products include:

- Netskope (*www.netskope.com/*)
- McAfee MVISION (formerly Skyhigh Networks)
  (*www.mcafee.com/enterprise/engb/products/mvision-Cloud.html*)
- BitGlass (*www.bitglass.com/*)
- Microsoft Cloud App Security
  (*www.microsoft.com/en-us/enterprise-mobility-security/Cloud-app-security*)

CASBs tend to provide similar functionality across the different products; this functionality is described below.

Discovery and risk assessment

The CASB identifies the Cloud services in use, alongside a view of the risk of using such services. CASB vendors maintain in-house catalogues of Cloud services – tens of thousands these days – with risk ratings scored using criteria such as 'hosting location' and 'certifications achieved'. Identification of the Cloud services in use will usually be achieved through analysis of web proxy and firewall logs or through running web traffic via the CASB for a period of time sufficient to identify normal usage.

Cloud access control

The CASB controls which Cloud services can be accessed by end users (authorised services) and which will have access to them blocked (non-sanctioned services). As always with security, a whitelisting approach is preferred to a blacklisting approach, though this comes with increased management overheads. CASBs can also control the actions that users can take within Cloud services through either the proxying of the connection or the configuration of the service via the APIs that the services expose.

Data loss prevention

CASBs can be used to prevent sensitive information leaking to Cloud services. CASBs work much as any other DLP solution, i.e. through pattern matching and/or heuristics. Some CASB products offer agents that can be installed on end user devices to prevent information leakage at source, i.e. on the device and prior to traversal of the CASB itself. Some CASBs will take a retroactive approach to DLP by scanning documents uploaded to Cloud services and removing them when they are found to contain controlled content.

Data tokenisation and/or encryption

CASBs can be used to tokenise or encrypt information being uploaded to Cloud services. Some SaaS providers offer downloadable pseudo-CASBs to enable this functionality, e.g. the ServiceNow Edge Proxy.[231]

Security assessment

CASBs often offer the capability to perform a security assessment of the Cloud services that they secure, e.g. through a check against relevant CIS benchmarks.[232]

---

[231] *https://docs.servicenow.com/bundle/london-servicenow-platform/page/administer/edge-encryption/concept/c_EdgeEncryptionOverview.html*.

[232] *www.cisecurity.org/benchmark/amazon_web_services/*.

Cloud monitoring

A CASB provides another source of logging and monitoring information to supplement that available from Cloud services. If all Cloud access is passed via the CASB, the CASB can provide a single point of visibility for user activity across an organisation's Cloud environment.

CASBs can be deployed either on-premises or in the Cloud, with the latter becoming a more common approach. However, if deployed on-premises, these products can offer extremely valuable functionality for the integrity of data and for compliance with data residency requirements. Consumers can use these products to encrypt or tokenise their sensitive data to ensure that it remains on-premises. If an organisation does not have strong regulatory compliance requirements to ensure that data remains on-premises at all times, then the Cloud-based model tends to be more appropriate for most organisations– for the same reasons that often make the Cloud model trump on-premises alternatives.

There are three main deployment approaches for using CASBs, illustrated in Figures 37-39. These figures depict the CASB as being hosted in the Cloud, but bear in mind that it could also be hosted on-premises.

Figure 38 illustrates the model you may be most familiar with: a CASB implemented in-line between the Cloud users and the Cloud services.

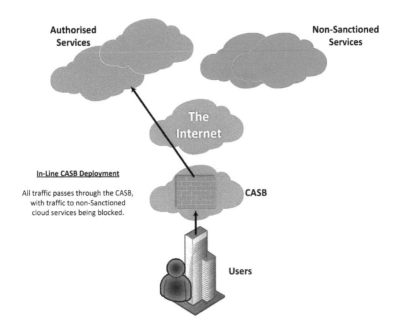

Figure 38: CASB in-line deployment option

In the *in-line* model, all user traffic is routed via the CASB. This is the only deployment model that allows organisations to actively block access to non-sanctioned Cloud services. This model allows proactive control of user activity and pre-emptive DLP, i.e. controlled content can be blocked prior to being stored within Cloud services.

Figure 39 illustrates the other common CASB deployment pattern: API only.

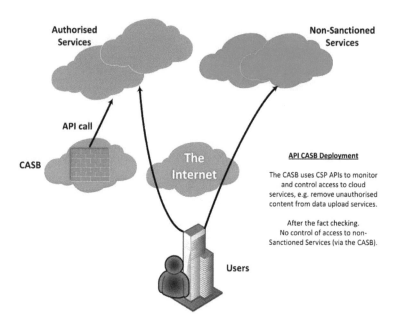

Figure 39: CASB API deployment option

With the API model, the CASB sits to the side of both users and the Cloud services that they access. The CASB is provided with credentials to the protected Cloud services and uses this access to control user activity via the APIs exposed by the various Cloud providers. In this model, the Cloud consumer is best able to control user activities within the Cloud services that the CASB product understands, i.e. there will be little value in this deployment approach if the CASB product has no ability to call the required APIs. In general, connectors can be configured as required, but this entails coding, testing and maintenance overheads. It is important to note that DLP operations are carried out retroactively in this model. For example, should a document containing controlled content be uploaded to One Drive, Dropbox, Box or a similar service, this upload will not be blocked in real time; however, the CASB will use its access to scan the uploaded content and will automatically remove it – as a result, there will be a polling window whereby controlled content will be hosted and available within the Cloud service. This may not be acceptable to some organisations.

The reverse proxy model is the final deployment model that I will discuss here (see Figure 40, below).

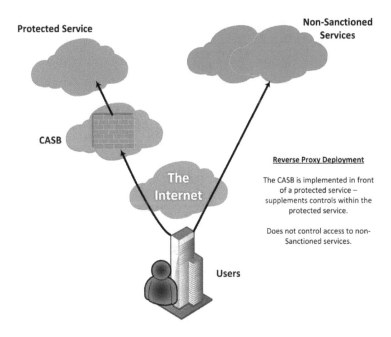

Figure 40: CASB proxy deployment option

In this model, the CASB is implemented to support a specific Cloud service by supplementing its access controls. This may be necessary if the SaaS service seems to lack adequate controls in areas like authentication, authorisation and security monitoring. In the reverse proxy model, as in the in-line model, the CASB is able to prevent the upload of controlled information into the protected Cloud service.

CASBs are typically considered within the SaaS context (which is why they are discussed in this chapter); however, they can also be used to control access to the major IaaS suppliers – the main CASB vendors understand the management APIs well enough to act as an additional source of access management capability. Note that these deployment models are not necessarily exclusive, i.e. it is perfectly reasonable, and indeed advisable, to deploy both the in-line and API models to control activities both within the Cloud service and in transit to the Cloud.

I mentioned encryption and tokenisation earlier in this section, and this subject is worthy of further discussion. Figure 41 illustrates how such technologies work.

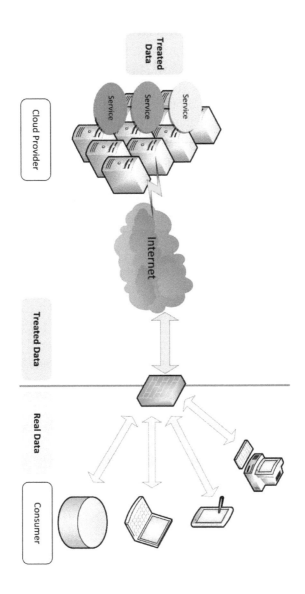

Figure 41: Encryption and tokenisation

On the left, we have our SaaS CSP and on the right, our consumer on-premises environment. In this scenario, the consumer is keen to take full advantage of the functionality and flexibility offered by their CSP, but they also have requirements that necessitate keeping their sensitive data on-premises. The solution illustrated in Figure 40 allows the consumer to meet both requirements, with certain restrictions relating to the difficulties of completing search and sorting operations on encrypted data. Users within the consuming organisation accessing their Cloud services are unaware of the device sat in-between themselves and the SaaS provider. This device (e.g. a CASB or other product) intercepts the sensitive data before it leaves the on-premises environment and replaces the sensitive data items with either encrypted or tokenised values. This treated data is then transmitted to the CSP and stored within the Cloud. Subsequently, when the user needs to access the SaaS application, the application processes the treated data that it holds and returns it to the end user. Before the response reaches the end user, the device replaces the treated data with the real data. End users can, therefore, take advantage of many of the SaaS application's capabilities whilst retaining complete control of their sensitive data.

The use of equality-preserving and/or order-preserving encryption algorithms can enable support for some logical operations and functionality on encrypted fields within the SaaS application; however, this comes with the security cost of encrypted fields always producing the same ciphertext for the plain text (as opposed to usual field-level encryption which would see different ciphertext being produced for each encryption operation). Equality-preserving encryption supports comparison operations, such as filtering, matching, and grouping. Order-preserving encryption algorithms support sorting and size comparison (less than/greater than) operations in addition to the capabilities enabled by equality-preserving algorithms.

Tokenisation is different to encryption: it replaces sensitive data with random values rather than relying upon encryption. When using tokenisation, a mapping between the real values and tokenised values must be retained on-premises so that the real values can be reinserted for presentation to end users.

Implementing products like CASBs or other tokenisation/encryption solutions has some downsides. For example:

- If their purpose is to keep data on-premises, the devices must be implemented on-premises. Implementing new physical hardware may not be compatible with the aims of moving to Cloud-based delivery.

- Hardware and software does not maintain itself: the products will require configuration and maintenance, e.g. patching, sanctioned application whitelisting, SaaS application level access control, et cetera.

- These devices can now act as a choke point and 'bump in the wire' for your SaaS access. Ensure that you can still meet required response times.

- It may be necessary to install a high availability or resilient pair, possibly at more than one location if the Cloud-based deployment option is not deemed adequate.

- Tokenisation or encryption will result in a degraded user experience within the SaaS applications: application capabilities that require access to clear text data will not function as expected with encrypted or tokenised data.

The above issues all point to a significant financial investment (in kit, hosting, CASB licensing and management) which may outweigh the financial benefit from moving to a pay-as-you-go model. In particular, consumers should ensure that they factor all relevant issues into their cost/benefit analysis with regard to adopting SaaS.

Availability

In a SaaS environment, the options for *business continuity (BC)* and *disaster recovery (DR)* are limited. If an organisation has fully bought into the SaaS philosophy and has little in the way of on-premises equipment, data or technical IT expertise then they will struggle to continue their business processes should their SaaS fail. Furthermore, if a SaaS (or the CSP) fails catastrophically, consumers may also struggle to retrieve their data from the CSP. On the positive side, one of the selling points of the SaaS approach is the relative speed to operation compared to an on-premises implementation. So, if there is a long-term outage a consumer could simply switch providers, assuming that the consumer has access to the underlying business data. Obviously, such a supplier switchover would not be a trivial undertaking and the feasibility of such an approach varies with the complexity of the service involved. It is also not just a technical issue, any switchover would also require users within the consuming organisation to be retrained to operate the new service and potentially implement changes to established business processes. So, whilst it may be a relatively trivial exercise to move from one vulnerability assessment as a service provider to another (e.g. from Qualys to SureCloud), it would be a much more painful exercise to switch your personal productivity suite from Google Apps to Office 365.

There are six concrete steps that a would-be SaaS consumer should take to ensure that appropriate business continuity and disaster recovery mechanisms are in place:

1. Ensure that you know the availability requirements of the business processes relying on the proposed SaaS application.
2. Investigate whether your proposed SaaS CSP can meet the identified availability requirements before signing up through examination of published availability statistics.
3. Examine the recompense on offer from the CSP should they fail to meet their published SLAs: service credits may not be much comfort when you are losing thousands of pounds an hour in lost business.
4. Consider the impact on your business processes should the SaaS provider undergo outages of minutes, hours, days or weeks. At which point (if any) is the outage unsustainable?
5. Consider storing a replicated copy of your business data either on-site or at a separate CSP to ensure that your data is always available, even if your SaaS application is not.
6. Plan for the worst-case scenario. Know what you will do if the SaaS is unavailable to the point of the associated losses being unsustainable. Options may include:
   - Falling back to a legacy on-premises system;
   - Falling back to manual processes (making use of the copy of your business data);
   - Switching to an alternative SaaS solution; and

- Having insurance.

The above steps are not intended to offer a comprehensive approach to business continuity; there are enough standards available, e.g. BS 25999/ISO 22301 that provide detailed advice in this area. My aim is rather to suggest some questions that should be in the back of your mind as you plan a SaaS implementation. You should also consider the comparative cost of implementing similar levels of business continuity and disaster recovery using physical, on-premises, systems. Whilst the levels of BC/DR available in the SaaS world may be limited, the SaaS approach may still represent a more feasible or cost-effective solution, particularly where an organisation does not possess geographically distributed redundant data centres or who have a poor track record of delivering available services.

As the Cloud model has matured, the number of organisations delivering complex business processes through a combination of many atomic Cloud services, sometimes integrated and managed via a service broker, has increased. For example, implementation of separate sales, CRM, storage, and authentication SaaS services to deliver a single overall business process. This approach offers great flexibility as you can switch in and out different CSPs as new 'best of breed' suppliers emerge – at least in theory. In practice, life is made more difficult through the lack of common standards in the area of portability and interoperability.

From an availability perspective, you can find the availability of your overall business process being less than you may imagine. Always remember that the availability of your overall business process is dependent upon the availability of each atomic service, i.e. failure at one element may take down the entire business process. A combination of four services offering 99.5% availability will only deliver a combined availability of 98% which may not meet your needs. Of course, similar concerns affect systems hosted on-premises where a failure of a critical server, database, switch, et cetera could also adversely affect the availability of a service. Always remember to step back and consider the overall requirements for your business processes and the impacts of those requirements not being fulfilled, regardless of your proposed delivery approach.

Cryptography

The delivery of the services within the *cryptography* grouping is firmly the responsibility of the SaaS CSP in most instances. Only the SaaS CSP can define the encryption requirements needed to access their service, albeit that such access is usually protected via TLS. Furthermore, it is the responsibility of the CSP to properly implement any encryption (and associated key management) of customer data should that be an element of their service. Given that the key management functions and the encryption implementation are both in the realm of the CSP, such a capability should not be viewed as offering protection from a threat actor within the CSP.[233] The only choice available to the consumer in a vanilla SaaS implementation may be whether or not to enable encryption on their communications and data. However, remember that SaaS consumers can still choose to encrypt data on-premises and only send encrypted

---

[233] Although some SaaS providers do allow a form of Bring Your Own Key, e.g. Salesforce Shield
www.salesforce.com/uk/products/platform/products/shield/.

(or tokenised) data into the Cloud should they decide to implement products such as a CASB.

Access management

Unlike with the IaaS and PaaS chapters (chapters 9 and 10), I am not going to explore the individual access management facilities available within a variety of different SaaS providers. I will instead provide some generic guidance as to how you can maintain control of your users and data when using SaaS providers.

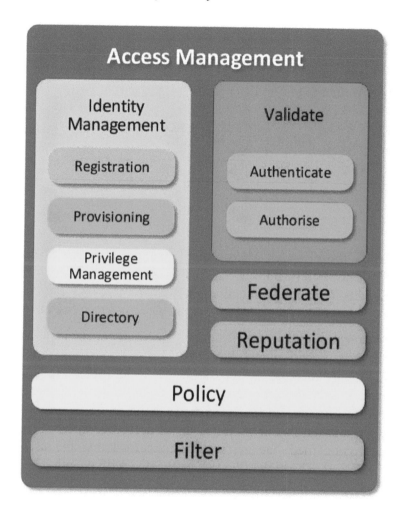

Figure 42: SaaS access management

Figure 42 shows the delivery responsibility split when you, as a SaaS consumer, adopt a standard implementation of a SaaS service. The CSP is responsible for how they authenticate your users to their service. The CSP is responsible for how they authorise access to your data and their functionality (on your data) within their application. The CSP provides the enforcement functionality (*filter*) to enforce their access controls. All that is left for you to do as a consumer is to:

- Register your users;
- Assign their access rights;
- Set an access management policy around users' access rights (if such a capability exists); and
- Decide whether or not to adopt federated identity management (if it is supported by the CSP).

Even those areas where the consumer still has some influence will be implemented using CSP-provided services, i.e. they remain a joint delivery responsibility.

For some consumers, this shifting of access management responsibilities may well count as one of the benefits of adopting a SaaS model. For others, it represents their worst nightmare of what can possibly go wrong with the Cloud model. As a SaaS consumer you need to decide which camp you fall within; there is no generic right or wrong answer. Your answer should be the result of a consideration of the data concerned, the application concerned and the users concerned. The higher the risk associated with unauthorised access to your data, the more likely it is that you will not be content to delegate so much of the access management functionality to the CSP. So what can you do if you are not content to rely solely upon your CSP? Once again, we have the option of implementing a CASB to control access, particularly in conjunction with a Cloud-based identity provider, e.g. Okta or Duo Security (now owned by Cisco).

At this point, consumers may also want to consider the adoption of a 'zero trust' approach towards access control –

this will be discussed further below, but see the *validate* section of chapter 9 for more.

Other than maintaining a level of control over the delivery of *access management* services, an equally important result of adopting a single sign-on and control approach is user convenience. Consider a situation where a normal enterprise user must access applications hosted across their on-premises environment and across multiple SaaS providers. From a user experience perspective it is undoubtedly preferable to only authenticate once and then be presented with access to all of your authorised applications rather than be constantly prompted to enter your credentials.

From an organisational perspective, supplementing this authentication with zero trust considerations, such as device health and behavioural anomaly detection, provides extra comfort. It should be noted that some CSPs do offer some of the characteristics associated with zero trust approaches out of the box, so not all consumers will need to add in new components, e.g. users of Office 365 can benefit from Azure AD Conditional Access.[234] Conditional Access allows authentication decisions to be supplemented with access control decisions based on a user's network location, the device they are using or the client application making the connection. Consumers should always inform themselves about native capability so they can make informed choices regarding user authentication and authorisation.

Now, one danger of adopting an approach in which you enforce control via some form of gateway, such as a CASB or an associated authentication provider, is that you must

---

[234] *https://docs.microsoft.com/en-us/azure/active-directory/conditional-access/*.

ensure that your users actually traverse that gateway. Easy enough when all of your users are based on-premises, but more often than not there will be a requirement to support mobile users, including users based on the Internet. In this scenario, you could choose to force your users to connect via your chosen gateway, e.g. by requiring your remote users to connect to your on-premises network before hopping back to the Internet to access the SaaS services. This is not a recommended approach: users are increasingly Internet-native, and zero trust approaches allow organisations to move away from this kind of old-world approach of VPNing into a corporate network prior to reaching out again to SaaS services. Alternative approaches include the installation of agents on end user devices (a functionality offered by some CASBs), or configuring the SaaS application to always redirect users to the gateway for authentication.

So, to summarise:

- Help your users (and yourself) by implementing single sign-on.
- Make use of appropriate federation technologies based on the levels of risk, e.g. OpenID Connect, OAuthv2, SAML, et cetera.
- Select an appropriate mechanism to act as a 'front door' to your SaaS services, e.g. Okta, Duo Beyond, Azure AD, Cloud App Security, et cetera.

Where you do not implement federated identity management, consider:

- Your *authentication* requirements (e.g. two-factor authentication). Ascertain whether they can be supported by your CSP.

- Your *provisioning* requirements. Ascertain whether it is sufficiently straightforward to create users, distribute their credentials, and remove or deactivate them when necessary.

- Your *authorisation* requirements. Ascertain whether the levels of control within the application are sufficiently granular. Make sure that it is sufficiently simple to maintain user privileges.

- Your data *privacy* requirements. Ensure you are legally entitled to populate SaaS-hosted user directories with the personal details of your employees (if relevant).

Another question that consumers should consider relates to the choice of Cloud deployment model. Some SaaS applications can be made available via a public or a community Cloud model, particularly where vendors are targeting government or other closed community clients (e.g. defence organisations); a number of SaaS CSPs are already offering community Cloud services aimed at delivering to government clients. Remember that Cloud does not always mean 'public Cloud'.

Security governance

The primary delivery responsibilities for the SRM *security governance* services for a SaaS application are shown in Figure 43.

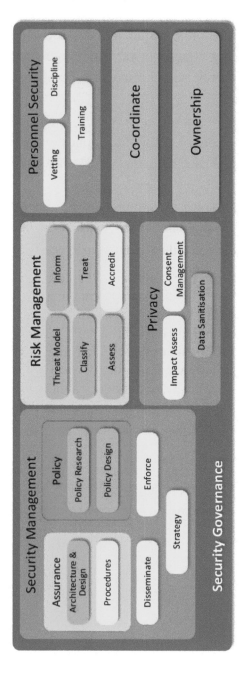

Figure 43: SaaS security governance

The *risk management* responsibilities for the application are now the primary delivery responsibility of the SaaS provider; it is their application and consumers have no control over how the application level risks are managed. However, consumers must still remember to consider their risk management responsibilities with regard to their data and their business processes that rely upon the SaaS application.

There are still some services within the *security governance* grouping that are a joint delivery responsibility, for example, the *disseminate* and *enforce* services and the *personnel security* services. With regard to the *disseminate* service, security policies and procedures must be disseminated to staff within both the CSP and the consumer. Similarly, both the CSP and the consumer must enforce those policies and procedures. In a SaaS environment, the CSP is primarily responsible for delivery of a base set of security policies regarding how their service may be used. The consumer must provide their own set of policies and procedures for their own users, but the primary delivery responsibility for security policy regarding the SaaS application itself sits with the CSP.

The *personnel security* service grouping remains a joint delivery responsibility with SaaS as it is with all Cloud models. Employees should be appropriately vetted and managed whether they are employed by the CSP or the consumer; both sets of staff may pose a risk to the confidentiality, integrity and availability of the service.

Security operations

The primary delivery responsibilities for the SRM *security operations* services are shown in Figure 44.

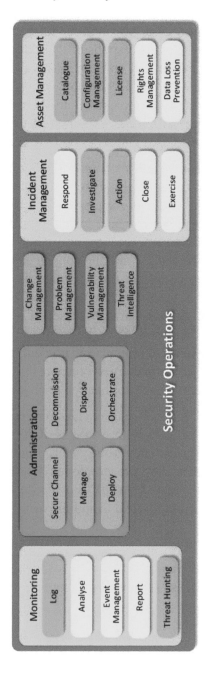

Figure 44: SaaS security operations

Always remember that the actual assignment of responsibilities for the SRM services will vary depending upon the actual application and CSP concerned. The assignments in this book are based on an abstract application that could be hosted on-premises, on an IaaS, or PaaS or SaaS Cloud rather than being based on a single real-world SaaS application. That said, you can see from Figure 44 that the *monitoring* duties are split between the CSP and the consumer. Whilst the *log* service is undoubtedly the delivery responsibility of the CSP, the *analysis* service is a joint delivery responsibility. After all, the consumer must analyse the relevant audit log information that the CSP is collecting.

The *event management* service is primarily the responsibility of the CSP; many of the events that are identified will be within the realm of the CSP such as problems with the underlying infrastructure or issues with the application itself. Consumers will mainly be interested in events specifically affecting their users, data or service. A service being described as the primary delivery responsibility of a CSP does not necessarily mean that there is no delivery responsibility for the consumer. This view of the SRM is primarily intended to help organisations understand where the bulk of the effort takes place and to identify where interfaces need to be established between the CSP and consumer.

Consumers that implement CASBs or other Cloud security gateways may well have a different split in responsibilities with regard to security *monitoring* services. Such devices (or services) increase the level of control and visibility that consumers retain of their users' interactions with Cloud services.

In terms of the *administration* services within the SRM, these services are, with the exception of *deploy*, completely within the remit of the CSP. The CSP is responsible for the management of their service (e.g. security patching), provision of mechanisms to manage their service and the subsequent decommissioning and disposal of their equipment upon failure or end of life. The one service within this grouping that is a joint delivery responsibility is the *deploy* service. Even in a SaaS environment, consumers must still undertake a set of activities to deploy the application to their users, e.g. provision of connectivity, access devices, user credentials, upload of business data and user training. It is these kinds of deployment activities that make *change management* a joint delivery responsibility.

SaaS CSPs often tout their rolling programme of tightly managed application upgrades as a major advantage of the SaaS service model. SaaS consumers do not need to worry about keeping up to date with service patches or costly upgrades to the latest versions of their business applications – this is all part of the service in SaaS. However, such changes can impact upon the business processes of the SaaS consumer. Consumers should monitor CSP roadmaps to ensure that they are aware of upcoming functionality to ensure that:

1. They take full advantage of new business opportunities that new functionalities may offer; and

2. They do not suffer a sudden unexpected drop in availability should a capability that their business users currently rely upon become deprecated in a scheduled update.

Problem management is similarly a joint delivery responsibility; problems may arise from a misconfiguration of the application by the consumer, as well as from issues with the application or service itself. Communication channels must be available for each side to notify the other of potential issues with the service.

Vulnerability management is firmly in the domain of the CSP in the SaaS environment, indeed there would be little point in consumers performing security testing as they would have no ability to fix any identified issues. Consumers should instead ensure that their CSPs have a thorough *vulnerability management* process in place including regular penetration testing by qualified organisations.

The *incident management* services are a joint delivery responsibility; both consumers and CSPs must be able to respond to a security incident and, in some cases, respond jointly. As in other areas where responsibility is joint (or where the CSP is primarily responsible) there must be a well-publicised communications facility available to, firstly, notify the other party of an incident and then to enable both parties to manage the incident through to closure. SaaS consumers should be aware of the potential difficulties of obtaining evidence that is admissible in court from SaaS CSPs. However, as many organisations often choose to manage such incidents in-house rather than involving law enforcement in order to manage potentially adverse publicity, this may not be a major stumbling block.

The *asset management* services are primarily the responsibility of the CSP as they are responsible for the physical assets and software licenses providing their service. The consumer remains responsible for managing the licenses that may be associated with their usage of the SaaS application.

Conclusion

The SaaS service model is likely the most widely adopted of the Cloud service models and is also the most diverse in terms of the services on offer. The SaaS CSPs are responsible for delivery of a secure application and there is little that a consumer can do to actively influence the security of the SaaS service. From an application perspective, consumers are often limited to controlling the data that they choose to upload to the CSP, configuring the access rights of their users and monitoring the usage of the SaaS application. Consumers must also consider the security of the mechanisms that they use to connect their users and their data to the SaaS application, particularly as such communications tend to involve the Internet as the bearer.

CHAPTER 12: SECURITY AND FUNCTION AS A SERVICE

In this chapter, I describe how the security services defined within the SRM, and depicted in Figure 7, may be delivered by consumers implementing a service using a FaaS Cloud.

FaaS is the latest evolution of the Cloud model and it takes abstraction to its ultimate form: the running of individual ephemeral functions. With FaaS, there is no monolithic application constantly running in the background, instead, functions are triggered and executed on demand. In many ways, FaaS is similar to PaaS: consumers must still code the individual functions that make up their service, but the ephemeral nature of functions drives a number of different considerations (explored in this chapter).

There are currently three main providers offering FaaS:

1. AWS Lambda (*https://aws.amazon.com/lambda/*)
2. Azure Functions (*https://azure.microsoft.com/en-gb/services/functions/*)
3. Google Cloud Functions (*https://cloud.google.com/functions/*)

Of the above, AWS Lambda remains by far the best known and most commonly deployed.

FaaS and the SRM

The rest of this chapter is dedicated to explaining how the services described within the SRM can be delivered when deploying services on an FaaS Cloud.

In order to provide some context for these discussions, it is worth considering a sample FaaS architecture such as that shown in Figure 45.

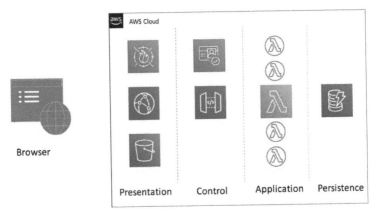

Figure 45: Example FaaS application architecture

Figure 45 shows an example of how a simple web application could be delivered using FaaS and other serverless technologies such as S3 and DynamoDB (a NoSQL database).[235]

I have split the AWS-hosted application into different zones; this is purely for the convenience of this discussion and is not driven by the network zoning that you may expect to see in a traditional n-tier architecture. All of these technologies are serverless, and consumers do not need to concern themselves with traditional network segregation issues; however, zones of trust remain relevant.

On the left of the diagram is the user's browser; it runs JavaScript that interacts with the various APIs exposed as

---

[235] *https://aws.amazon.com/dynamodb/*.

Lambda functions by the hosted application. The web application itself is presented to the Internet via the AWS CloudFront Content Delivery Network (CDN) service and protected by the AWS WAF service. Static website content is held within, and presented by, S3. The 'control' zone includes AWS Cognito, for the provision of user identities and access rights,[236] and the API Gateway, which controls access to the APIs offered by the various Lambda functions in the 'application' zone. These Lambda functions are triggered on demand by HTTPS invocations via the API Gateway – there is no continually running application per se.

However, Lambda functions are ephemeral and, consequently, there is a requirement for a mechanism[237] to store items like user state – DynamoDB acts as this mechanism in the 'persistence' zone of our example architecture. The Google Cloud Functions service has a similar requirement for state information to be stored externally. It should be noted that Azure has an option of using Durable Functions[238] which removes this restriction for users of that platform.

---

[236] *https://docs.aws.amazon.com/cognito/latest/developerguide/role-based-access-control.html*.

[237] AWS has provided a method of passing state through a series of Lambda Functions, using Step Functions to describe a state machine: *https://docs.aws.amazon.com/step-functions/latest/dg/tutorial-creating-lambda-state-machine.html*.

[238] *https://docs.microsoft.com/en-us/azure/azure-functions/durable/durable-functions-overview*.

I will frequently refer to this example application in this chapter, so it is worth familiarising yourself with it before we move on.

Secure development

The FaaS environment shares multiple qualities with the PaaS environment in relation to development: the consumer codes their own application and so has the freedom – and responsibility – to develop as they choose. However, the FaaS paradigm does impose some constraints in terms of maximum execution times and 'cold-start' speed, i.e. the time it takes to spin up the micro-VM[239] and run-time within which your function will run. Applications must be correctly coded to limit the number of cold starts, otherwise user experience will suffer due to poor response times.

It is worth noting that a serverless function will stay active (i.e. 'hot') as long as it is executing an application call and for a short period afterwards, in which it remains ready and available for another execution. However, after a period of inactivity, the Cloud container/run-time environment will timeout and your function will become inactive. The next function call will require another cold start. Users for whom performance is a key concern can 'warm up' their functions by calling them in advance of user needs and by continuing to call them on a regular basis to ensure that the functions stay active.

The situation is more complicated when working with multiple chained functions, such as AWS, because they can reuse a container for different functions; functions must, therefore, be called in the right order, e.g. CloudWatch Event

---

[239] *https://firecracker-microvm.github.io/* in the case of AWS Lambda.

'pings' could be used to maintain the right functions in the right state. There are tools available to help keep functions warm (e.g. *https://github.com/jeremydaly/lambda-warmer*), but pinging functions at the wrong time or in the wrong order can have an adverse performance impact. Testing is important, though these approaches do, of course, incur a degree of cost as FaaS charges per execution.

Significantly, FaaS consumers do not have access to the underlying host, so many traditional security tools cannot be used, e.g. host-based intrusion prevention systems (IPSs) and most runtime application self-protection (RASP) products.[240] RASP is in an interesting area as there are different deployment models available, and some *may* be suitable for use with FaaS whereas others will not; as ever, the nature of the application and supporting architecture will also impact upon the suitability of a specific RASP approach. An illustrative RASP architecture is shown in Figure 46.

---

[240] Custom run-times can provide FaaS consumers with more control, enabling support for some of these technologies, see *https://docs.aws.amazon.com/lambda/latest/dg/runtimes-custom.html*.

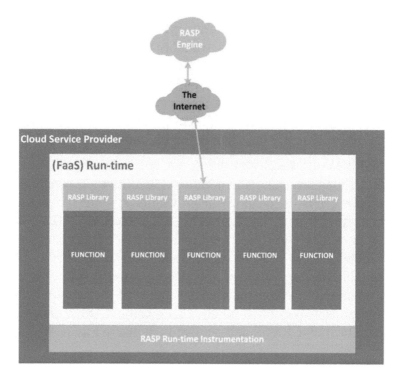

Figure 46: RASP architecture

At a high level, RASP products can be viewed as providing WAF capabilities within the protected application, as opposed to these being abstracted out to a separate WAF capability. RASP can protect against common vulnerabilities such as SQL injection, cookie tampering, cross-site scripting as well as more generic (i.e. not just web application) issues. Figure 46 illustrates how and where RASP tools can provide security capability. RASPs can either be included, within the function requiring protection, through the provided RASP libraries or by instrumenting the run-time (e.g. the Java Virtual Machine), with the latter option providing more general protection to all hosted functions. RASP products are often designed to call out to Cloud-hosted machine learning based decision engines, which require such functionality to complement the necessarily more basic controls provided locally.

Now, a type of RASP tooling – one that simply allows security controls to be compiled into the functions through the inclusion of the provided libraries – may well be suitable for use in FaaS environments to provide some simple security capabilities. For example, Puresec provide a free security library for AWS Lambda and Google Cloud Functions, called FunctionShield[241]; this offers some basic security capabilities, such as the ability to disable outbound Internet access and to execute child processes. More complex RASP solutions also include the ability to make decisions based on anomaly detection, but this will often require a call-out to a Cloud-hosted decision-engine and this comes with two disadvantages from an FaaS application perspective:

1. A performance hit due to the latency associated with traversing the Internet and awaiting a synchronous response; and

2. A need to open outbound Internet access for each protected function.

The other RASP deployment mechanism illustrated in Figure 46 relates to instrumentation of the run-time itself, e.g. the Java Virtual Machine. This mechanism is clearly not available where the Cloud service provider controls the run-time and the provider has no capability to add in the required instrumentation. However, this is a rapidly evolving area,

---

[241] *www.puresec.io/function-shield.*

with the RASP vendors evolving their products to provide better support for FaaS offers; for example, the Twistlock RASP Defender tool can be deployed as a Lambda Layer which allows it to be reused across functions.[242]

Developers building with FaaS need to be cognisant of the security controls that they can implement within their application via RASP-like functionality and those which they must abstract outside of their application, for example, through the use of API gateways and WAF capabilities.

Integrity

With a FaaS approach, you are buying into the integrity of the run-time and storage services offered by the Cloud provider. FaaS architectures will typically be adopting the microservices paradigm, i.e. adhering to the following design principles[243]:

- Autonomy
- Loose coupling
- Reuse
- Composability
- Fault tolerance
- Discoverability
- APIs alignment with business processes

---

[242] *www.twistlock.com/2018/11/29/introducing-lambda-layers/*.

[243] Taken from the NIST document: "Security Strategies for Microservices-based Application Systems", *https://nvlpubs.nist.gov/nistpubs/SpecialPublications/NIST.SP.800-204-draft.pdf*.

FaaS consumers need to concern themselves with the integrity of the overall application, the individual functions and any orchestration capabilities, e.g. API gateways or service mesh components. Individual functions should be subject to signed cryptographic hashing so that their integrity can be assured. The maintenance of service integrity will be explored further in the next section, on *availability*.

With respect to *content checking*, FaaS consumers should follow the approaches outlined earlier for PaaS services, i.e. they should consider using third-party content checking tools for files and WAFs for web traffic to preserve service integrity.

Availability

For organisations adopting FaaS, one major driver is the ability to handoff the responsibility for service availability – both infrastructure and run-times scale up automatically, albeit subject to the cold start concerns described earlier.

Using the microservices approach and its associated design principles – in particular those relating to reuse, autonomy and loose coupling – developers are able to update each microservice as they see fit as long as they do not make any breaking changes to the API (unless these are carefully managed). However, the overall application functionality can be affected by changes within the individual functions that comprise the service. This being the case, it is recommended that updates to individual functions are introduced via the canary approach, i.e. organisations should run both the old and new versions of the function in production by diverting a small percentage of traffic to the new API; in addition, performance should be tracked until sufficient confidence has been established to withdraw the older version of the function. In the FaaS model, the canary approach can be implemented via the API gateway or a service mesh (see the 'control' section of Figure 45).

Where response times are of critical importance, it may be possible to run functions closer to the user. The AWS Lambda@Edge[244] capability allows Lambda functions to be executed via Lambda infrastructures co-located with their CloudFront content distribution network; this significantly increases response times when the main Lambda service is hosted in a region geographically remote from the end user. In this model, the Lambda functions are triggered by specific CloudFront events.

Cryptography

The delivery of the services within the *cryptography* grouping is split between the provider (responsible for the *encryption* services offered by the underlying serverless platform) and the consumer (who will maintain joint responsibility for *key management* if they choose to implement using their own keys).

In general, FaaS consumers will rely upon the encryption services offered by the underlying platform, e.g. the encryption of access control tokens, network encryption via TLS and storage encryption via default encryption (e.g. S3 encryption or Azure Storage encryption) will all be performed by the platform. Application developers may need to be careful when passing information via HTTP headers if they choose not to enable encryption on the safe side of any API gateway. Developers may wish to encrypt such

---

[244] *https://aws.amazon.com/lambda/edge/*.

information so that it does not pass in the clear even if the HTTP traffic itself is unencrypted at the network level.

Access management

The *identity management* approach for applications delivered through FaaS is similar to that for PaaS applications: FaaS developers can make use of the identity services provided by the Cloud platforms, such as AWS Cognito or Azure AD, to control access to their applications. However, developers must be aware that they retain responsibility for the provision of appropriate access rights for the functions themselves, e.g. they must ensure that they grant appropriate access rights for the functions to call the platform services that they require – and only the platform services that they require. The principle of 'least privilege' is as applicable to FaaS as it is to any other IT delivery model: functions should only be able to access the data and services that they require.

Functions can be triggered in a variety of ways, e.g. AWS Lambda functions can be triggered synchronously, asynchronously or via scheduling.[245] The full list of triggers can be found here:

https://docs.aws.amazon.com/lambda/latest/dg/lambda-services.html.

AWS services that can send events directly to Lambda include:

- Amazon Kinesis
- Amazon DynamoDB

---

[245] *https://docs.aws.amazon.com/lambda/latest/dg/services-cloudwatchevents.html*.

- Amazon Simple Queue Service

AWS services that can trigger Lambdas synchronously include:

- Elastic Load Balancing (Application Load Balancer)
- Amazon Cognito
- Amazon Lex
- Amazon Alexa
- Amazon API Gateway
- Amazon CloudFront (Lambda@Edge)
- Amazon Kinesis Data Firehose

Whilst those AWS services that can trigger Lambdas asynchronously include:

- Amazon Simple Storage Service
- Amazon Simple Notification Service
- Amazon Simple Email Service
- AWS CloudFormation
- Amazon CloudWatch Logs
- Amazon CloudWatch Events
- AWS CodeCommit
- AWS Config

Each of these different scenarios for triggering a Lambda function requires a slightly different approach to granting access. For example, if developers are reading events from a stream or a queue, they must ensure that the Lambda function's execution role[246] can access the relevant source. Conversely, if the Lambda function is being triggered by another AWS service, such as S3, then it is the service that must be granted access to call the Lambda function via the relevant Lambda resource-based policy.[247] For example, should a developer wish to trigger an AWS Lambda function when an item is uploaded to an S3 bucket, then that Lambda function must be configured to allow S3 to invoke it.

In summary, if Lambda is actively monitoring a stream for a trigger event, it must have access to that stream; conversely, if Lambda is passively awaiting the notification to execute, the notifying service must be given the permission to trigger that execution.

Azure Functions take a slightly different approach and uses the concepts of both triggers and bindings. Each Azure function must have only one trigger, and this must be selected from the various options available. The available triggers include:

- Timer
- HTTP
- Blob
- Queue
- Azure Cosmos DB
- Event Hub

---

[246] *https://docs.aws.amazon.com/lambda/latest/dg/lambda-intro-execution-role.html.*

[247] *https://docs.aws.amazon.com/lambda/latest/dg/invocation-eventsourcemapping.html.*

Bindings are different to triggers: Azure functions can have multiple bindings, and these allow data to be exchanged with Azure services on either an inbound or an outbound basis (depending on their function). Functions can establish bindings with the services listed at:

https://docs.microsoft.com/en-us/azure/azure-functions/functions-triggers-bindings.

The mechanism that launches the execution of Google Cloud Functions relies upon events and triggers. Cloud Functions supports events from:

- HTTP
- Cloud Storage
- Cloud Pub/Sub
- Cloud Firestore
- Firebase (Realtime Database, Storage, Analytics, Auth)
- Stackdriver Logging

A trigger is the means to tell functions to execute in response to an event of interest. For example, the command below could be used to create an HTTP trigger which would execute the function 'helloworld' when the function's URL receives an HTTP request:

> gcloud functions deploy helloworld --runtime nodejs8 --trigger-http

The Google Functions identity model is quite blunt by default: all functions operate under the service account (*PROJECT_ID@appspot.gserviceaccount.com*). This approach makes it more straightforward for the function to obtain the security credentials it requires to operate (the service identity has 'Editor' permissions by default); however, it makes it harder to implement least privilege because it is a shared account. Fortunately, it is possible to choose non-default identities and, consequently, to have a different identity for each function. This approach is more secure but it does require more effort in terms of provisioning the right permissions per identity.

Cloud Functions identity is described more fully here:

https://cloud.google.com/functions/docs/securing/function-identity.

For the purposes of this book, we are focussing on the hosting of a web application (illustrated in Figure 45). In this case, the functions – whether Lambda, Azure Functions or Cloud Functions – would most likely be triggered by HTTP requests, so some traditional capabilities will be available to secure access, namely web application firewalls and API gateways. For example, in the case of AWS and Figure 45, you would potentially have AWS WAF in the 'presentation zone', alongside CloudFront, acting as the first line of defence. Should an HTTP request be deemed valid by AWS WAF, and be unfulfillable by CloudFront, then the request would be passed to the API Gateway which would then check whether the request is authorised, potentially by using the Cognito identity services. Both API Gateway and Cognito sit in the 'control' zone. Interestingly, API Gateway can also use custom authorisers (now known as Lambda authorisers) that call out to specific Lambda functions designed to provide authorisation decisions – so you may find yourself using Lambda functions to control access to other Lambda functions.

If the request is authorised, the API Gateway will call the Lambda functions with the relevant parameters and return the results post-execution. This example illustrates the power of the serverless model: basic web applications can be up and running in short order, with no need to procure hardware security devices or security services with all elements delivered natively on the Cloud platform.

Security governance

From a *security governance* perspective, there are few specifics to worry about when it comes to using FaaS platforms, with the notable exception of those areas relating to maintaining cohesiveness of the overall application, i.e. the *security architecture, coordination* and *ownership* services. FaaS applications should be stateless and decoupled: organisations should be able to update each function independently of the other elements of the application. This approach relies on organisations having an agreed and tightly managed set of APIs that front each individual function and that may be registered with a relevant API gateway.

Providing that the interface for interacting with each individual function remains unchanged, the code delivering the functionality can be updated or replaced as required. This allows each function to be owned by different project teams, with the responsibility for maintaining the overall API sitting with an adequately empowered architect/owner. The maintenance of tightly controlled APIs also reduces the amount of work needed to secure the application as it does not require regular updates to any API gateways or WAFs protecting the service.

Control of the API is vital: it is easy to introduce breaking changes by making API updates without informing the project teams that use that API. Amazon's overall philosophy regarding the management of APIs is that "two is better than none"; however, this is balanced by the view that "none is better than five."[248] Accordingly, there may be a 'Goldilocks zone' somewhere between one and five. The point is that teams should not feel pressured to immediately deprecate an old API upon the introduction of a new version, although regular clean-ups should be performed to prevent the sprawl of different APIs providing the same capability. FaaS is the ideal service model for using canary deployments in combination with workloads that are easily distributed via an API gateway.

Security operations

DevSecOps and FaaS go hand in hand: both the application and the relevant security controls should be articulated as code, enabling the application to be deployed as a whole with embedded security (e.g. WAF rule sets).

The ephemeral nature of functions makes the security monitoring of FaaS a potentially problematic capability to provide; enterprises do not get to implement host-based intrusion detection systems (HIDS) or similar. As an underlying principle, FaaS seeks to limit the number of dependencies that must be incorporated into the application at launch (due to the cold start problem described earlier); consequently, using security agents is rarely the right answer, particularly if they require registration with any central management station as a result of the short-lived nature of their functions. This leaves FaaS consumers with the following options for security monitoring:

---

[248]*www.theregister.co.uk/2019/05/14/amazons_away_teams/?page=3.*

- Concentrating on the instrumentation of the application itself, i.e. making certain that the functions emit the security events required to provide observability;

- Using a lightweight RASP-type capability, such as FunctionShield;

- Closely monitoring the security support services, e.g. the API gateways and WAFs; and

- Closely monitoring the other serverless services being accessed by the FaaS platform, e.g. storage services, pub-sub services, notification/messaging services, et cetera.

Ideally, all of these options should be considered and implemented so as to provide a cohesive and comprehensive approach towards security monitoring. Each of those elements can be configured to log to a central repository which can then be analysed and reported upon as per other service models.

As discussed in the *governance* section, change management is an important element of operating an FaaS-based application – whilst the underlying functions can be changed by the owning project teams, the APIs those functions provide must only be changed via a formal change management process so that relying services do not find themselves facing breaking changes. Handling the change management process correctly is critical: enterprises do not want to find themselves reintroducing waterfall-style governance gateways and inhibiting agility.

There are approaches better suited to the DevOps ways of working; these include coupling the multiple API approach with an adherence to a versioning scheme, such as Semantic

Versioning (SemVer),[249] and performing contract testing on each release. Clients should be able to hit a specific version of a published end point, such as v2, knowing that behind the scenes there are a number of minor releases, e.g. v2.x.x. In this scenario, v2.6.2, for example, is guaranteed to be backwards compatible with v2.5.4, with breaking changes only being introduced when the end point moves to v3. (The latest ~2.x.x behind the v2 end point would be kept available for a documented and agreed time.)

As with all utility services, *asset management* is key with respect to delivering cost control. Organisations using serverless technologies need to keep track of their use of any relevant technologies and make sure that they perform regular housekeeping duties, e.g. deleting old S3 buckets when they are no longer needed rather than paying for unnecessary storage.

Integration

Integration is key to the successful implementation of FaaS approaches. The use of triggers to launch the execution of functions, and the potential use of WAFs and API gateways to mediate access, were all discussed in the *access control* section of this chapter. Cloud workload protection platforms may become more relevant to functions as the technology matures, but these technologies are currently much more focussed on securing containerised microservices than FaaS offerings.

CASBs are not particularly applicable in the FaaS space; they may be used to control access to the management plane,

---

[249] *https://semver.org/*.

though this may add an extra level of complexity for little security gain.

Conclusion

The FaaS service model is probably the Cloud service model with the most potential for future growth. As the various offers mature (e.g. as cold start times decrease and security product vendors take a greater interest), FaaS may well become a threat to the current Kubernetes-dominated on-premises world of containerised microservices. In the meantime, functions are an excellent means for automating discrete pieces of functionality and for gluing together other serverless components (e.g. for acting on a security log event to update a firewall rule) as part of a move towards a true DevSecOps approach.

Part 3: Conclusion

INTRODUCTION

Part 3 presents a look ahead to the future of Cloud computing and the likely impacts of future changes on the security of Cloud consumer data and services. Finally, I conclude with a summary and some closing thoughts on the security of Cloud computing.

CHAPTER 13: LOOKING AHEAD

This book primarily concerns the current state of Cloud computing. I believe an appropriate way to finish is to engage in a look to the near future of Cloud computing and the attendant security implications. This chapter is purely my personal opinion on the likely evolution of Cloud computing, and you may well have different opinions.

Overview

There can be little doubt now that Cloud computing is here to stay: the agility and flexibility that Cloud offers cannot be matched by traditional delivery models; in addition, many global enterprises have materially reduced their in-house data centre footprints, so they could not bring workloads back on-premises even if they wanted to (at least not within reasonable time frames).

Over the next few years, the challenges for organisations will primarily be cultural and organisational: finding the right structures to take full advantage of the differing Cloud models. In some cases, this will entail organisations restarting their initial Cloud efforts as these may founder during attempts to transplant legacy processes and tooling into the Cloud.

One unfortunate factor that cannot be discounted is the current drift towards protectionism; this may impact upon the fortunes of the major Cloud providers and lead to a 'balkanisation' of the Cloud market, with national security agencies becoming increasingly wary of non-sovereign Cloud providers.

Enterprise perspective

In 2011, I stated my view that the emergence of Cloud computing would hasten the adoption of service-oriented architecture (SOA) among enterprises. I believe this prediction has stood the test of time, though the SOA terminology has fallen out of favour, and the term 'microservices' is more commonly used when discussing this approach. Both SOA and microservices architectures promote loosely coupled services that work together to deliver business capability. This is a perfect fit with the different models of using best-in-breed Cloud services to deliver a business capability (in a SaaS-First model), using containerised infrastructures to do the same, hosting upon IaaS Clouds or using serverless technologies in the FaaS world.

One area where enterprises are currently struggling with their adoption of Cloud is culture change, which relates to culture, governance and organisational structure. This issue will continue to impede Cloud adoption for the next decade or so: culture change is rarely a short-term job. Cultural issues are contributing to the increase in the number of organisations that are revisiting their initial Cloud efforts. Some organisations need to make adjustments because they initially viewed Cloud as 'just another data centre' and simply migrated architecture principles, tooling and processes into the Cloud – clearly, such an approach cannot support the more exciting opportunities offered by Cloud. Enterprises will spend the next few years becoming more comfortable with the shifting Cloud security paradigms around automation, security as code and embedded security. This culture change will likely have to be organic and driven by those who 'grow up' with the Cloud, and Cloud ways of working, gradually progressing through organisational hierarchies.

How can organisations accelerate their culture change? Given my career as a consultant, my answer may be biased; however, there is often value in bringing in external expertise to demonstrate the art of the possible and to provide the required transfer of knowledge. Many enterprises will establish 'centres of excellence' (COEs) to drive their Cloud endeavours, but it is common for these COEs to be largely staffed with consultants and independent contractors who then linger in post for an indeterminate period of time.

Whilst I believe that the external perspective is useful, I do not believe that Cloud-native organisations should be building long-term dependencies upon external advisors. Such advice and assistance should be extremely tightly scoped and, ideally, time bound, with specific requirements regarding knowledge transfer. One of the ideals of Cloud adoption should be for organisations to become self-sufficient from an IT delivery perspective, with that delivery being indistinguishable from the business projects it supports. Supported by Cloud, agile delivery could enable a true symbiosis of IT and the organisation as a whole.

However, some organisations – particularly if going down the SaaS-only route – may decide to completely outsource their IT to a Cloud broker. I am aware of one financial services organisation that is completely SaaS-based, with the exception of an IaaS-hosted Active Directory that serves as an identity provider. Such organisations may decide that IT is a utility and an overhead that could be outsourced. It should be noted that this is a prediction and not a recommendation: there will be something of a culture war between those who view IT as a non-core capability suitable for outsourcing and those who see business and IT as inseparable in a digital world.

Over the last few years, we have seen the Big 3 Cloud providers of Amazon, Microsoft and Google come to dominate the Cloud market. Whilst other players will continue to serve niche markets or seek to maintain their revenues by cannibalising on-premises revenues through offering Cloud-based replacements, it is unlikely that the dominance of the Big 3 will be challenged. However, there is one caveat: the Chinese market should not be ignored. Alibaba[250] and Tencent[251] both offer IaaS Cloud services and have the range of services and scale of backing to emerge as genuine global contenders. Whilst Western organisations may be reluctant to adopt Chinese technologies due to security concerns and/or poorly disguised protectionism, these concerns may not be as relevant to enterprises elsewhere across the globe. The West would be wise not to focus solely on its own backyard: should the rest of the world find itself operating on Chinese technology, much of the soft power of the West will dissipate. I firmly expect Alibaba, Tencent and other Chinese providers to become increasingly prominent, and one day they may even challenge the dominance of the Big 3.

Regarding the enterprise architecture perspective, it is important to note that we are still seeing enterprises roll out their own Kubernetes and OpenShift containerised microservices architectures, sometimes hosted on hybrid Clouds. These architectures are often complex and difficult to secure. Those organisations that have yet to invest in

---

[250] *https://eu.alibabacloud.com/*.

[251] *https://intl.cloud.tencent.com/product*.

building their own similar architectures must decide on the most appropriate route forward. Would such organisations be better off moving towards FaaS and serverless technologies rather than building their own functional equivalent? In many ways, this discussion mirrors the discussions we had back in 2008, 2009 and 2010 about the relative benefits of control versus utility with respect to on-premises hosting versus hosting on the public Cloud.

In the future, I would not be surprised to see the result of the FaaS versus containerised microservices discussion resulting in an outcome and a move to a Cloud-based FaaS that resembles the changes we have seen among more traditional workloads since 2010. However, I recognise that before this vision can be realised, Faas has some technical shortcomings that must be addressed and that hybrid approaches may also emerge and prove popular, as they did with Cloud.[252]

From an end user organisation perspective, the Cloud, in its widest sense, will continue to have a major impact on working practices. More and more ICT users will spend most of their working hours on the Internet, accessing support services and business applications that are hosted within the Cloud. There will be increasing adoption of 'bring your own device' (BYOD), whereby organisations provide their staff with an allowance to purchase their own preferred IT equipment rather than managing a central pool of standardised equipment.

Cloud is a great leveller in terms of its ubiquitous support for a multitude of different client access devices such as laptops, mobile phones and tablets. Remember, all that is needed to

---

[252] See *https://knative.dev/* for example, a Kubernetes-based platform for the delivery of serverless workloads.

access a large number of Cloud services is a browser, an Internet connection and an appropriate set of access credentials. The security implications here are interesting:

- You cannot trust the network bearer (the Internet), so all sensitive traffic should be encrypted.
- You cannot trust the end point without the addition of suitable agents providing secure enclaves.
- You cannot necessarily trust the end point or the network so you must ensure that your user authentication mechanisms are suitably robust.

An increasing number of organisations will adopt data-centric access controls and federated identity management to promote collaboration with their partners. This brings us towards the idea of zero trust networking discussed in chapter 9. The idea of de-perimeterisation – moving away from a hard network perimeter protecting a relatively unprotected centre – had been around for decades, following on from work by the Jericho Forum.[253] However, Google's BeyondCorp papers updated the principles of de-perimeterisation; they focussed more on the pragmatic delivery of identity-based perimeters and identity-aware proxies and on bringing those principles into operation.

This focus created the concept of zero trust networking. It is important to recognise that zero trust networking does not just replace one hard perimeter layer (network) with another (identity). A move to zero trust networking must be accompanied by defence in depth, e.g. security monitoring, the principle of least privilege, privileged access control,

---

[253] *https://publications.opengroup.org/w124.*

secure coding, patching, et cetera. Done well, zero trust is a suitable model for a workforce that is increasingly Internet-native and which does not see the need to have to VPN into a network to be able to access the services it hosts. I envisage zero trust picking up momentum over the next few years as organisations become more comfortable with the level of security it provides, as well as the associated terminology and capabilities. This will have implications for the consumption of Cloud services: those organisations that have implemented on-premises control points – and, consequently, force their users to connect into their corporate networks prior to accessing Cloud services – will have to revisit their security approaches to account for direct device to Cloud access via the Internet.

The need for security in the Cloud will increase because the Cloud will be a growing market. Tools like those of Zscaler[254] look well-positioned in this market, alongside some of the CASB products described earlier in this book.

In this zero trust scenario, does it not make more sense for federated identities and shared data to reside within the Cloud rather than locked away behind leaky firewalls? In the future, will individuals really want to constantly have to switch identities in order to work? Perhaps there may even be an increased use of OpenID Connect-style authentication for business purposes where there is a low level of risk and where organisations choose to trust social media logins. This leads on to a gradual merging of social and business identities whereby individuals can log on to low-risk business services using their Facebook or Gmail or Windows Live (or other) identities.

---

[254] *www.zscaler.com/products/zscaler-internet-access.*

Individuals may decide to formalise their holding of multiple identities – we all have multiple identities at the moment whether we choose to recognise it or not. We have our work identities (usernames, payroll numbers, etc.), we have our financial identities (bank account details, credit card numbers) and we have our social identities (Facebook IDs, email addresses, etc.). Would it not be good to be able to use these identities as we see fit rather than having to provide the same information to a multitude of organisations? Often it is a user's entitlement to access data or service that is of importance to a business rather than their actual identity; users could choose to use different identity and attribute providers to hold different personal details. They could then use OpenID Connect and OAuth2 to only provide the personal information they are comfortable with sharing with the relevant party, be that their employer, their bank or their government.

Whilst this may seem a little far-fetched, I should note that the UK government are currently attempting to create a market in identity providers under their HMG Verify programme.[255] It is fair to say that Verify has had a troubled existence so far, with uptake far below that predicted within the initial business case. The government is spinning Verify out to the private sector where it faces something of an uncertain future. However, I believe there is a need for trusted identity and if HMG and Verify cannot deliver it then the market will: there are already other functional identity

---

[255] *www.gov.uk/government/publications/introducing-govuk-verify/introducing-govuk-verify.*

verification and validation providers out there, such as Yoti.[256]

If such a market can be successfully established, then the idea of individuals using different identities for different purposes, in a more formal and educated manner than is currently the case, becomes less far-fetched. From a security perspective, there are issues with this approach. The following questions should be considered:

- Which identity providers do you trust?
- How do you verify that the identity providers operate as they claim?
- How do you know how strongly verified a user identity was at the point of registration?
- If you are only using attributes rather than identities, how do you track transactions? Do you need to track all transactions?

So far, I have outlined a fairly rosy view of the future, one in which empowered users get to work in a flexible, collaborative environment empowered by the Cloud. A future in which businesses benefit through lower costs of operation, easier collaboration with their partners, more intimacy with their clients and more resource to allocate to improving their business rather than looking after their IT. However, I do not expect everything to be so straightforward. Let's look forward from a security perspective.

---

[256] www.yoti.com/.

Cyber security perspective

I expect at least one major Cloud provider will see their management systems hacked within the next five years (perhaps sooner, if the current trade war between the US and China intensifies), with unauthorised access granted to customers' data, and I anticipate that this event will be publicly exposed. This will again raise the question of the security of the Cloud model.

Why so negative a prediction? Primarily due to the well-known modus operandi and targets of some established advanced persistent threat (APT) actor groups. APT10, also known as Stone Panda and believed to be of Chinese origin, compromised a series of managed security service providers (MSSPs) from 2017,[257] with its primary aim being the onward compromise of their customers. This incident is also known as Cloud Hopper. Considering the motivation to attack MSSPs for onward compromise, it is highly likely that the major Cloud providers would also be high priority targets for such threat actors.

Similarly, it is not hard to envisage the major Chinese Cloud providers facing similar threats from Western groups. I would suggest that a compromise is inevitable at some point in the future. Cloud commentators will again forget quite how many on-premises IT systems are currently hacked on a daily basis.[258] My advice is to expect such a hack to take place and to design your services and business processes to be able to cope with such an event when it does, primarily

---

[257] www.ncsc.gov.uk/news/apt10-continuing-target-uk-organisations.

[258] See the Verizon Data Breach Investigations Report (DBIR) for an example: https://enterprise.verizon.com/en-gb/resources/reports/dbir/.

through strong integrity controls that ensure that any compromise of your data or Cloud-hosted applications can be identified.

The Cloud also promises to fundamentally alter the way that we approach security: it is not just about the move from the old models of perimeterisation towards zero trust, from waterfall towards agile or from the rigid segregation of duties towards DevSecOps; it is much more about mindset and the real fundamental of cyber security: trust. At its heart, cyber security is all about trust: trust in your service providers; trust in your application vendors; trust in your hardware providers; and trust in your staff. In every solution, there is always a basis or 'root' of trust, and, primarily out of practicality, most people do not seek more assurance than this provides.

How many organisations will really choose to strip down the hardware they receive in order to look for implants? Most will simply choose to trust their providers and associated logistics providers. Yes, we talk about 'trust, but verify' but we cannot get away from trust at the root. (There is an interesting side discussion here about threat models which would probably sit better in a different book.) Currently, we are at a point where the Cloud providers are building trust. Major organisations and governments trust their Cloud providers to host their services and data. They may not yet trust the CSPs to secure that data, so you will still see a lot of third-party tooling in use – indeed, this book has pointed you towards many examples of such third-party tooling.

I envisage this will change as we move forwards. We can already see the Cloud service providers moving into the security space, offering identity services, encryption services and monitoring services, amongst other capabilities. The

Azure Sentinel SIEM represents a step change in this approach by offering a genuinely competitive solution that can stand on its own merits. Whilst many of the native Cloud security tooling is selected due to cost and convenience, sentinel may be the first to challenge traditional security vendors on capabilities as well. Security vendors will need to be very clever in their marketing and research in order to prevent being swallowed by Cloud service providers offering similar functionality at a more competitive cost (in order to tie customers to their platform).

What should security vendors be doing? Perhaps playing on the trust point will work for a few years yet, but I am not convinced that it is a play that will work forever. Once the Cloud service providers are also trusted to adequately secure data with native tooling, the drivers for the use of additional third-party tooling diminish. Regulation and compliance drivers may be the only things that save the wider security industry in the long run. Perhaps I am being too harsh on the innovation and capabilities provided by security product vendors and too optimistic about the capabilities of Cloud native tooling. We shall see.

I have called out the difficulty of business continuity in the Cloud in a number of places in this book. The Cloud providers offer highly available services from disparate data centres across different geographies. As consumers become more comfortable with the Cloud, the traditional approach of having data and backup services in other environments becomes less appealing. Attempting to have an Azure-hosted backup of an application usually hosted in AWS ready to pick up the load in the event of an outage is a nontrivial exercise.

However, hosting a business on a single provider does not come without risk, particularly if that provider decides, rightly or wrongly, that you are misusing or otherwise endangering their wider service and closes you down.[259] Cascade failures are also a reality and, although unlikely, the potential for a Cloud provider to suffer a major and prolonged outage is not beyond the realms of possibility.

The issue of business continuity is even more pronounced with SaaS (as noted in chapter 11) – of course, Cloud consumers can maintain a copy of their data in another location, but said data will do them little good without an application to process it. This is a problem that will persist in the future, so other solutions will be required. In this instance, I can see a strong growth in the use of cyber insurance services as a more cost-effective mechanism for managing risk than attempting to build duplicate services to provide true business continuity.

My other major concern with the Cloud model relates to data privacy and wider regulatory issues. The major Cloud providers all offer AI and ML capabilities, alongside offers to support the IoT and associated connected devices. The EU GDPR is now in force and it is more aligned to the digital age than the previous iteration of EU privacy law. However, I still have concerns about the appropriateness of the GDPR when it comes to inferred data, AI and the ability of the major Cloud providers to profile our personalities and daily lives. We have all seen the influence of targeted content and 'bot' interactions on social media. The only issue of dispute is the effectiveness of such interactions, with the potency of its

---

259

www.theregister.co.uk/2019/05/31/digitalocean_killed_my_company/.

influence most commonly being dismissed by those who benefit from it and their supporters. The Cloud will only make these capabilities available to a wider range of threat actors, providing them with an increasing number of channels through which they can both obtain data (to refine their targeting) and disseminate their messages.

We have a problematic situation in which 'bad' actors' usage of technology is evolving much more quickly than the regulators can act to counter such behaviour. It is key for governments across the globe to educate the general public on the dangers of misinformation or, if they choose not to, for privacy professionals to step up and do so.

Privacy issues also have wider geopolitical ramifications and they could be yet another weapon to be deployed in trade disputes. A Cloud service that is acceptable in one jurisdiction may be illegal in another. Furthermore, Cloud services in one jurisdiction may not be able to legally target users in another. There are also concerns regarding the use of Cloud services hosted within repressive regimes, or regimes that are viewed with suspicion by other national governments. Unless mechanisms can be agreed to standardise upon regulatory requirements, the Cloud model could well fracture rather than be global in nature. This will have negative consequences for the scale, and so volume-driven prices, that CSPs will be able to offer. In addition, as the broker model of delivering capabilities matures, organisations will have to take even more careful account of their supply chain to ensure that they are content with the base location (and ultimate ownership) of all of their suppliers.

I do not want to end this chapter on a negative note. Despite the preceding arguments, I still believe that the Cloud model offers unprecedented opportunities for enterprises, e.g. to refocus on their core business activities rather than on their IT operations. Business stakeholders are no longer beholden to IT departments to provide them with IT services. The move to Cloud will be accompanied by a growing acceptance by security professionals of the need to accept risk in order to increase benefit and to retain their own relevance (and employment). The role of the security professional will morph over the next few years into that of someone able to:

- Accurately describe risk in business terms;
- Put forward pragmatic solutions to manage identified risks;
- Recognise that it is no longer acceptable to just say no to risks that they don't understand; and
- Actively help to embed, automate and delegate security throughout their organisations.

My predictions may be wrong, and the Cloud may burst like other bubbles before it. However, I believe that the current economic uncertainties will sustain the Cloud model for the foreseeable future. There will be little cash available within government or enterprises for major capital expenditure in IT infrastructure for a number of years yet. Businesses will not stand still during this time and so must adopt new ways of working. The future for Cloud computing, at least, looks bright.

CHAPTER 14: CONCLUSION AND SUMMARY

The purpose of this book has been to act as a guide to the possibilities open to those looking to adopt Cloud computing in a risk-managed manner. In order to do so, I have adopted a fairly standard format; an introduction to the problem space, a review of past work, a suggested approach and then examples of how that approach can be implemented.

I have not tried to be exhaustive, overly comprehensive or dictatorial in tone. My aim has been to suggest an approach and a set of controls for your consideration: only you, your business stakeholders and security subject matter experts can decide which controls are appropriate for your particular application or service (with help from your regulators where applicable). I view this book as being something akin to a travel guide: I have suggested areas that may be of interest, but it is up to you define your own itinerary based upon your own needs. Alternatively, but still on a geographical theme, you could also view this book as a map, but certainly not as a set of directions.

In summary, if we strip out the technical content, we can condense this book's advice into the following ten principles of guidance:

1. Establish your governance and ownership (e.g. strategy, risk and assurance) structures as soon as you possibly can.

2. Define a manageable set of core Cloud principles and then stick to those principles as rigidly as you can. Revisit these principles regularly and review them for currency.

3. Define your set of core 'shared services' (e.g. identity, monitoring, encryption, etc.) and use these as key building blocks.

4. Decide upon the guardrails that you want to implement to protect your developers and operations staff (and, consequently, the organisation itself) from mishaps, whilst empowering your staff to work within those guardrails. Remember, guardrails do not necessarily need to be technical.

5. Use security architecture approaches to help define both the core building blocks and the individual project components.

6. Remember, security architecture approaches work in agile environments as well as in traditional waterfall models – they can be iterative and work on different scales (enterprise, business unit, service, application, etc.).

7. Define your security requirements in relation to the risks you face – threat modelling, attack surface identification and risk assessment remain key aspects of cyber security in the Cloud world.

8. Embed security into your development lifecycle and operations via the adoption of DevSecOps approaches where appropriate.

9. Build governance processes to maintain enterprise and project architectures during their lifecycles; make use of change management processes, continuing requirements analysis, regular security assessments, et cetera.

10. Bring your people with you on the Cloud journey. Cultural change is a hard but necessary aspect of adapting to the digital world.

Does the above approach guarantee a 100% secure Cloud application? Of course not, as there is no such thing as 100% secure (which is itself a fairly meaningless term). However, what this approach does provide is a mutual understanding between all parties within the consumer of the level of risk associated with a Cloud deployment, and the expected approach towards secure usage of the relevant Cloud services. The appropriate stakeholders (either centralised, embedded or a hybrid thereof) can then decide if that level of risk is acceptable when balanced against a perceived business benefit. Always remember that it is the role of the business to decide upon whether a risk is acceptable; it is the role of the security professional to ensure that the business take such decisions from an informed position.

I hope that my view on the security of Cloud computing has become apparent over the course of the last couple of hundred pages. However, I will conclude this book with a series of bullet points to highlight some key messages:

- Cloud computing is an evolution, not a revolution, in terms of the delivery of information systems.
- Cloud computing has the potential to be a revolution, not just an evolution, in terms of the business approach to, and use of, information systems.
- Cloud computing increases the attack surface of applications and services – multi-tenancy can occur at any level of the technology stack but, wherever it occurs, there is a boundary between your service and something

else that would not be present in a siloed on-premises implementation.

- Cloud computing can be secured to a level appropriate to the business requirements of most, but perhaps not quite all, organisations.

- The public Cloud is not the only Cloud. Community and private Clouds have their own valid use cases, particularly for those with strong compliance or assurance requirements.

- Security architecture methodologies should be used to link the business requirements, appetite for risk and compliance requirements to the delivery of security services.

- Traceability is important: you must be able to demonstrate why a security control is in place, the risks it mitigates and/or the business requirement(s) it delivers.

- The primary delivery responsibility for security services shifts from the consumer to the CSP as you move from IaaS to SaaS. This can be a good thing or a bad thing depending on your existing in-house security capabilities.

- PaaS and FaaS are often the most troublesome service models to secure due to the high number of services that must be delivered by both consumer and CSP; gaps are likely to appear between the two unless they are very carefully managed.

- Cloud services will get hacked, possibly even completely and utterly compromised. The same could be said of your on-premises equipment or your existing technology providers. Factor the risk of Cloud compromise into your decision-making process. Supply chain compromise is not a new issue, just a very difficult one to resolve.

- The business benefits that Cloud offers in terms of moving IT departments and security teams 'out of the way' of business delivery – including, increased agility, elasticity, mobility and collaboration – means that it is here to stay; security professionals must either adopt a pragmatic mindset or prepare for retirement.

- Shifting security left via approaches like DevSecOps offers us the opportunity to embed and automate security controls; placing each application within its own Cloud account offers true segmentation and enables blast radius reduction. In addition, the major Cloud providers get insight into industry-wide vulnerabilities and will often patch their infrastructures prior to wider industry notification. A move to the Cloud represents an opportunity to address many long-standing security concerns.

- 'Secure' means delivering services that do not exceed the risk appetite set by the business. It does not mean delivering 99.99% hacker-proof (but unusable) services.

Finally, we work in a business environment that has mostly accepted the need for informed risk management in preference to ignorant risk avoidance.

14: Conclusion and summary

I hope that this book helps to inform and, therefore, enable the pragmatic adoption and operation of Cloud services. Good luck with your continuing Cloud journeys!

APPENDIX A: SRM SECURITY SERVICE ASSIGNMENTS

Table A1: Service Assignments

Service Name	Level	IaaS Rationale	PaaS Rationale	FaaS Rationale	SaaS Rationale
Secure Development	0	Consumers are responsible for the security of any in-house developed applications that they host on an IaaS Cloud.	A PaaS will typically include a set of provided APIs for the consumer's use. The provider is responsible for the secure development of those APIs; the consumer is responsible for the security development of any applications that use those APIs.	A FaaS provider will offer a set of back-end services that a consumer can utilise as part of a serverless application. The consumer is responsible for securing their code, whilst the provider is responsible for the security of the back-end services.	The SaaS provider is responsible for the delivery of a secure application.
Coding Standards	1		The consumer must implement a set of coding standards to ensure that they use the CSP-provided	The consumer must implement a set of standards to ensure consistency across their serverless	

Service Name	Level	IaaS Rationale	PaaS Rationale	FaaS Rationale	SaaS Rationale
			APIs correctly. The provider must implement a set of coding standards to ensure that they code secure APIs for their consumers' use.	application architectures.	
Code Review	1				
Repository	1				
Automate	1	Infrastructure as code enables the automated provisioning of environments and testing by the consumer.	The consumer can automate their build and testing activities. The provider must do the same for the elements under their control.	The consumer can automate their build and testing activities. The provider must do the same for the elements under their control.	
Build	1	Infrastructure as code must be instantiated as a working infrastructure at some point.			
Secrets Management	1	The consumer is responsible for any operating	The consumer is responsible	The consumer is responsible for the	

Appendix A: SRM security service assignments

Service Name	Level	IaaS Rationale	PaaS Rationale	FaaS Rationale	SaaS Rationale
		level system credentials necessary to configure the environment.	for the management of any application secrets required by their code.	management of any application secrets required by their code.	
Mitigate	1				
Test	1			The consumer remains responsible for the testing of their own application code.	
Integrity	0	Consumers are responsible for building any integrity checking mechanisms into the services they host on an IaaS Cloud.	The provider is responsible for the integrity of the operating system and any provided APIs. The consumer is responsible for the integrity of the hosted application.		The provider is responsible for the integrity of the data that they host and the service(s) that they offer.
Non-Repudiation	1				
Content Check	1				Depending on the nature of the SaaS, consumers may be required to set up data

Appendix A: SRM security service assignments

Service Name	Level	IaaS Rationale	PaaS Rationale	FaaS Rationale	SaaS Rationale
					validation rules.
Snapshot	1				
Hosting	0	The provider is responsible for the physical hosting of their service.	The provider is responsible for the physical hosting of their service.		The provider is responsible for the physical hosting of their service.
Physical Security	1				
Environ-mental Security	1				
Storage	1				
Communi-cations	1				
Compliance	0	The risks and penalties associated with breaches of compliance cannot be outsourced. Whilst the compliance status of the provider can be helpful, the primary responsibility for compliance remains with the consumer.	The risks and penalties associated with breaches of compliance cannot be outsourced. Whilst the compliance status of the provider can be helpful, the primary responsi-bility for compliance remains	The risks and penalties associated with breaches of compliance cannot be outsourced. Whilst the compliance status of the provider can be helpful, the primary responsibility for compliance remains with the consumer.	The risks and penalties associated with breaches of compliance cannot be outsourced. Whilst the compliance status of the provider can be helpful, the primary responsibility for compliance remains with the consumer.

Appendix A: SRM security service assignments

Service Name	Level	IaaS Rationale	PaaS Rationale	FaaS Rationale	SaaS Rationale
			with the consumer.		
Audit	1				
Test	1				
Regime	1				
Identify	2				
Translate	2				
Availability	0	The responsibility for delivering availability requirements is shared between the consumer and the provider. The provider must provide a resilient service; the consumer must build a resilient application upon that service.	The responsibility for delivering availability requirements is shared between the consumer and the provider. The provider must provide a resilient service; the consumer must build a resilient application upon that service.	The responsibility for delivering availability requirements is shared between the consumer and the provider. The provider must provide a resilient service; the consumer must build a resilient application upon that service.	The responsibility for delivering availability requirements is shared between the consumer and the provider. The provider must provide a resilient service; the consumer must build appropriate business continuity processes to ensure that it can survive any outages at the provider.
Business Continuity (BC)	1	The consumer must ensure that its critical business processes can continue in the event of the application failing.	The consumer must ensure that its critical business processes can continue in	The consumer must ensure that its critical business processes can continue in the event of the	The consumer must ensure that its critical business processes can continue in the event of the

Appendix A: SRM security service assignments

Service Name	Level	IaaS Rationale	PaaS Rationale	FaaS Rationale	SaaS Rationale
			the event of the application failing.	application failing.	application failing.
BC Planning	2				
BC Implement	2				
BC Test	2				
Disaster Recovery (DR)	1	Disaster recovery is a joint responsibility. The provider is responsible for ensuring that any hardware or data centre failure can be recovered. The consumer is responsible for designing their service so that it can be recovered in similar circumstances.	Disaster recovery is a joint responsi-bility. The provider is responsible for ensuring that any hardware, data centre failure or shared service failure can be recovered. The consumer is responsible for designing their service so that it can be recovered in similar circum-stances.		Disaster recovery is a joint responsibility. The provider is responsible for ensuring that any hardware, data centre or application failure can be recovered. The consumer is responsible for ensuring that their service can be recovered in the event of a DR invocation.
DR Planning	2				

Appendix A: SRM security service assignments

Service Name	Level	IaaS Rationale	PaaS Rationale	FaaS Rationale	SaaS Rationale
DR Implement	2				
DR Test	2				
Resilience	1	Resilience is a joint delivery responsibility. The consumer must design their services so that they can failover effectively – either within different containers (e.g. AWS regions or Availability Zones) within a single IaaS or, alternatively, across different IaaS Clouds. The provider must ensure that hardware failures are transparent to their consumers.	The consumer must code their application so that it takes advantage of the failover capabilities of the Cloud platform. The provider must ensure that their services failover gracefully in the event of a system or application fault.	The consumer must code their application so that it takes advantage of the failover capabilities of the Cloud platform. The provider must ensure that their services failover gracefully in the event of a system or application fault.	The provider must ensure that their services failover gracefully in the event of a system or application fault. The consumer remains responsible for ensuring that their connectivity to their provider can failover gracefully in the event of a hardware or ISP failure.
Copy	2				The consumer should still ensure that their business data is replicated so as to enable business continuity in the event of a provider failure.

Service Name	Level	IaaS Rationale	PaaS Rationale	FaaS Rationale	SaaS Rationale
Reliability and Chaos	2	Consumers are responsible for enabling the scoped automated failure of infrastructure and application components.	Consumers are responsible for automating the failure of application components. The provider is responsible for automating the scoped failure of the underlying infrastructure.	Consumers are responsible for automating the failure of individual functions. The provider is responsible for automating the scoped failure of the underlying infrastructure and back-end services.	
Evergreen	2	Consumers are responsible for building parallel environments to enable evergreen approaches to configuration management.	Providers offer application deployment mechanisms that enable consumers to adopt evergreen approaches.	Providers offer application deployment mechanisms that enable consumers to adopt evergreen approaches.	Providers are fully responsible for the patching status of their environments.
Content Distribution	2				
DoS Prevention	2				
Cryptography	0	The consumer retains primary delivery responsibility for cryptography	The consumer is responsible for the appropriate use of the	The consumer is responsible for the appropriate use of the cryptography	The provider now has primary responsibility for the implement-

Service Name	Level	IaaS Rationale	PaaS Rationale	FaaS Rationale	SaaS Rationale
		services, e.g. data encryption and the encryption of traffic between end users and the hosted application.	cryptography services provided by the platform. The consumer can also develop their own cryptographic services to run on the platform. The provider is responsible for the delivery of the cryptographic services they offer.	services provided by the platform. The consumer can also develop their own cryptographic services to run on the platform. The provider is responsible for the delivery of the cryptographic services they offer.	ation of cryptographic services. The consumer retains responsibility for ensuring the security of the keys and certificates used to access the SaaS.
Encryption	1	The consumer is responsible for the design and implementation of encryption services from the operating system upwards. This includes the use of encrypted network protocols within their virtual environment. The provider is only responsible for the provision of the encrypted	The consumer is responsible for the appropriate use of the cryptography services provided by the platform. The consumer can also develop their own cryptographic services to	The consumer is responsible for the appropriate use of the cryptography services provided by the platform. The consumer can also develop their own cryptographic services to run on the platform. The provider is responsible for the	The provider is responsible for the design and implementation of encryption at network and data levels. Typically, the consumer can only decide whether to access the service using http or https.

Service Name	Level	IaaS Rationale	PaaS Rationale	FaaS Rationale	SaaS Rationale
		channel used to administer the service.	run on the platform. The provider is responsible for the delivery of the crypto-graphic services they offer.	delivery of the cryptographic services they offer.	
Key Management	1	Key management is primarily the responsibility of the consumer.	Key manage-ment can be a joint respon-sibility in a PaaS, e.g. where keys or certificates are imported into the authenti-cation and authori-sation services offered by the provider.	Key management can be a joint responsibility in an FaaS, e.g. where keys or certificates are imported into the authentication and authorisation services offered by the provider.	Key management remains a joint responsibility in a SaaS environment as the consumer retains responsibility for the secure management of the certificates used to access the service.
Access Management	0	The consumer is responsible for access management relating to the hosted application. (The provider secures access to the IaaS administration features.)	Many platforms provide access manage-ment services. The provider is responsible for the security of these	Many platforms provide access management services. The provider is responsible for the security of these access management services; the	The provider is responsible for the provision of access management services. The consumer is limited to use of the access management

Service Name	Level	IaaS Rationale	PaaS Rationale	FaaS Rationale	SaaS Rationale
			access management services; the consumer is responsible for the secure use of these services. Consumers can also develop their own access management services.	consumer is responsible for the secure use of these services.	services, e.g. deciding which roles should be assigned to their users.
Identity Management	1	The consumer is responsible for designing and implementing the identity management services used by their application.	The consumer may be responsible for the development of the identity management services used by their application. The consumer may use the shared identity management services provided by the PaaS. The provider is responsible	The consumer is responsible for the secure implementation of identity management, which may involve using the services offered by the platform provider. The provider is responsible for the security of the identity management services that they offer.	The provider has primary responsibility for the provision of identity management services. Typically, the consumer will only make use of the services made available by their provider.

Service Name	Level	IaaS Rationale	PaaS Rationale	FaaS Rationale	SaaS Rationale
			for the security of the identity manage-ment services that they offer.		
Registration	2		The consumer is responsible for ensuring that they have a suitable user registration process. This may involve using services provided by the PaaS.	The consumer is responsible for ensuring that they have a suitable user registration process. This may involve the usage of back-end identity services provided by the wider platform.	The consumer is responsible for ensuring that they have a suitable user registration process. Either users must be registered in the SaaS, or the SaaS must be configured to use federated identity management.
Provisioning	2	Application users will be provisioned using mechanisms that the consumer controls.	Depending on the application, users may be provisioned indepen-dently of the Cloud provider. Typically, application users will be configured using APIs provided by the Cloud provider.	FaaS developers will typically use identity services made available by the Cloud provider.	Application users are provisioned using the tools provided by the SaaS provider. (Provisioning is, essentially, a technical service, unlike registration.)

Appendix A: SRM security service assignments

Service Name	Level	IaaS Rationale	PaaS Rationale	FaaS Rationale	SaaS Rationale
Privilege Management	2				The consumer will still be responsible for the allocation of application administeration privileges.
Directory	2				The user directory is provided by the SaaS provider.
Validate	1	The consumer is responsible for the delivery of validation services, e.g. delivery of application authentication mechanisms.	The provider offers authentication and authorisation APIs that should be reused by the consumer. The provider is, therefore, primarily responsible for the delivery of these services.	The consumer will typically reuse authentication and authorisation services offered by the platform. The provider is, therefore, primarily responsible for the delivery of these services.	The shared application includes the validate services.
Authenticate	2	The consumer decides on and implements the authentication mechanisms used by their application.	The consumer will typically use the authentication services delivered	The consumer will typically use the authentication services delivered by the provider.	The consumer must use the authentication mechanisms supported by the shared application.

Service Name	Level	IaaS Rationale	PaaS Rationale	FaaS Rationale	SaaS Rationale
			by the provider.		
Authorise	2	The consumer decides on and implements the authorisation mechanisms used by their application.	The consumer will typically use the authorisation services delivered by the provider.	The consumer will typically use the authorisation services delivered by the provider.	The consumer must use the authorisation mechanisms supported by the shared application.
Federate	1	The consumer is responsible for any federation mechanisms, e.g. the establishment of trust frameworks.	The consumer has primary responsibility for any federation mechanisms, e.g. the establishment of trust frameworks.	The consumer has primary responsibility for any federation mechanisms, e.g. the establishment of trust frameworks.	The consumer has primary responsibility for any federation mechanisms, e.g. the establishment of trust frameworks. The provider's application must be able to support federation.
Policy (AM)	1	The consumer sets the access management policy for the hosted service.	The consumer sets the access management policy for the application. The provider sets the access management policy for the	The consumer sets the access management policy for the application. The provider sets the access management policy for the shared APIs.	The provider sets the overall access management policy for the service. The consumer may set the specific access management policy for their implementation.

438

Appendix A: SRM security service assignments

Service Name	Level	IaaS Rationale	PaaS Rationale	FaaS Rationale	SaaS Rationale
			shared APIs.		
Filter	1	Delivery of the filter service is a joint responsibility. The provider is responsible for the provision of filter capabilities relating to the underlying IaaS. The consumer is responsible for filter services protecting the hosted application.	Delivery of the filter service is a joint respons-ibility. The provider is responsible for the provision of filter capabilities relating to the underlying PaaS. The consumer is responsible for filter services protecting the hosted application.	The consumer is responsible for filter services protecting the hosted application, e.g. API security.	The provider is responsible for the filter services protecting the shared application.
Security Governance	0	The consumer must provide the security governance frameworks under which the hosted application is delivered and operated.	The consumer and provider must jointly provide the security governance frameworks under which the hosted application is delivered and operated.	The consumer and provider must jointly provide the security governance frameworks under which the hosted application is delivered and operated.	The consumer and provider must jointly provide the security governance frameworks under which the shared application is delivered and used.
Security Management	1	The consumer must design the technical	The consumer must design	The consumer must design the technical	The consumer must design the operating

Service Name	Level	IaaS Rationale	PaaS Rationale	FaaS Rationale	SaaS Rationale
		architecture and operating procedures for the hosted application; this includes the associated security management capabilities.	the technical architecture and operating procedures for the hosted application. The provider must do the same for the shared services.	architecture and operating procedures for the hosted application. The provider must do the same for the shared services.	procedures for their use of the hosted application. The provider must provide the security management of the hosted application.
Assurance	2				
Architecture and Design	3	The consumer is responsible for the architecture and design of their application and its hosting environment. The provider is only responsible for the design of the underlying hardware.	The provider is responsible for the architecture and design of the shared services. The consumer is responsible for the architecture and design of the hosted application itself.	The provider is typically responsible for the architecture and design of the run-time and back-end services. The consumer is responsible for the architecture and design of the serverless application itself.	The provider is responsible for the architecture and design of the service. The consumer may be responsible for small levels of customisation, e.g. 'skinning' the application with corporate colours and logos.
Procedures	3				Consumers remain responsible for the creation of the procedures governing

Appendix A: SRM security service assignments

Service Name	Level	IaaS Rationale	PaaS Rationale	FaaS Rationale	SaaS Rationale
					application usage.
Policy (SM)	2	The consumer is responsible for producing the security policies relating to the hosted application.	The provider is responsible for setting the security management policies for the usage of their shared services. The consumer is responsible for the security management policies regarding how those shared services are to be used and how the application itself must be used.	The provider is responsible for setting the security management policies for the usage of their back-end services. The consumer is responsible for the security management policies regarding how those back-end services are to be used and how the application itself must be used.	The provider is responsible for the application's top level security management policy. The consumer can only set policies governing their usage of the application.
Policy Research	3				
Policy Design	3				
Disseminate	2	Dissemination of security policy regarding the application is primarily the responsibility of the consumer.	Dissemination of security policy is a joint responsibility; both the consumer	Dissemination of security policy is a joint responsibility; both the consumer and provider must	Dissemination is a joint responsibility; both the consumer and provider must disseminate the security

Service Name	Level	IaaS Rationale	PaaS Rationale	FaaS Rationale	SaaS Rationale
			and provider must disseminate the security policy to their respective users.	disseminate the security policy to their respective users.	policy to their respective users.
Enforce	2				
Risk Management	1	The consumer remains responsible for ensuring that risks to the application are identified and appropriately managed.	The consumer must ensure that risks to their own application are identified and managed. The provider must ensure that risks to their shared APIs are identified and managed.	The consumer must ensure that risks to their own application are identified and managed. The provider must ensure that risks to the serverless APIs are identified and managed.	The provider is responsible for ensuring that risks to the application are identified and appropriately managed. The consumer may wish to assure themselves that the provider is managing risk appropriately.
Threat Model	2				The consumer is responsible for modelling threats to their data and service. The provider is responsible for modelling threats to the application itself.
Classify	2				

Service Name	Level	IaaS Rationale	PaaS Rationale	FaaS Rationale	SaaS Rationale
Inform	2				
Assess	2				
Treat	2				
Accredit	2				
Personnel Security	1	Personnel security is a joint responsibility: the consumer is responsible for the vetting, discipline and training of their end users and administrative staff; the provider is responsible for their own staff.	Personnel security is a joint respon-sibility: the consumer is responsible for the vetting, discipline and training of their end users and admini-strative staff; the provider is responsible for their own staff.	Personnel security is a joint responsibility: the consumer is responsible for the vetting, discipline and training of their end users and administrative staff; the provider is responsible for their own staff.	Personnel security is a joint responsibility: the consumer is responsible for the vetting, discipline and training of their end users and administrative staff; the provider is responsible for their own staff.
Vetting	2				
Discipline	2				
Training	2				
Coordinate	1	It is the consumer's responsibility to coordinate all aspects of the security of their service.	It is the consumer's respon-sibility to coordinate all aspects of the security of their service.	It is the consumer's responsibility to coordinate all aspects of the security of their service.	It is the consumer's responsibility to coordinate all aspects of the security of their service.

Appendix A: SRM security service assignments

Service Name	Level	IaaS Rationale	PaaS Rationale	FaaS Rationale	SaaS Rationale
Privacy	1	The consumer remains primarily accountable for managing their privacy requirements.	The consumer remains primarily accountable for managing their privacy require-ments.	The consumer remains primarily accountable for managing their privacy requirements.	The consumer remains primarily accountable for managing their privacy requirements.
Impact Assess	2				
Consent Management	2				
Data Sanitisation	2				The consumer may use tokenisation, encryption or anonymi-sation to prevent data entering the platform. Once it is within the provider platform, the provider is responsible for data sanitisation.
Security Operations	0	Security operations primarily remain the consumer's responsibility but the provider must play its part.	The provider is responsible for security operations up to and including the operating	The provider is responsible for security operations up to and including the run-time. The consumer is responsible for security	The provider is responsible for security operations up to and including the application. The consumer may choose to implement

Appendix A: SRM security service assignments

Service Name	Level	IaaS Rationale	PaaS Rationale	FaaS Rationale	SaaS Rationale
			system layer. The consumer is responsible for security operations at the application level (with the exception of the shared APIs).	operations at the application level (with the exception of the shared APIs).	some security operations services on-premise.
Monitoring	1	The consumer is responsible for the security monitoring of the hosted application. The provider is responsible for the monitoring of the underlying IaaS. For example, the provider must be able to recognise distributed denial of service attacks against its service.	The consumer is responsible for the security monitoring of the hosted application. The provider is responsible for the monitoring of the underlying hardware and also of the shared services (e.g. authentication and authorisation).	The consumer is responsible for maintaining the observability of the serverless application. The provider is responsible for the monitoring of the underlying hardware and also of the shared services (e.g. authentication and authorisation).	The consumer is responsible for monitoring the application's use by their end users. The provider is responsible for monitoring the security of the application and the supporting platform.
Log	2	The consumer must decide which (virtual) network, operating	The consumer must decide which events their	The consumer must decide which events their	The provider is responsible for deciding which events the

Service Name	Level	IaaS Rationale	PaaS Rationale	FaaS Rationale	SaaS Rationale
		system and application level events they wish to capture.	application must log.	application must log.	application can log. The consumer may have some flexibility regarding which of these events they log.
Analyse	2	The consumer must put in place the capability to analyse security logs.	The analysis tasks are split between the consumer and the provider. Both parties must implement analysis capabilities.	The analysis tasks are split between the consumer and the provider. Both parties must implement analysis capabilities.	The analysis tasks are split between the consumer and the provider. Both parties must implement analysis capabilities.
Event Management	2	The consumer has the access to manage most events, with the exceptions of hardware and physical network issues.	The consumer has the access to manage application level events.	Events are used to trigger functions. Event management has different connotations in the FaaS environment. Event triggers are often provided by the platform.	Events affecting the application as a whole or the underlying platform must be managed by the provider. Traditional misuse of authorised access by end users must still involve the consumer.
Report	2	The consumer has access to most of the	The consumer can	The consumer can instrument	The consumer must work with the

Service Name	Level	IaaS Rationale	PaaS Rationale	FaaS Rationale	SaaS Rationale
		information required to report on security events.	instrument their application to deliver most of the information required to report on security events.	their application to deliver most of the information required to report on security events.	services offered by the provider to gather the necessary information to produce the report.
Threat Hunting	2				
Administration	1	The consumer is responsible for the administration of all aspects of the hosted application from the operating system upwards.	The provider is responsible for the administration of everything except the application itself.	The provider is responsible for the administration of everything except the application itself.	The provider is responsible for all system administration.
Secure Channel	2	The consumer must choose appropriate management channels for their virtualised environment.	The provider must ensure that appropriate out-of-band management channels are used.	The provider must ensure that appropriate out-of-band management channels are used.	The provider must ensure that appropriate out-of-band management channels are used.
Decommission	2	Decommissioning is a joint responsibility: the consumer must decommission its hosted services, whilst the provider	Decommissioning is primarily the responsibility of the provider: both virtual images and physical	Decommissioning is primarily the responsibility of the provider: both virtual images and physical hardware are within their	Decommissioning is the responsibility of the provider.

Appendix A: SRM security service assignments

Service Name	Level	IaaS Rationale	PaaS Rationale	FaaS Rationale	SaaS Rationale
		must ensure that released resources do not expose consumer data to other IaaS users.	hardware are within their scope of provision.	scope of provision.	
Manage	2	The consumer is responsible for the management of their virtual environment from the network upwards.	The provider is responsible for server management and the management of any shared services. The consumer is responsible for application management.	The provider is responsible for server management and the management of any shared services. The consumer is responsible for application management.	The provider is responsible for all management of the service (with the exception of any user-configurable elements such as 'skinning').
Dispose	2	The provider is responsible for the secure disposal of decomm-issioned hardware.	The provider is responsible for the secure disposal of decomm-issioned hardware.	The provider is responsible for the secure disposal of decomm-issioned hardware.	The provider is responsible for the secure disposal of decomm-issioned hardware.
Deploy	2		The consumer is responsible for the code to be deployed and has a degree of control over how	The consumer is responsible for the code to be deployed; the provider is responsible for actual deployment.	

Appendix A: SRM security service assignments

Service Name	Level	IaaS Rationale	PaaS Rationale	FaaS Rationale	SaaS Rationale
			the code is deployed.		
Orchestrate	2				
Change Management	1	The consumer retains primary responsibility for managing change to the hosted application and the supporting operating system.	The consumer retains responsibility for managing change to the application but must consider the effects on any shared services. The provider is responsible for managing change to the underlying platform.	The consumer retains responsibility for managing change to the application but must consider the effects on any back-end services it relies upon. The provider is responsible for managing change to the underlying platform.	The provider is responsible for technical change management to the application. The consumer is responsible for changes to the user-configurable elements of the service (e.g. data types, access rights, 'skinning') and associated business processes.
Problem Management	1	Problem management is a joint responsibility: problems with the underlying IaaS must be communicated and managed jointly.	Problem management is a joint responsibility: problems with the underlying PaaS must be communicated and managed jointly.	Problem management is a joint responsibility: problems with the underlying FaaS must be communicated and managed jointly.	Problem management is a joint responsibility: problems with the application must be communicated and managed in a coordinated manner.

Service Name	Level	IaaS Rationale	PaaS Rationale	FaaS Rationale	SaaS Rationale
Vulnerability Management	1	The provider must identify and manage vulnerabilities within their IaaS. Consumers must identify and manage vulnerabilities to their hosted services (operating system and application).	The provider must identify and manage vulnerabilities within their PaaS. Consumers must identify and manage vulnerabilities to their hosted application.	The provider must identify and manage vulnerabilities within their FaaS. Consumers must identify and manage vulnerabilities to their hosted application.	The provider must identify and manage vulnerabilities within their application and supporting infrastructure.
Threat Intelligence	1				
Incident Management	1	The consumer retains primary responsibility for incident management since the main source of incidents will usually be users, the application or the underlying operating system.	Incidents may occur within the shared services or within the consumer-specific application, or in some combination of the two. Consumers retain responsibility for user-initiated incidents.	Incidents may occur within the shared services or within the consumer-specific application, or in some combination of the two. Consumers retain responsibility for user-initiated incidents.	The provider is responsible for managing incidents affecting their service. The consumer must still manage incidents affecting their users, data and business processes.
Respond	2				
Investigate	2				

Appendix A: SRM security service assignments

Service Name	Level	IaaS Rationale	PaaS Rationale	FaaS Rationale	SaaS Rationale
Action	2				
Close	2				
Exercise	2				
Asset Management	1	The consumer is responsible for ensuring that they understand the assets they are operating in the Cloud, including whether or not they hold the appropriate licenses.	The consumer is responsible for ensuring that they understand the applications they are operating in the Cloud. The provider is responsible for ensuring that they understand their service portfolio and the underlying assets.	The consumer is responsible for ensuring that they understand the applications they are operating in the Cloud. The provider is responsible for ensuring that they understand their service portfolio and the underlying assets.	The provider is primarily responsible for managing the assets that provide the service.
Catalogue	2				
Configuration Management	2	The consumer has primary responsibility for the configuration management of their virtual environment. The provider must provide suitable	The consumer has configuration management responsibility for their	The consumer has configuration management responsibility for their deployed application. The provider has configuration	The provider is responsible for the configuration management of the application and its supporting physical hardware.

Service Name	Level	IaaS Rationale	PaaS Rationale	FaaS Rationale	SaaS Rationale
		configuration management of the underlying physical hardware.	deployed application. The provider has configuration management responsibility for the underlying platform and its supporting physical hardware.	management responsibility for the underlying platform and its supporting physical hardware.	The consumer may retain responsibility for any user-configurable aspects.
License	2				
Rights Management	2				
Data Loss Prevention	2				
Integration	0	The consumer is responsible for the integration of their Cloud services.	The consumer is responsible for the integration of their Cloud services.	The consumer is responsible for the integration of their Cloud services.	The consumer is responsible for the integration of their Cloud services.
CASB	1	The consumer is responsible for Cloud security brokerage.	The consumer is responsible for Cloud security brokerage.	The consumer is responsible for Cloud security brokerage.	The consumer is responsible for Cloud security brokerage.
API	1	The consumer is responsible for	The consumer is responsible	The consumer is responsible	The provider is responsible for the APIs it

Service Name	Level	IaaS Rationale	PaaS Rationale	FaaS Rationale	SaaS Rationale
		the APIs they expose. The provider is responsible for the APIs it exposes.	for the APIs it exposes. The provider is responsible for the APIs it exposes.	for the APIs it exposes. The provider is responsible for the APIs it exposes.	exposes. The consumer can only choose whether or not to use the APIs offered by the provider.
Cloud Workload Protection	1	The consumer has almost complete control over which security controls are implemented on their workloads and over their portability.	The consumer has a large degree of control over which security controls are implemented on their workloads and over their portability.	The consumer has a significant degree of control over which security controls are implemented on their workloads and over their portability.	Not applicable. There is no opportunity to put a consistent security tooling wrapper around a SaaS workload within a SaaS platform.

FURTHER READING

IT Governance Publishing (ITGP) is the world's leading publisher for governance and compliance. Our industry-leading pocket guides, books, training resources and toolkits are written by real-world practitioners and thought leaders. They are used globally by audiences of all levels, from students to C-suite executives.

Our high-quality publications cover all IT governance, risk and compliance frameworks and are available in a range of formats. This ensures our customers can access the information they need in the way they need it.

Other publications you may find useful include:

- *Data Protection and the Cloud – Are you really managing the risks? Second edition* by Paul Ticher, *www.itgovernancepublishing.co.uk/product/data-protection-and-the-cloud-are-you-really-managing-the-risks*
- *Availability and Capacity Management in the Cloud – An ITSM Narrative Account* by Daniel McLean, *www.itgovernancepublishing.co.uk/product/availability-and-capacity-management-in-the-cloud*
- *Information Security Risk Management for ISO 27001/ISO 27002, third edition* by Alan Calder and Steve G Watkins, *www.itgovernancepublishing.co.uk/product/information-security-risk-management-for-iso-27001-iso-27002-third-edition*

For more information on ITGP and branded publishing services, and to view our full list of publications, visit *www.itgovernancepublishing.co.uk*.

To receive regular updates from ITGP, including information on new publications in your area(s) of interest, sign up for our newsletter at *www.itgovernancepublishing.co.uk/topic/newsletter*.

Branded publishing

Through our branded publishing service, you can customise ITGP publications with your company's branding.

Find out more at *www.itgovernancepublishing.co.uk/topic/branded-publishing-services.*

Related services

ITGP is part of GRC International Group, which offers a comprehensive range of complementary products and services to help organisations meet their objectives.

For a full range of resources on cyber security solutions visit *www.itgovernance.co.uk/cyber-security-solutions*.

Training services

The IT Governance training programme is built on our extensive practical experience designing and implementing management systems based on ISO standards, best practice and regulations.

Our courses help attendees develop practical skills and comply with contractual and regulatory requirements. They also support career development via recognised qualifications.

Learn more about our training courses and view the full course catalogue at *www.itgovernance.co.uk/training*.

Professional services and consultancy

We are a leading global consultancy of IT governance, risk management and compliance solutions. We advise businesses around the world on their most critical issues and present cost-saving and risk-reducing solutions based on international best practice and frameworks.

We offer a wide range of delivery methods to suit all budgets, timescales and preferred project approaches.

Find out how our consultancy services can help your organisation at *www.itgovernance.co.uk/consulting*.

Industry news

Want to stay up to date with the latest developments and resources in the IT governance and compliance market? Subscribe to our Weekly Round-up newsletter and we will send you mobile-friendly emails with fresh news and features about your preferred areas of interest, as well as unmissable offers and free resources to help you successfully start your projects. *www.itgovernance.co.uk/weekly-round-up*.